EAST EUROPEAN MONOGRAPHS, NO. XXIX

Frank L. Kaplan is Assistant Professor of Journalism
at the University of Colorado

Library of Congress Catalog Card Number 77-071387
ISBN 0-91470-22-2

Printed in the United States of America

WINTER INTO SPRING: THE CZECHOSLOVAK PRESS AND THE REFORM MOVEMENT 1963-1968

FRANK L. KAPLAN

EAST EUROPEAN QUARTERLY, BOULDER
DISTRIBUTED BY COLUMBIA UNIVERSITY PRESS
NEW YORK

1977

To the Memory of my Father
and
To my Mother . . .

whose love of literature has instilled in me a lasting appreciation for the printed word and a deep respect for those individuals who throughout history have devoted their efforts to preserving its truth and its freedom.

PREFACE

This work is a study of the Czechoslovak press and its involvement in the reform movement of 1963-68 which culminated in what has generally been referred to as the Prague Spring. In pursuing this goal, the book also focuses on the journalist and writer as political actors in their society and as transmitters of those basic humanistic and democratic values imparted to the nation by early patriotic leaders who, in the main, were not professed politicians or statesmen, but poets, writers, journalists or scholars propelled into the political arena by necessity and a steadfast adherence to their beliefs.

Since its emergence as a sovereign state following World War I, Czechoslovakia has frequently been in the spotlight of European and world affairs. This has come to pass due to the repeated crises which its people have experienced and, also, because of the prominent geographic position the nation occupies in East-Central Europe, one generally regarded as a bridge between East and West. As a result of this position, and because it has been subjected to distinctly different forms of political ideology and rule during its brief existence as an independent state, Czechoslovakia represents a cogent example for the study of political behavior and, more recently, of the role played by a traditionally Western-oriented and pluralistic press in a society subjugated to one-party rule.

In the light of events antecedent to 1968, the experience of the Prague Spring itself and the oppression that followed, one is reminded of the cyclical evolution of history. The Russian writer Yevgeny Zamyatin, in his futuristic novel *We,* stated it clearly:

> *Human history ascends in circles . . . The circles differ — some are golden, some bloody. But all are equally divided into three hundred and sixty degrees. And the movement is from zero — onward, to ten, twenty, two hundred, three hundred and sixty degrees — back to zero.*

This, then, represents a study which critically examines the press during the latest such completed historic cycle of a nation whose people have repeatedly expressed the desire to be governed not by despots or absolute ideologies, but by principles inherent in the rational thinking and actions of man.

In conducting research for and writing this book, I have been fortunate in obtaining much valuable assistance from persons too numerous to mention here. I am especially indebted, however, to Professor William A. Hachten who provided valuable guidance during the initial phases of the venture. Research for this project was supported by grants from the American Council of Learned Societies and Social Science Research Council awarded through the Foreign Area Fellowship Program (FAFP). Without this generous assistance, I would never have been able to travel to Munich and spend the time needed at the library of the Collegium Carolinum and at Radio Free Europe (RFE) where most of the research was undertaken.

In this regard, I owe much gratitude to the staff of the Evaluation and Research Department of the Czechoslovak Unit at RFE whose members never failed to assist me during my stay. Also, to the Czechs and Slovaks who answered my questions and discussed with me their experiences during the liberalization process and Prague Spring, I extend my sincere appreciation.

Additional insight into problems of Eastern European states in general and Czechoslovakia in particular was gained through three visits to the area. In summer 1969, I stayed in Prague for more than three weeks, experiencing firsthand the country's trauma during the demonstrations marking the first anniversary of the Warsaw Pact invasion, while during fall 1971 I had the opportunity to travel through Hungary, Rumania and Yugoslavia. The latter month-long trip was made possible through the original FAFP grant. I visited Prague again in July 1975.

My greatest debt is to my wife, Phyllis Ann, whose understanding and occasional justly deserved prodding has enabled me to complete this project. Without her willing support, editorial assistance and undeserved patience in indulging my idiosyncrasies, this work would most likely never have passed beyond the state of a mere wistful dream.

Boulder, Colorado
Fall 1976

CONTENTS

ABBREVIATIONS

BBC	British Broadcasting Corporation
CPSU	Communist Party of the Soviet Union
CSM	Czechoslovak Union of Youth
CSSR	Czechoslovak Socialist Republic
CTK	Czechoslovak News Agency
HSTD	Chief Authority for Press Supervision
IOJ	International Organization of Journalists
K-231	Club 231 (organization of former political prisoners)
KAN	Club of Committed Non-Party People
KSC	Communist Party of Czechoslovakia
KSS	Communist Party of Slovakia
MI	Ministry of Information
POSN	Prague Branch of the Union of Journalists
RFE	Radio Free Europe
ROH	Revolutionary Trade Union Movement
SCN	Union of Czech Journalists
SCS	Union of Czech Writers
SCSN	Union of Czechoslovak Journalists
SCSS	Union of Czechoslovak Writers
SSN	Union of Slovak Journalists
SSS	Union of Slovak Writers
TASS	News Agency of the Soviet Union
UNCSSR	Center of the Journalists of the Czechoslovak Socialist Republic
UPS	Central Publication Authority (formerly HSTD)
VOA	Voice of America

INTRODUCTION

Within the quaint Italian town of Bressanone (Brixen), in the alpine province of South Tyrol, stands a large and weather-aged house with a small vineyard bordering one of its tall protective walls. The two-story structure looks like many of the other domiciles that dot the town's sloping outskirts and would not warrant any special notice by the casual passer-by were it not for the bronze plaque adorning its narrow front facade. This modest memorial, however, honors neither an Italian patriot nor a historic event. Instead, it commemorates a nineteenth-century Czech journalist, poet and political activitist, Karel Havlicek Borovsky, who took up quarters in the house after being exiled in 1851 by Austrian authorities for his journalistic and political activism during and after the revolutionary years 1848-49. He was interned in Brixen (then part of the Austrian Empire) until 1855 and only allowed to return to die in his native land the following year.

For more than a century, Havlicek's legacy — his prominent role in the Czech national awakening, inspirational writing and eventual martyrdom at the hands of the absolutist regime of Minister of the Interior Alexander Bach — has served as a vivid symbol for ensuing generations of Czech journalists and writers who have repeatedly found themselves struggling against demagoguery and tyranny while being politically and culturally oppressed under totalitarian forms of rule.(1) L'udovit Stur, the nineteenth-century educator, journalist and prominent leader of the Slovak movement opposing forced Mygarization, has served as a similar symbol for generations of his countrymen.

Most recently, following the August 1968 Soviet-led invasion of Czechoslovakia, approximately 1,580 (or more than 36 percent) of the nation's journalists were expelled from their professional organization, which also meant from their editorial positions.(2) Furthermore, at least 150 journalists and writers sought exile in the West. In many instances, the dismissed journalists who remained in the country were allowed to accept only jobs of manual labor, while some experienced serious difficulty in merely securing a livelihood.

Accompanying this cleansing of media personnel (which in several cases included court proceedings brought against individual journalists who had actively supported the liberal program) was the reimposition of rigid political censorship and the abolition of those popular newspapers and periodicals which had most vigorously backed the democratization process of 1968. Such actions were part of the normalization program(3) of the new Communist Party leadership which in April 1969, with the active support of the Soviet regime, took over the reins of power from Alexander Dubcek's reformist government and returned the nation to its "proper" course of Socialist construction.

It is the intent of this book to closely examine the role of the print media during the liberalization and democratization phases of this reform movement, that is, from the onset of de-Stalinization(4) in December 1962 until the Warsaw Pact invasion of August 1968. In brief, this is a study of press activism during the nation's cultural, economic, social and political revival of the 1960's as embodied in the print media's transformation from a uniform, rigidly controlled and centrally directed communication system into distinct focal centers and channels of dissent, and later into a generally united force which not only opposed the status quo and advocated change but, unknowingly, also began setting the stage for the military intervention that nullified the nation's experiment of pursuing a new road toward socialism.

The gradual transformation of this uniform mass communication system — stimulated by gross failures on virtually all fronts in Czechoslovakia's development under communism, changing trends within the Soviet Union and Communist world, and effects of the communications boom of the early 1960's — helped to undermine the centralized and bureaucratic regime of Antonin Novotny, leading ultimately to its downfall in January 1968. In its place, the Dubcek administration began to construct a Socialist democracy in which the merger of Masaryk's humanism and Marx's socialism was to prevail.

The essence of this experiment, conducted during the first eight months of 1968, was contained in the new Action Program and reflected in the free and wide-ranging public exchange of ideas and in the spirit of the people. The Action Program, which incorporated positive concepts from both Capitalist and Socialist societies, was to serve as the main instrument in furthering the nation's economic, cultural and political development. By reviving the nation's democratic traditions, including freedom of expression, the new leadership attempted to establish conditions for a more pluralistic society in which public opinion was a determining factor in the formation of public policy. As Milovan Djilas so aptly stated in his assessment of Czechoslovakia's experiment:

> *For the first time the policy of a communist party in power became public and subject to criticism, and the ideas of its top leaders ceased to be directives for the entire society. The visions of reformists of communism about the union of collective property with personal freedom became a reality, and Czechoslovakia, in mediating between East and West and in bringing them together, found her true being and realized her mission. (5)*

Prompting this realization no doubt were the dominant forces of history and nationalism, as well as a democratic press tradition rooted in the nation's renaissance of the last century and coming to full fruition during the country's democratic phase of the interwar period, 1918-1938.

A prominent aspect of the Czechoslovak press tradition has been the relationship between culture and politics, an alliance perhaps best reflected in the figure of the activist writer. Besides his status as a man of letters, he also traditionally has been a political actor, both as an individual and in the collective sense. For the writer, especially in the latter case, has established himself as a leading force among the heterogeneous intellectual community. Due to his achievement of this position and because of his prominence in the reform movement, it is appropriate to define the concept of the writer in the context of Czechoslovak society. Moreover, since the writer is a member of the intelligentsia which, historically, has been recognized as possessing "perhaps greater prestige in Eastern Europe than anywhere in the world," (6) the following definition can apply not only to Czechoslovak writers but also to most writers in the other states comprising today's Eastern Europe.

Accepting the notion of Herbert Passin's literary "continuum," (7) one can readily visualize that at one end of this imaginary scale is the author, who deals almost exclusively with belles-lettres or scholarly output, while on the opposite side rests the journalist, personified by the reporter covering a beat for his newspaper. Drawing within the middle range, however, a blending of the two occurs in the form of the writer who can and frequently does function within *both* fields interchangeably.

The writer in this sense does not initially have to be either an author or a reporter but, understandably, can come to the literary-journalistic field from any discipline or profession. The determining factor, it seems, is the individual's desire to become actively engaged in the political process by promoting his or her views, or the ideology to which he or she adheres, through journalistic endeavors. In this sense, however, the individual is not just a reporter but a commentator, essayist, critic, feuilletonist, satirist, polemicist, and/or publicist — simply, a writer. The meaning of publicist, interestingly enough, further amplifies the close relationship between literature and politics. The term can be generally defined as "a political writer or journalist who, in the public interest, informs (or comments) on timely questions."(8)

The phenomenon of the *engage* writer has become an intrinsic feature of Czechoslovakia's cultural-political scene where the "pure" author, in the strictly Western sense, has been a rare specimen indeed. For those who write creatively are also closely and frequently officially associated with a newspaper, magazine or journal, not to mention radio, television, theater and the film-making industry. As one Slovak writer has observed: "In our country, for instance, the writer is least professionalized. Predominantly, everyone has his civil occupation which has its own demands and draws upon his capabilities. Only after his employment can the writer devote himself to creative work."(9)

Thus, only a very few of the most popular (and government accepted) authors gain sufficient financial rewards from their writing to sustain their literary habit. Three prevailing factors account for this duality in roles. These are tradition, the desire for continued access to a mass medium (since such access has tended to be limited and controlled) and the need for a steady income, a cogent point when considering the economics of smaller nations.

This is not to imply, of course, that no journalists as such exist. That would be an erroneous assumption. The explanation is meant only to stress the point that, traditionally, the relationship between literature and politics in Czechoslovakia has been much closer than is the case in some Western states. The part played by liberal-minded writers and the cultural press in the drive toward reform during the 1960's is a relevant example. "Writers and artists," according to Djilas, "have taken foremost places among those devoting their creative activities to destroying rigid formulas and attitudes, and they were the first to set about a spontaneous demolition of Stalin's and Lenin's (and indeed other Marxist) dogmas."(10)

It should also be noted that newspapers as primarily financial ventures are foreign to Czechoslovakia's journalistic tradition. Even during periods when certain papers did serve such a purpose, as was the case during the 1920's and 1930's, they never completely cut the cord that bound them to a political party or interest group. This is a direct outgrowth of the practice developed during the formative years of modern Czech and Slovak journalism when newspapers served as the primary voices of the forerunners of the nation's political parties and special interest groups.

Traditionally, then, Czechoslovak writers have utilized the print media to a far greater degree as a means of expressing personal opinion, social criticism and political commentary than has been the case in the West, especially in the United States, where a deeper awareness of professional separateness exists and more numerous and diverse communication channels have developed.

The foregoing provides a historical perspective and a point of departure for the central problem under consideration: press activism in Czechoslovakia's reform movement. There remains the question of method or form of analysis to be employed in dealing with the process of change in a one-party system; that is, the analytic framework through which one is able to examine the political process, or at least a significant aspect of it.

For some time now, the notion of interest and pressure groups influencing power holders and decision-making in Western political systems has generally been accepted and widely studied under the rubric of group theory. Only during recent years, however, has the concept been adopted by scholars for the study of Soviet and East European politics. No doubt the outmoded monolith concept and the challenges which have been issued against the totalitarian approach (which tends to view group conflict primarily as a struggle among factions within the top leadership) have stimulated a wider search for new analytic tools in the study of Communist systems and societies.(11) And while the interest group approach has gained support from among area specialists, it has not done so without facing opposition.

One such skeptical view is based on the belief that Communist monism and Western pluralism are so diverse in principle as to defy the application of an analytic concept based on one system in the study of the other — in this case, using the interest group theory developed from Western pluralism in analyzing Communist politics.(12) Although the criticism may not seem altogether groundless in terms of the Soviet Union where a pluralistic tradition is virtually absent, it fails to hold true when considering those East European states whose historical development is based on Western principles and thus includes a pluralistic tradition. Czechoslovakia stands out as a good example.

For added support, one can turn to the writings of East European scholars, such as the Slovak legal theorist Michal Lakatos, who have taken up the issue of interest groups in institutionalized mass organizations and, hence, have acknowledged their presence. As Lakatos explained in a 1965 article:

> *The reality that interest groups are an inseparable element of the whole course of our socialist structure demonstrates the existence of interest organizations. This institutional expression is an admission of the influence of these interests within the political sphere. Socialist society could not function if there wasn't here the integrative element and if the directive leadership (the Party) of society did not adapt to this function of interest groups.(13)*

Not only did Lakatos acknowledge the existence of a conflict of interests in Communist society, which he viewed as normal, and the emergence of interest groups within social organizations, but he also argued that the various social interests should be given political expression by the creation of an electoral system which would allow these interests, through existing social and professional organizations, to be represented in legislative bodies.(14) (Increased representation in the decision-making process was one of the basic aims of the intellectuals in their effort to reform centralized political rule.)

Further, the rigid controls which characterize Communist countries and hamper scholarly research were generally absent in Czechoslovakia during a good portion of 1968, thus enabling the heretofore diffuse and unclear aspects of one-party politics in that country to rise closer to the surface and come into sharper focus. This openness was enhanced considerably by an unfettered press which did much during its period of freedom, brief though it was, to bring to light that which previously had been hidden in the secrecy of a closed society.

It should be clear that the intent here is not so much to defend the interest group approach per se — such a task would be superfluous because it has already been accomplished quite adequately by a number of scholars(15) — as to underscore the validity of its application in a study focusing on Czechoslovak politics and the print media. By its very nature, such a study must also include the changing status and role of the most prominent associations involved, namely the Union of Czechoslovak Journalists (SCSN) and the Union of Czechoslovak Writers (SCSS), which Lakatos described in 1968 as "two of the most significant interest organizations of intellectuals."(16)

This is not to say that the political process of a given Communist society can be explained solely on the basis of the relationship between interest organizations and those in power. Nevertheless, when considering Lakatos' remarks and recognizing the evident changes in the status and activities of institutionalized organizations in Communist societies, the interest group approach does appear a valid method by which to examine the process of the aggregation and channeling of societal demands and dissent. From the standpoint of historical experience, this process has represented a key aspect of political development in those East European societies with a propensity toward nationalism and pluralism. As Djilas commented about the Czechoslovak experiment with democratization: "All these changes . . . are organically linked to the history, culture and character of the Czechs and Slovaks."(17)

Finally, support for the interest group approach can also be found in a study by a former deputy chairman of Warsaw's Press Institute who concluded that "since 1956, the writers and journalists (of Poland, Hungary and Czechoslovakia) have become an intermediary body between the Party and the people, a pressure group which exercises its influence as well on the Party as on public opinion."(18) This influence has been evident on a number of occasions during past years, most recently in Poland where the mass media and Roman Catholic Church have gained substantial concessions from the Edward Gierek regime.

Inherent in the Communist system is the built-in provision whereby the Party *apparat* or state administration, for purposes of self-interest, provides official professional groups and public organizations with means of internal communication, primarily newspapers but often periodicals as well, and encourages national congresses and local meetings. During the Stalinist years, such institutionalized associations, with their publications acting as transmission belts, were used for the specific purpose of disseminating and interpreting policies from above. De-Stalinization, however, served as an impetus for altering this regimented one-directional channeling process, encouraging some of these organizations to take advantage of the feedback potential of their respective publications.

The freer atmosphere, in essence, stimulated the use of these ready-made communication channels for the purpose of stating demands and interests, whether such articulations constituted self-interests (pertaining only to a given group) or ones which would benefit the public at large (i.e., easier travel abroad, freer access to information or cessation of injustices). By expressing their interests, organizations were in effect attempting to change established policies, either within their own domain or on a broader societal level.

Due to the ethnic complexity of East European nations, organizations are at times divided along national lines. In Czechoslovakia this takes the form of Czech and Slovak sections, each publishing newspapers and/or periodicals in its respective language. Similarly, one can assume that a national organization can be grouped, whether in institutionalized form or not, by other criteria such as geographic (urban and rural), demographic (prewar generation and postwar youth), political (conservatives and liberals) and occupational (editors handling economic materials and those concerned with foreign affairs) considerations. The emergence of such divisions or factions within an organization can possibly result in friction and, taken to the extreme, a struggle for control of the organization. This becomes more evident with the formation within a given association of subgroups along political or ideological lines.

No less significant is the ideological outlook or direction taken by the editorial staff of a newspaper or periodical which a given organization has at its disposal, for such publications are not necessarily restricted in influence to the sponsoring group's membership but can (especially during periods of crisis) affect a much larger audience, one encompassing representatives from various groups and social strata. This was clearly outlined by Professor Ghita Ionescu in his discussion of periodicals as important centers of dissent: "Their effect is to concentrate the vague and sometimes ineffectual currents of thought which, once thus reduced to essentials, are then disseminated to wider public spheres."(19) Thus, a publication has the *potential* of becoming a powerful focal center of dissent by being able to aggregate and channel popular demands and grievances.

However, a major key to becoming such a center, and concomitantly for interest groups to be successful in exerting influence, is the strength and authority of those in power. Once the leadership's authority is undermined and becomes subject to question, other elements and forces of interest are afforded the opportunity to make themselves felt in the political process. (20) Such a situation developed in Czechoslovakia during the 1960's as the Novotny regime's vulnerability became increasingly exposed. This progressive exposure served to heighten the criticism voiced against the Party leadership and its dysfunctional policies, increasing the frequency and boldness with which demands for change were expressed.

By analyzing the print media in this light, one hopefully can determine the actual role the press played in Czechoslovakia's reform movement and detect the sources of pressures brought to bear on the Novotny leadership as reflected in the formation of centers of dissent and the channeling of grievances.

Furthermore, the mass media's key role in the nation's effort to construct a Socialist democracy warrants close examination because the media's very success during the democratization process — especially the abolition of political pre-censorship — constituted a prime factor in the ultimate negation of the Czechoslovak experiment.

Since the Warsaw Pact invasion, numerous studies (some excellent and valuable) have been published on various aspects of the Prague Spring, as well as on antecedent events leading up to this period. Few, however, have focused primarily on the mass media. Certainly, the part played by the press should not be overestimated, but neither should it be diminished by submerging the press' role into the background of the overall political milieu. For practically all works dealing with this period stress the importance of the communication media.

Major publications which focus on Czechoslovakia's reform movement and include material pertaining to the mass media can be classified into three basic categories: works utilizing primary sources, writings based on personal experiences of Western observers and accounts by Czechoslovaks who were personally involved in the struggle for reform in their country.

The most pertinent sources in the first category include Vladimir Kusin's *Political Grouping in the Czechoslovak Reform Movement* (1972) and Galia Golan's comprehensive studies *The Czechoslovak Reform Movement* (1971) and *Reform Rule in Czechoslovakia* (1973). Both Kusin's study and Golan's first book include sections on the mass media, while the latter's second work has an extensive section on censorship. Also in this category would be Robin A. Remington's *Winter in Prague* (1969), a compilation of important speeches and documents pertaining to democratization, the invasion and its aftermath; and Andrew Oxley's, et al., *Czechoslovakia: The Party and the People* (1973), containing translations of relevant Czech and Slovak press articles.

The best sources in the second category are Tad Szulc's *Czechoslovakia Since World War II* (1971), Harry Schwartz's *Prague's 200 Days* (1969) and Z. A. B. Zeman's *Prague Spring* (1969). Although their main emphasis is on general history and politics, these works do include some discussion concerning the writers and the press.

The most enlightening accounts dealing with various aspects of the struggle for reform are those found in the last category mentioned with the following perhaps the most representative of this group. Dusan Hamsik's *Writers Against Rulers* (1971) describes the events surrounding the Union of Writers' Fourth Congress of June 1967 and the consequences that ensued. The author, a former editor of the Union's chief weekly paper, also offers his justification for the Prague Spring. In *The Seventh Night* (1969), Ladislav Mnacko interweaves his account of the invasion with a series of revealing flashbacks to key periods in the nation's history, the Communist movement and the struggle for reform. He includes many interesting insights into the problems and realities of Communist rule based on information gained while working as a journalist. Antonin J. Liehm's *The Politics of Culture* (1972) is primarily a composite of interviews conducted between 1965 and spring 1968 with some of Czechoslovakia's leading writers and thinkers, most of whom were prominent figures in the nation's reform movement. In the introductory chapter, Jean-Paul Sartre analyzes Soviet socialism in Czechoslovakia and concludes that the reform leaders could not have acted in any way other than adopting the course they chose to pursue.

Other sources in this group include *A Year Is Eight Months* (1970), written by Josef Maxa under the pseudonym Journalist M, and *"Svoboda" The Press in Czechoslovakia 1968* (1969), published by the International Press Institute. While the latter discusses the press, radio and television during the 1967-68 period (through chapters written anonymously by people involved in such activities), Maxa's book focuses more generally on events that transpired during the democratization phase.

This study of the Czechoslovak press was undertaken with the conviction that it would help elucidate the status, function and effect of the press in a Communist society under various political conditions. The democratization process of 1968 presented a unique situation in that a free press (one unrestrained by prior political censorship) was functioning in a Communist state and was able to reflect public opinion openly. Such an experience deserves close examination to determine not only what actually occurred during the political regeneration, but why.

Moreover, this examination was pursued to further support the premise that East European states and their institutions, including the mass media, should be studied as separate entities, from the perspective of national development and traditions, and not as appendages to studies about the Soviet Union as has tended to be the general practice. Similar pleas have been voiced by area specialists in other disciplines who recognize that, as one observed, "in the majority of instances the principal factors to be regarded in comprehending a Communist country or party or system are no longer its 'communism' but rather its origin, traditions and patterns of development."(21) One is reminded of Djilas' words, quoted above, concerning the organic link between the democratization process and the Czech and Slovak national character, cultural heritage and historical tradition. And once again it was the journalist-writer and the press which helped to facilitate this linkage by reuniting the nation with its past.

PART I

YEARS OF STRUGGLE FOR REFORM

A major task of any Communist party after seizing and consolidating power has usually been the creation of a mythology of the newly instituted order so as to provide it with a legitimate sense of continuity along certain progressive and revolutionary lines. By so doing, the leadership hopes to make the new directive force in society appear as the inevitable culmination of a phase in the class struggle and a manifestation of the nation's historical development. This generally has been achieved by rejecting existing predominant national, so-called bourgeois, traditions and initiating new methods and trends in directing the nation. But an undertaking of such magnitude has never been an easy one, especially in those states where the national heritage is based on Western principles of political rule, i.e., pluralism and individual freedom, which are accepted and valued by the people.

In the case of the Czechs and Slovaks, their historical experiences and traditions, stemming from decades of struggle for cultural and political autonomy, have repeatedly served as a vital ingredient of national cohesiveness. This is reflected in the people's national consciousness and their almost religious devotion to a cultivation of historical awareness. (The meticulous reexamination of the nation's role in history initiated at the Union of Writers' Fourth Congress in 1967 and continued during 1968 is a recent case in point.)

The Communists well realized the people's close attachment to their past and attempted to take advantage of this attribute in creating the new order. However, in their initial efforts to purify society of its bourgeois characteristics, Party leaders felt the need to reinterpret history which resulted in the exclusion or at least total refutation of many progressive elements representing an integral and, therefore, inseparable part of the nation's past. The field of journalism was no exception in this respect, especially those aspects which reflected the Western traditions, standards and practices adopted during its formative years and pursued by the nation's press following independence. Thus, after February 1948, many past traditions were condemned as degenerate and many former practices abandoned, including the press system of the interwar period which was replaced by one based on the Soviet system of mass media regulation.

The promulgation of and steadfast adherence to the established myth lasted into the second decade of Communist rule in Czechoslovakia, reaching its apex during 1960 when a new Socialist constitution was adopted and the triumphant declaration made that socialism was victorious in the nation, the class struggle had been won. The Party leadership, perhaps a bit heady due to its own delusions, even went so far as to prophesy that the final stage of socialism — communism — would be achieved in their country within the next twenty years. Nothing could have been further from the truth.

By fall 1962, failures much too evident to be concealed, or simply brushed aside by some inane excuse or arbitrarily placed blame as had been the common practice in the past, finally forced the Novotny leadership to face reality and begin the process of de-Stalinization. Thus, the last stringent vestiges of Stalinism gave way to serious inquiry, with the social sciences and the arts serving as the primary analytic tools. This introspection enabled Czechoslovak society to become increasingly aware of the scope and extent of its inner malady, which affected every vital organ of the system, and even to probe the very theory upon which the system was based.

The main thrust of the four chapters comprising Part I is to examine this introspective process and determine how the method of diagnosis led to improvements and, eventually, to the proposed cure which began to be administered in earnest during spring 1968. One of the most important first steps leading to improved conditions entailed the rejection of the more stringent Soviet methods and tactics which had been imposed on society. Initially, this was undertaken in the cultural field, i.e., literature, journalism and the arts, by reviving national traditions, a process which increasingly placed the writers and liberal journalists at odds with the regime. Also, the confrontation stimulated centers of dissent among the intelligentsia which formalized into an oppositional force after de-Stalinization was initiated and, eventually, contributed to the regime's downfall.

The expansion of liberalization from above, combined with the demands for more relevant information by the awakening public opinion from below, served to professionalize the news media. The Party hoped to compete more effectively with the West in disseminating information on the domestic front while at the same time carrying the message of socialism more convincingly to the nation's masses. The press, with its rediscovered professionalism, however, soon diverted its attention from merely transmitting sterile propaganda to joining the growing reform movement and heralding its message of change.

The gradual transformation of the press into a medium of information helped to intensify dissent against the Notovny regime and, thus, to broaden the movement for reform. This was especially the case of the cultural press which formed a major center of opposition by increasingly confronting the Party leadership on key issues in an attempt to extend the liberalization process and create a freer climate within the nation, an atmosphere that would facilitate the desired revival process.

CHAPTER I
ON THE ROAD BACK TO REALITY

After seizing control of the country in February 1948, the Communist Party of Czechoslovakia (KSC) made a concerted effort to reorganize the mass communication system and mold the nation's press to the pattern existing in the Soviet Union. This meant abandoning prevailing traditions and practices and transforming the press into the Party's propaganda instrument.

The negative aspects of media performance which resulted from this reorganization were openly repudiated by the writers and journalists as soon as conditions for criticism were afforded them. Such an opportunity occurred during the brief thaw that followed the denunciation of the Stalinist cult at the Twentieth Congress of the Communist Party of the Soviet Union (CPSU) held in February 1956. It was during this short period of a relaxed atmosphere in spring 1956 that the theoretical framework for reform was conceived.

Repudiation of the Personality Cult

The initial effect of the Twentieth Congress of the CPSU was traumatic for the Czechoslovak nation, for Nikita S. Khrushchev's condemnation of the most gruesome aspects of Stalinism signaled the release of the pent-up fears and pressures which had lingered after the dictator's death. Pure relief following the exhaustive experience of nearly seven years of terror was evident everywhere. The response to what promised to be a more hopeful future, however, was not uniform among the rulers and those ruled; the former realized only too well what uncertainties and personal dangers the relaxation might bring. The Communist Party leadership, therefore, attempted as best it could to ride out the period of confusion created by Khrushchev's strategic move, while the rest of the nation breathed more freely in the fresh and reviving atmosphere pervading Eastern Europe.

The KSC leaders dutifully reiterated Moscow's call for waging a decisive battle against the personality cult. But they did so in cautious and defensive tones, maintaining that the cult was not as deeply rooted in Czechoslovakia as in other Socialist states and thus implying that no real need existed to decultivize.(1) Most of the intelligentsia, on the other hand, responded more positively to the opportunity which Moscow's ukase presented. Repulsed by what they had witnessed and experienced during the early 1950's, they began to reconsider the paramount principle (which many of them had actually helped to bring about) of the Party's infallibility.

Initially, this reevaluation was most evident among the nation's writers whose Second Congress was held April 22-29, 1956, only two months after Khrushchev's well-known secret speech. Those present at the meeting apparently took to heart the words of the Soviet writers' representative, Boris Polevoj, who proclaimed during the opening ceremonies: "God grant you, comrades, that your discussion be intense, creative and held in a spirit of camaraderie. . . . Let your congress be as stormy and happy as a spring thunderstorm."(2) Stormy and thunderous the discussions proved to be, pervaded by eloquent and passionate speeches by such individuals as Frantisek Hrubin, Vaclav Kaplicky and Jaroslav Seifert. Speaker after speaker denounced the abuses and humiliations of the Stalinist era and revealed how they had been forced to distort reality in order to have their works published. They advocated change and avowed their future responsibilities. At the same time, excerpts of these speeches appeared in *Literarni noviny* (Literary News), the writers' weekly.

What the writers achieved, in essence, was to revive a feeling for national cultural traditions and to reaffirm the time-honored concept that the Czechoslovak writer is his nation's conscience, not merely an engineer of human souls as the Soviet dictum would have it. (Both themes later were major cornerstones in the reform movement.) By so doing, the writers attempted to regain their readers' trust which had waned ever since literature became regimented and utilized primarily as a tool of exhortation and propaganda.

Judging from the nature and tone of letters published in *Literarni noviny* after the Congress, the writers made a positive start in this endeavor. The gist of these emotion-filled letters was perhaps best expressed by a Moravian teacher who, after admitting her initial doubts and skepticism about the Congress, wrote: "You cannot imagine with what animation we are analyzing your newspaper here! How the wilted, almost dead, flower of trust again rises in our hearts — we again have our writers! After all, they are the ones in whom we place our trust."(3) The Congress, and the peaceful student demonstrations that followed both in Prague and Bratislava, thus constituted the first overt effort to have the Party relinquish its rigid control over cultural affairs.

In more subdued tones and in a much less public sphere, the journalists undertook the task of reexamining the performance of the nation's press and reviewing their status as newsmen. Their criticisms and analyses came to light during the discourse conducted prior to their Second Congress scheduled for June 1956. The journalists readily took advantage of a chance for an open discussion about their profession, the first since the initial euphoric days of the Communist victory, which the Central Committee of the SCSN was obliged to sanction. "The second congress, and the preparatory period for it," wrote one discussant, "is a useful opportunity for us to more critically ponder the phenomena which are dulling the edge of our press."(4)

The phenomena proved to be many and in virtually every aspect of journalistic endeavor as evidenced by the relatively frank outpouring of grievances, primarily on the pages of the Union's official monthly magazine, *Ceskoslovensky novinar* (Czechoslovak Newsman). In fact, the criticism was so blatant and extensive that the SCSN leadership, fearful of the apparent developing trend, postponed the Congress until the following year. The journalists' discontent focused on the sterility of the press created by the drab writing, content uniformity and scarcity of timely news which resulted from the centrally controlled dissemination of information. They also expressed concern over their low status, both professional and material. In essence, the journalists criticized the lack of professionalism existing in the print media and the strict controls to which they were being subjected.

In light of this expressed discontent, brief though it was, it is useful to examine some of the practices and policies enforced during the preceding years when, as one journalist phrased it," 'with the best of intentions,' human themes (were transformed) into theses, newspapers into bulletins, and journalists into clerks."(5)

Russification of the Press

An extensive reorganization and reorientation of all the mass media occurred after the Communist Party gained complete power during the closing days of February 1948. This transformation, which amounted to a degradation of established journalistic standards, continued with varying intensity and scope until about 1954 when the trend was arrested and then gradually reversed. A major feature of the initial changeover was the implementation of assurance of compliance measures whereby the main criterion for work in the journalistic profession was absolute, or at least simulated, allegiance to the KSC. The Party delegated to Communists all positions considered important and every leading post was included in the Party Central Committee's nomenclature.(6)

At the onset, emphasis was given to purging remnants of the bourgeois press by either suppressing individual papers outright or simply altering their staffs and incorporating them into the Party-designed press network. To complete the cleansing of "compromising elements" in the information field, begun soon after the end of World War II, the Union of Czech Journalists (SCN) alone expelled 106 of its members, "those who were the leading proponents in the services of the reaction."(7) Similarly, the Union of Slovak Journalists (SSN) eliminated non-Communists from its ranks, especially members of the Democratic Party and those who had worked on its publications.

The next area of concern was the Party press itself which the KSC progressively attempted to mold into a mirror image of the Soviet press. The worst period in this campaign occurred between 1949 and 1954, coinciding with the nation's first Five Year Plan. In his 1961 study on press development, a Czech journalist used a candid and telling analogy from an earlier article appearing in *Novinarsky sbornik* (Journalistic Review) to describe the status of the press during this period:

> *Karl Marx once characterized the press as 'paper money of public opinion.' As far as our press following the victorious February 1948 is concerned, its future historians, were they to evaluate it from the same standpoint, will undoubtedly conclude that the period of its highest 'inflation' coincided roughly with the years 1949 to 1953. . . . Trust in the press of this period is analogous to the people's confidence in devaluating currency.(8)*

The regime also took steps to further consolidate the nation's press. Thus, the number of dailies declined from 18 to an all-time low of 11 during 1952 (44 daily newspapers had been published in 1945), while 350 periodic publications were suppressed during the same period. These were primarily organs of the National Socialist and Populist (Catholic) Parties in the Czech lands and Democratic and Freedom Parties in Slovakia.(9) (The number of periodic publications at the time was inflated by including many factory papers and other such house organs. This was reflected in an increase in the total number of periodic titles as indicated in Table I. See Appendix I.)

To fill the vacuum created by this purification process, some 300 Soviet newspapers, periodicals and reviews were made available to the Czechoslovak reader, including *Pravda* (Truth), *Novoye vremya* (New Times) and *Ogonyok* (Small Fire).(10) Moreover, names of some existing papers were again altered so that, for example, the daily *Svobodne noviny* (Free News) was once more given the name of its highly regarded predecessor of the interwar period, *Lidove noviny* (People's News), and during a 1952 reshuffle was reorganized into the weekly *Literarni noviny.* (The names of several prominent newspapers had already been changed following the nation's liberation in 1945.)

Law No. 184, ratified in December 1950, reaffirmed the control of the Ministry of Information (MI) over the nation's mass media and, further, provided that only the following possessed the legal right to publish newspapers and periodocials: political parties of the National Front; state organs; individual professional organizations; leading organizations of culture, economics, special interests (hobby groups as opposed to interest groups in the Western sense), social welfare and physical education.(11)

The act also increased the SCSN's power, by delegating to it full disciplinary control over its members, and authorized the Ministry to draft the Union's statutes.(12) These the MI issued the following May. During the same year, Law No. 68 was passed which attempted to organize every adult and school-age child into "voluntary" cultural, scientific, professional and sports associations as well as organizations for women and youth.(13) These groups were supervised directly through appropriate Party organs.

The SCSN, meanwhile, had undergone significant organizational and role changes in terms of its status as a transmission belt and supervisory body for the nation's press. This transformation and the Union's major tasks in the new order were outlined during the journalists' First Congress, held October 23-24, 1948, which also saw the unification of its two sections into a single national body. (The Slovak section continued to exist but the central leadership, headquartered in Prague, held decisive sway by issuing directives and setting guidelines.)

It is interesting to note that during the months prior to the Congress, when the euphoria of victory still permitted personal views and opinions to be voiced, individual Communist editors advocated maintaining modern journalistic practices and methods which, according to them, were demanded by the times to make the press attractive and responsive to its readers. However, any hope of continuing practices similar to those adhered to by the Western press was stifled by President Klement Gottwald when, in a letter addressed to the journalists' First Congress, he stated:

> *It is the end, the definite end, of the past. . . . Today the tasks of our press are completely different. In our new democratic order the press should be one of the main agents of national, state and moral education of the people, an effective aid in our development. This means an end to wild sensations and the whipping up of readers' nerves, an end to the competitive chase to see who is first.(14)*

The entire scope of the Congress and the tasks delegated to the SCSN by the Party leadership increased the Union's influence considerably, not only over its members but on the entire press as well. So much so in fact that Vojtech Dolejsi, Union chairman during the latter part of the 1950's, was later forced to admit that the Congress' decisions, combined with the law governing journalists, resulted in "some incorrect methods" being practiced, "namely in the Union's commission for the control of editorial operative plans, which assumed the right to interfere with editorial content and to direct the press."(15)

The commission, composed of active newsmen, demanded that major editorial offices submit monthly schedules, so-called mirrors, for their respective papers. Commission members evaluated them and recommended changes whenever they deemed it necessary. The operative plans had to not only include major articles and commentaries, but also indicate virtually every headline and the substance of each piece of copy the editors planned to use during the month. Despite the evident unwieldiness of such a scheme, the practice was continued until 1952 when it was modified due to the simple fact that not a single daily was able to adhere to its approved mirror plan.(16)

Another aspect of this era of regimentation was the creation of secretariates in editorial offices. These entities, designated as political secretariates so as not to be confused with administrative bodies, undertook the supervision of every imaginable aspect of newspaper production. Their bureaucratic tentacles soon reached into every department. The members changed the meaning of articles at will, often unbeknownst to either the chief editor or the writer involved, and made certain that all directives and new regulations, which sprang up like mushrooms at the time, were observed regardless of workability.

Similar bureaucratic practices existed in the operation of the national wire service (CTK) which, as a result, lagged hopelessly behind in furnishing news to its subscribers. The CTK was the primary source of foreign news for the nation's media; yet as late as 1955, eighty percent of its international news was taken verbatim from TASS.(17) During discussions prior to the journalists' Congress in the mid-1950's, the agency's slipshod reporting and lack of initiative were criticized in several articles. The authors of one of these pointed out that news about a meeting between Czechoslovak and Nepalese trade representatives was contained in a CTK dispatch which cited the *Hindustan Times* as its main source. What is also revealing is that *Rude pravo* (Red Right) and the Army's *Obrana lidu* (People's Defense) published the agency's report verbatim, while only *Zemedelske noviny* (Agricultural News) reworte it without giving any source.(18) The dispatch in question, the article continued, was issued only two days after the CTK was reproved for learning from a New York source about flood conditions in neighboring Austria.

Inherent in the Communists' creation of a new society was the mania for gearing individual work and overall production to explicit norms established by central planners who, in many cases, knew little if anything about the specific job or process involved. Such was the case, for example, in preparing copy for typesetters. Planners established norms designating the exact numbers of lines per page, precise length of each typewritten line and number of corrections allowed on every page of copy.(19) While much effort and time were wasted on such ventures, these norms were hardly ever fulfilled.

The bureaucratic measures described, plus other similar restrictions which gradually infiltrated the journalistic field, diminished the value of reporting to such an extent that the basic reporting of news was considered "beneath the dignity of journalists" who concentrated their efforts instead on propaganda, cultural affairs and other similar matters.(20) Investigative reporting could not even be contemplated for, under the existing state security laws, the practice was tantamount to spying. Only on special occasions, when events warranted the presence of journalists — public Party celebrations, political show trials or completion of major construction projects — did newsmen leave their desks. As a result, basic editorial departments, such as domestic political affairs, ceased to exist and were replaced by information departments whose members handled the sparse amount of hard news allowed to appear in the nation's daily press.

Implementation of Prior Censorship

Initially, the Party's influence (as opposed to direct control) over the press was maintained by the aforementioned compliance measures, or cadre safeguards, which proved sufficient at the time because the views of Party-appointed editors and Party leaders generally coincided. Top Party figures did not shield themselves from the public as much as they were to do in future years, making it possible for a relatively easy exchange of ideas and opinions between them and press representatives. Also, public opinion, in terms of the victorious class at least, remained in unison with that of the KSC vanguard during its initial months in power.

The apparent harmonious situation, however, began to deteriorate as Stalinist bureaucracy became more deeply entrenched, police terror spread and the principle of the Party's infallibility was more frequently proclaimed. A certain tension developed between the Party's leading circles and the press so that cadre safeguards and directives from above no longer sufficed. A method had to be found to control the press, radio, newsreel films and, eventually, television (experimental TV programing began in May 1953). The decision reached amounted to prior censorship which was enacted by a secret government ordinance, No. 17, on April 22, 1953.(21) The censorship agency, known as *Hlavni sprava tiskoveho dohledu* or HSTD (Chief Authority for Press Supervision), first became part of the general government administration but during 1954 was attached to the Ministry of the Interior.

The agency's authority was so extensive that it reached beyond the mass media to include in its scope publicly displayed photographs and posters, exhibitions, and publicity slogans. The HSTD, in the name of the Party, controlled virtually everything that was written or said for public consumption, even stage comics' "impromptu" remarks.(22) Outside of a small circle who knew the HSTD existed, the general public was oblivious of the agency's operations and, initially at least, tended to believe that writers, publicists and artists actually were expressing their own ideas. This was indeed true in certain cases; some of these individuals, a number of whom were later to become very much involved in the reform movement, did support the orthodox course pursued by the Party at the time. Such individuals were joined, of course, by older Communists afraid to oppose the trend and young opportunists whose careers were launched or advanced during this unstable period.(23)

Writer Ladislav Mnacko later described the metamorphosis of his own convictions from fully supporting the regime to opposing it: "I was a pioneering agitator, convinced about the fact that I was doing the right thing. But what broke me was the Slansky trial, in such a way that from that time onward I began to be a rebel. At least on a level that was possible."(24) The trial referred to by Mnacko was the most publicized of the political show trials conducted in Czechoslovakia during 1951-52. Party Secretary-General Rudolf Slansky, the alleged leader of a conspiracy against the Party and state, was sentenced to death along with ten of his thirteen codefendants, all Party functionaries. The other three were given life sentences.

The question that comes to mind is how could all this have happened? How was it possible for the highly developed fields of literature and journalism to be completely transformed, and writers and journalists coerced to such a degree as to allow the media to no longer be responsive to society but exist almost solely for the perpetuation of an adulterated ideal and the glorification of Party leaders? An explanation, understandably, lies not in a single reason alone but in several factors which all coalesced to create the oppressive situation that evolved. Some of the most important elements are:

1) One must understand, first of all, that a new order and an accompanying regimentation of society were implemented after the Communist victory. The Party leadership attempted to destroy almost overnight what remained of the Western-oriented political, economic and social systems but possessed only vague idealistic notions of what to construct in their place. "They were men of destruction," wrote Mnacko in describing the KSC leaders of this period, "and their historic role was to destroy the evil old world." They set out to remold their country with a "power neither their character nor training had prepared them for, power they did know how to use."(25) These leaders turned to the Soviet model to seek solutions for the creation of their people's democracy and the new Socialist man. The result was a profusion of pamphlets, disseminated by the thousands after 1948, on how to achieve goals and how to do things in a Socialist society. This mass of micro-literature, some of which dealt with various aspects of journalism, amounted to translations of outdated materials of Russian origin which were not applicable to the actual needs of Czechoslovak society.

2) Once realizing that the transplanting of Soviet concepts to Czechoslovak society was not producing the desired results, the new leaders became even more determined to succeed. This led them to use force and invoke the principle of Party infallibility in order to safeguard their positions and disguise their own ineptitudes and mistakes. The ultimate consequence for the entire society was rule by police terror which held everyone, including many leading functionaries, immobile in a grip of fear and led to the atrocities (such as the show trials) later described as breaches of Socialist legality and negative features of the personality cult. Moscow's direct interference in this state of confusion could not but help to make matters worse.

3) The nation's journalists and writers had undergone a series of purges. Starting during the German occupation and continuing after the Communist victory, this cleansing process greatly depleted the number of experienced working journalists. The few who did manage to endure were for the most part relegated to secondary positions with the vacuum filled by unseasoned journalists or *apparatchiki* who knew little and cared even less about professional practices but excelled in following orders. "Seldom did anyone ask about professional qualifications and still fewer times was concrete proof about journalistic experience requested," a critic wrote about the methods used to co-opt loyal Party members into editorial offices. "A cadre verification to the extent of 'He has a positive outlook toward the people's democratic order, and he hangs out flags,' often sufficed."(26) By 1956, fully 66.6 percent of the approximately 3,000 active SCSN members were no more than thirty-five years old and less than 11 percent had any journalistic experience prior to 1945.(27) Furthermore, editorial offices were filled with bureaucrats who never wrote for publication, resulting in classifications such as "writing" and "non-writing" journalists. The nation's press corps, therefore, proved to be malleable, readily dominated from above.

4) Adding to this situation was the simple but salient reality of job control. The state was the sole employer of all journalists and the SCSN the agency which kept them employed. Expulsion meant being deprived of one's livelihood. The Union, therefore, was able to easily dissuade any of its members from criticizing the status quo. There simply was nowhere else to turn. As a *Reporter* staff writer later explained:

> *This system demanded obedience. That means reliable people who will value the trust placed in them. And who values trust more, a talented person or one who otherwise would find it difficult to support himself? As it turned out, there was more 'reliability' in those who didn't want to lose their positions. Thus, professional revolutionaries were born. People are not stupid; they will learn the ropes.(28)*

The above factors combined to degrade the level of cultural output in general and the press in particular. As a result, people lost faith in the mass media and regarded journalists with indifference or contempt. The vast majority of the Czechoslovak public, once regarded as among the most avid press consumers in Europe, no longer read the daily press. The people turned their attention instead to books or concentrated their efforts, at great personal risk, on tuning in Western radio stations such as Voice of America (VOA), British Broadcasting Corporation (BBC) or Radio Free Europe (RFE).

The maxim "we don't need journalistic personalities," proclaimed as early as 1948 by Party spokesmen, prevailed and was reflected in newspapers which "lost above all their individuality, spoke the same language, published the same news, printed articles of an identical nature as it were (and) organized the same campaigns."(29) Most crucial for all concerned, perhaps, men and women working in editorial offices ceased to be journalists in the traditional sense and became instead merely transmitters of Party directives and propaganda.

End of an Era

Josef Stalin's death on March 5, 1953, followed by that of Gottwald within eight weeks, signaled the end of this oppressive era, even though remnants of the personality cult continued to plague the nation for years. The deaths of these men, nonetheless, proved to have a psychological effect on both the general public and the Party hierarchy. The elimination of these symbolic pinnacles of power served to diminish the people's fear (as seen, for example, in the outbreak of worker unrest in Pilsen during early June 1953(30)) and demoralized the Party hierarchy now headed by the lusterless figure of Novotny. Two other resultant changes were the KSC's modified view toward intellectuals and a reshuffle in government which saw the Ministry of Information replaced by the newly created Division of Press, Recording, Publishing and Book Distribution supervised directly by the cabinet.

The rather sudden change in the Party's attitude toward the intelligentsia became apparent during a speech given at the Central Political School of the Communist Party by Deputy Premier Vaclav Kopecky. He said in part:

> *We are now confronted by a situation where we have an insufficient number of people with college education and not enough graduate students. . . . I mention this in order to prove that we should respect the intelligentsia, and that we must, by all means, discard the damaging tendencies in our relationship with the intelligentsia. (31)*

Thus, certain events occurred which, though unheralded at the time, proved to be significant preconditions for the future improvement of journalistic standards and, what is more, the liberalizing course that later unfolded. During 1953, for instance, a department of journalism was created on the university level and the Institute for the Study of Journalism established in Prague. Its Slovak counterpart commenced activities the following year in Bratislava. The Institutes' basic tasks included the study of press history, press theory and the practical aspects of journalism, as well as cooperation in journalism education both at home and abroad. This new attitude also stimulated the dissemination of individual studies and the publication of new journals, namely *Novinarsky sbornik* and *Otazky zurnalistiky* (Questions of Journalism). The former was first issued in May 1956, the latter by the end of the decade. The journals, containing articles in both Czech and Slovak, constituted a forum for more or less scholarly discussions of problems pertaining to mass communication.

The department of journalism, later the Faculty of Enlightenment and Journalism of Charles University, had a definite impact on professionalizing the field. Started under the guidance of press historian Vladimir Klimes, the school provided the Czech media with people who knew not just how to follow directives and adhere to norms, but how to think and work like effective journalists. Though hindered at first in fully utilizing their acquired knowledge, such individuals eventually gained responsible positions which enabled them to assert a certain degree of influence during the 1960's, not only in terms of journalistic practices but in the orientation of their respective newspaper and broadcasting departments as well.

One of the university graduates, later active in Czechoslovak Radio, pointed out that journalism students were required to study at least two foreign languages, which afforded them the opportunity to absorb information from foreign sources. If students had the desire to read about certain aspects of the press abroad, he added, the necessary materials could nearly always be obtained. Besides, the scope of class lectures went beyond mere Marxist-Leninist dicta, including substantive information on Czech and Slovak press history and traditions.(32) (This of course became more pronounced as the teaching profession divested itself of some of the more stringent restrictions so prevalent during the early 1950's.) A Faculty of Journalism was also established at the Comenius University in Bratislava.

Another significant occurrence in the mid-1950's affecting the media was the fact that Czechoslovak authorities again permitted Western journalists to enter the country. None had been allowed to remain following the July 1951 trial of Associated Press correspondent William N. Oatis and his three Czech codefendants. Oatis had been arrested on April 23, charged with having conspired in acts of espionage and, at the conclusion of a two-day trial, sentenced to ten years in prison.(33) The American newsman did not regain his freedom until May 15, 1953.

Certain changes, limited as they were, also appeared in the nation's press. A few new publications were offered in the kiosks while individual journalists attempted to supplement the sterile gray diet tendered by the press with more interesting and realistic copy. In September 1955, for instance, the monthly *Kveten* (May) began publication as a voice of the less regimented younger generation of writers. The following year another monthly, *Svetova literatura* (World Literature), offered translations of foreign literary works. The publication served as a valuable source of creative trends abroad, including the West.

An example of the new type of journalism was a nine-part series published in *Kvety* (Blossoms) toward the end of 1955. The writer was a soft-spoken young Prague journalist who during 1968 became editor-in-chief of *Student,* weekly of the young intelligentsia. Alexej Kusak had embarked on a walking tour of the eastern-most part of his country, reporting on what he saw and experienced. One article in particular caused some stir and brought Kusak the undesirable distinction of official attention.

The article in question described life in a small village, situated just a few miles from the Soviet border, where the inhabitants existed in a rather primitive state. The village was not receiving any formal assistance from the local administration and only recently, with the help of a newly arrived teacher, had the villagers managed to dig a well. Previously, the only water source was the river. The former teacher, Kusak reported, had taken bribes so that village children did not have to attend school but could help in the fields instead.(34) As a result of his candid reporting, Kusak was called before the Party Central Committee's press section and reprimanded for failing to stress the positive aspects of Socialist society and told never to write such negative reports again. Just prior to this series, Kusak attempted to revive the traditional feuilleton genre, which had disappeared from the pages of the press, in an article dealing with the work of journalists.(35)

Meanwhile, the journalists' organization also began to stir. The SCSN statutes specified that the Union's highest body was the national congress to be convoked every four years. Since the last such congress had been held in 1948, the Union's leadership could stall no longer and during its annual membership meeting in September 1955 announced the scheduling of the Second Congress for the following June.

Actually, after the Party's closer supervision of the media and the introduction of censorship, the SCSN's role as a professional organization had deteriorated considerably so that only fifteen of the sixty-four officers elected some years earlier remained active.(36) The Union's Central Committee called for contributions from members in a discussion to determine the agenda for the upcoming Congress.

Signs of change seemed evident and an atmosphere of apprehensive anticipation spread throughout Czechoslovakia, as it did in all of Eastern Europe, waiting for some guideline from Moscow. Khrushchev obliged in due course with his denunciation of the personality cult.

The Brief Thaw and Its Aftermath

The day prior to the scheduled April 1956 writers' Congress, *Literarni noviny* published an article which served as an icebreaker in cutting through the blockage created by the freeze of the cult. The much discussed "What Wasn't in the Newspapers" represented Mnacko's personal confession, but it also constituted the symbolic testimony of all journalists and writers who had remained silent while knowing that the lives of innocent people were being ruined due to the incompetence of planners and highly placed Party *apparatchiki*.

To illustrate his point, Mnacko described events surrounding the construction of a foundry in Slovakia (where he served as a reporter at the time) which resulted in the loss of millions of crowns, disgrace for the chief engineer and the suicide of a young work brigade leader who had "lost faith in that for which he fought." Mnacko concluded his disclosure by beseeching his readers not to condemn and reproach him for becoming wise too late, but instead to "ask — as readers you have that right — demand of the journalist and writer: 'You are the public conscience! You are the public control! Once more we want to believe you. We are waiting — for your truthful word.' "(37) Mnacko's plea no doubt helped to bolster the courage of the writers participating in the Congress.

The previously discussed trend of criticism established during the writers' meeting continued after the Congress concluded. The students took up the cry for change by presenting to the Minister of Education a resolution which demanded improvements in the educational system, a more responsive and informative press, the importation of more periodicals from non-Socialist states and a halt to the jamming of foreign broadcasts.(38) For the first time in eight years, the students again were allowed to hold their traditional *Majales* (May Festival). Their procession in Prague included a group of gagged and blindfolded marchers representing the editors of the youth daily *Mlada fronta* (Young Front).

Although the national press reported the student activities and made references to the resolution, it failed to mention the specific provisions dealing with ideological questions or the students' quest for academic freedom. (Censorship was eased but not abolished during the brief thaw.) This shortcoming and other oversights by the press, however, were treated with typical Czech sarcasm in an article published by the writers' weekly: "If there were a contest for press 'modesty' and 'carefulness,' there is no doubt our press would win a place of honor. On numerous occasions when there were burning problems in the minds of people our press just blushed and said there was nothing to explain, (to) solve or to discuss."(39)

A similar barb, though less sharp in tone, was included in an article concerning the need for upgrading the press. "Problems, after all, do not fall from heaven. All those surrounding the Prague students' Majales, their discussions and mistakes certainly did not," the author wrote. "But our reader, if he is not a listener of western broadcasts, found out about them only because of a question posed by a foreign correspondent to the premier of our government."(40)

Criticisms of past actions, reevaluations of Party policy and attacks against the personality cult continued throughout the late spring and summer months, although Party leaders, once having recovered from the initial shock and confusion, never lost control of the situation as was the case in Hungary, for instance. Almost from the beginning, they urged caution and warned against the liberalizing trend going too far. This was aimed especially at the press, most pointedly the cultural press, as indicated by Novotny's statement in June 1956: "We definitely deny the independence of the press from the Party and its ideas."(41) Thus, gradually but firmly the regime began tightening the reins of control on the writers and those periodicals attempting to sustain the trend of change. The Hungarian uprising and subsequent Soviet intervention strengthened the Party's efforts in this direction.

Moreover, the journalists' Congress scheduled for June was postponed until the fall and, later, until the following spring because, as its chairman noted in 1960, "the atmosphere of 1956, as was sufficiently shown by the writers' congress, wasn't favorable."(42) At the time, however, the excuse provided by the Union's Central Committee was that "even though the pre-congress discussion has unfolded to an appreciable degree, preparations . . . are not of such a nature as to assure full success for the congress." The official announcement went on to specify that "little attention has been given to questions of ideology and the main tasks of the press, broadcasting and newsreel films have not been sufficiently examined."(43) When the Congress finally did convene, not one dissenting voice was raised. Novotny made certain by his presence.

Throughout the 1957-58 period, the Party, in an effort to reassert its full authority, launched a program designed to limit the liberalizing trend. And while the campaign helped to silence some of the more damaging criticism voiced against the regime, mere verbal threats failed to completely still the rumble of dissent. Individual writers and publications continued to utilize the personality cult issue as a protective shield to expose the Russification program faithfully executed by the KSC during the early 1950's.

When verbal admonitions failed to bring the more recalcitrant spokesmen to heed, the Party leadership demanded public self-criticism and statements of apology from them. The ultimate method used was dismissal from important posts. Thus, in preparation for the scheduled Congress of Socialist Culture in June 1959, a two-day writers' conference was hurriedly convened in March of the same year, the results of which not only served to halt liberalization but even reversed the trend, for the time being at least. Changes initiated during the meeting saw the revamping of the Union of Writers' Central Committee and its Presidium by dropping the liberal-minded writers elected to those bodies three years earlier and replacing them with hardliners, including some who had lost their posts in 1956. Similarly, a new chief editor was appointed for *Literarni noviny,* the writers' publishing house came under new management and the orientation of *Svetova literatura* was changed to conform with the Party's outlook. Finally, *Kveten* and *Novy zivot* (New Life), SCSS monthlies which had pursued the liberal trend, were abolished. The neo-Stalinist line sanctioned by the 1958 Party Congress was being fully implemented.

One may well ask why spring 1956 did not produce a phenomenon similar to that evident twelve years later. It should be remembered, though, that the outpouring of criticism and demands for change at the time were the products of a relatively small group of writers, journalists and students who failed to gain overt support from the still weary and apprehensive public. Nor did a viable liberal faction exist within the Party as was the case later. What is more, the Novotny regime maintained a firm grip on all the levers of power. Censorship, for example, had not ceased to function, enabling the Party to keep the nation's press, especially the dailies, under control, which was also the case with radio and television (the latter still in its infancy).

Further, the Soviet intervention in Hungary served as a major deterrent against any overt actions on the part of the dissenters who were decentralized and lacked the group cohesion which they later acquired. Novotny, therefore, was able to launch an effective counteroffensive against the liberalizing trend, thus squelching the possibility for any movement before it had a real opportunity to develop, gain momentum and, above all, attract wide public support. Nevertheless, the experiences of 1956, not only occurrences inside the country but also events in Poland and Hungary, proved to be a valuable lesson for the dissenters. It is true that repression continued for a time, but its force never again reverted to the level witnessed during the 1949-1954 period.

The new ideas and values brought forth by writers, journalists and students during the brief thaw that prevailed in spring 1956 served as the nucleus for the later reform movement. During the ensuing years, the idea of reform developed in the minds of men and women who, both as individuals and members of small groups, played a part in the overall exertion of influence and pressure against those in power while at the same time being subjected to varying degrees of repression from them. This conflict, which gradually unfolded and surfaced during the next decade, was most apparent in the broad field of culture, the nation's traditional battleground during periods of political oppression.

CHAPTER II
DE-STALINIZATION AND THE CULTURAL PRESS

By the onset of the 1960's, conditions had increasingly deteriorated inside the country, especially in the economy, with mismanagement, general inefficiency and public apathy caused by low morale all contributing to the stagnant national development. At the same time, a new liberal wave was emanating from Moscow where Khrushchev was proclaiming the principle of "peaceful co-existence" with the West and allowing the publication of anti-Stalinist works. Thus, both internal and external pressures gave rise to de-Stalinization in Czechoslovakia, accompanied by a liberal trend introduced from above in an effort to rejuvenate an inertia-plagued society. Along with the regime's decision to de-Stalinize came the revelation that the political purge trials of the early 1950's had represented a deformation of Socialist legality, and eventually scores of individuals condemned at the time were rehabilitated.

Taking full advantage of the Party leadership's defensive position, the intelligentsia spoke out against the remnants of dogmatism which had caused such aberrations and demanded that changes be implemented in the bureaucratic and centralized system impeding progress. At the forefront of this expressed discontent were the writers and liberal, primarily Slovak, journalists who, through their forthright criticism, opposed the regime's inept policies, especially those affecting culture and the literary and journalistic fields.

Through speeches and actions at their 1963 Congresses, the writers and journalists gave expression to demands for a more liberal atmosphere which would enable greater freedom in their work, thus setting in motion the reform movement which ultimately culminated in the Prague Spring. This, then, marked the beginning of a cultural revival which gradually adopted political overtones as the pressures for reform increasingly clashed with the regime's attempts to contain the introduced liberalism within the Party's designated boundaries.

Impetus for Change

The Twelfth Congress of the KSC, held during December 1962 (after being postponed in September), proved to be the signal, albeit a weak one, instituting the long-awaited de-Stalinization process in Czechoslovakia. Its importance can justifiably be compared to that of the epoch-making Fifth Congress in 1929, because the Twelfth Congress marked the start of a new era by opening the way for the reform movement just as the Fifth Congress had assured intensification in Bolshevizing the Party. Initially, however, the main thrust of the Twelfth Congress was the Party's reluctant consent to review the political trials of the 1949-54 period by officially acknowledging the earlier appointment of a commission, chaired by Presidium member Drahomir Kolder, for this purpose. The real issue concerned the rehabilitation of Slansky and his codefendants plus the public rehabilitation of scores of lesser purge trial victims, most of whom had been unostentatiously released from prison during preceding years.

Review of the trials represented the first major crack in the Novotny regime's defensive wall guarding the Stalinist past. For it should be noted that as late as November 1961, Novotny had rejected their review on grounds that a revision of the verdicts reached would be unjustified.(1) And, not until October 1962 did the Party leader see fit to order the removal of Stalin's statue, the largest of its kind in the world, which overlooked Prague from its massive pedestal high on a bank of the Vltava River. Its demolition, requiring the use of dynamite, was conducted only during night hours so as not to attract an excessive amount of public attention. Apparently, even top Party representatives could be afflicted with schweikism which at the time had "spread like a pest," according to the venerable writer Marie Majerova.(2)

Both internal and external pressures to de-Stalinize had intermittently been applied earlier, but the regime had stalled as long as it possibly could due to the fear that by relaxing control it would virtually open a Pandora's box. (This fear was well grounded as is evidenced by events that followed.) The main stimuli for ultimately permitting liberalization inside the country were the growing unrest on the domestic front,caused in the main by the regime's inability to adequately handle the pressing economic and political crises(3), and prodding from Moscow to fall into step with the more liberal line adopted at the Twenty-second Congress of the CPSU.

During the months prior to the Twelfth Congress, then, a certain amount of discussion focused on the consequences resulting from the persistent dogmatism of the personality cult era. This was evident, for instance, in a number of articles published during early spring which openly criticized the policy of film censorship even though the agency responsible, the Artistic Council of the Czechoslovak State Film, had been abolished. The author of one such article contended that concrete results of the agency's abolition would be realized by the public only in two or three years since all scripts for 1962 and some for 1963 had already been screened by the Council.(4) The general criticism concerned the censorhip of both domestic and foreign films.

On May 1, Prague students assembled at the statue of the nineteenth-century romantic poet Karel Macha to honor his memory as author of the poem "Maj" (May). The poetry reading, part of the traditional *Majales* festivities, turned into a demonstration during which students, along with young workers and onlookers, chanted anti-regime slogans. The protest, dispersed by police, constituted the first open sign of student unrest since the nonviolent demonstrations of May 1956 and prompted other similar spontaneous outbursts of dissent.

Among early indicators of a possible policy change was a critical article in the June 1962 issue of the Party's theoretical journal, *Nova mysl* (New Thought), which reviewed the course pursued by the nation following the adoption of the Socialist constitution less than two years earlier. Although the writer attempted to maintain a positive tone and preached the need to act responsibly within a framework of democratic centralism, the article nevertheless was apologetic for the "difficulties" and "inadequacies" incurred and spoke of "errors" having been committed. More important, it acknowledged the growing domestic unrest by citing the thousands of letters and personal appeals for redress directed by working people to local and top Party organizations and personalities, including Novotny himself. Many of these appeals were also sent in the form of letters to the Party press. Stating that self-criticism alone was insufficient to correct mistakes, the article called for the creation of proper conditions for general criticism and suggested that its suppression constituted an intolerable vice, citing instances where people, for criticizing correctly, were harassed and transferred to other jobs.(5)

While the Twelfth Party Congress proved to be disappointing to those anticipating an immediate and extensive expurgation of the residue of Stalinism from the established system, its general aura nonetheless had a delayed reaction on Czechoslovak society so that during 1963 it "produced an even greater confidence of public utterance and an even broader and deeper stream of criticism." This meant that "Party members, notably the writers and journalists, courageously asserted their own viewpoints, in opposition to that of the leadership, and began to give sharper . . . expression to their feelings of guilt and remorse and their outrage at the slowness of change."(6) During the month of the Party Congress, *Nova mysl* again assailed the evident formalism and bureaucracy in state organizations, while some three months later the same writers teamed up once more to support the already enunciated need to provide trained non-Party comrades with responsible positions in various aspects of general production.(7)

In the meantime the cultural press, taking full advantage of the wedge created by the KSC Congress, intensified its criticism of the dogmatic practices still evident in everyday life and, especially, in the field of culture. Beginning with articles carried by the writers' publications at the onset of 1963, the flow of criticism continued through the early spring and peaked during the meetings of Slovak writers and journalists held in April and May, respectively. The trend progressed through the remainder of the year and into 1964 when the Novotny regime, mindful of the intensity and scope which the criticism had reached, once again employed administrative methods to ease the pressures being applied against it. This confrontation between pressures from below and repression from above established the wave-like pattern which saw the distance between trough and crest gradually increase as the reform movement, coalesced primarily around the writers and their publications, began resolutely testing the limits of its confines.

Ferment Among the Writers

Preparations for the writers' Third Congress, scheduled for May 22-24, 1963, were initiated during the previous summer and coinsided with final arrangements for the Party's Twelfth Congress. The discussion which unfolded was unmistakably liberal in tone and reflected an expectation for change in the regime's orientation. The writers hoped for some movement toward a more relaxed atmosphere, similar to that sanctioned by Khrushchev in the Soviet Union.

It should be recalled that during the Soviet Party's Congress in October 1961, the chief editor of the liberal journal *Novy mir* (New World), poet Aleksandr Tvardovsky, had called upon his fellow writers to state the whole truth. It was this appeal which encouraged the then unknown teacher Aleksandr Solzhenitsyn to submit his memorable manuscript *One Day in the Life of Ivan Denisovich* to Tvardovsky's magazine. The poignant account of life in a Stalinist concentration camp was published in *Novy mir's* December 1962 issue as "the first totally uncensored work of high literary standard with a controversial content critical of the (Soviet) society."(8) It was a time when literary realism and anti-Stalinist poetry and prose were on the ascent inside Soviet Russia, a situation not overlooked by the writers of Eastern Europe.

The pre-Congress discourse by Czechoslovak writers peaked during the prepartory meeting of the Slovak section held in Bratislava on April 22, 1963, less than three weeks after the KSC's Central Committee had convened to hear and act upon the Kolder Commission report which declared that the political trials constituted a breach of Socialist legality. (The report was not made public until the latter part of August. However, by means of Party meetings, its contents became known to the rank and file and soon filtered to the general public.) As a result, the Party leadership initiated a major reshuffle in its hierarchy which saw Dubcek replace Karol Bacilek as First Secretary of the Communist Party of Slovakia. Bacilek, who during 1952-53 had served as Minister of State Security, was deeply implicated in the political trials. Also dropped from the Presidium was deputy secretary Pavol David, whom Mnacko later described as the real ruler of Slovakia and the writers' greatest adversary.(9)

The nature of the speeches heard at the Bratislava conference, as well as the organizational matters dealt with, clearly indicated that the Slovak writers were setting forth on a new path. Laco Novomesky, expelled from the Union in 1951, was fully reinstated while poet Karol Rosenbaum, a liberal, attained the chairmanship of the Union of Slovak Writers (SSS). The writers' publishing house came under new management and a new chief editor was named for *Kulturny zivot* (Cultural Life), the Slovak writers' official weekly, which printed articles about the meeting as well as texts of the main speeches presented.

Setting the tone for this coverage of the conference, the new chairman referred to events surrounding the April Party plenum as having "a significant meaning for the moral healing of both society and literature" and a character, "let's not be afraid to say it, of revolution." Rosenbaum concluded by telling his readers that voices raised during the conference were "our soul, our conscience. We promised ourselves. . .that we want to be socialist people, and socialist writers of our people. We all wish that the wave of enthusiasm and activity won't fall by the wayside but will change into a significant creative act."(10) His introductory commentary was followed by contributions from Novomesky, Mnacko, academician Michal Chorvath and Czech representative Jiri Hajek, all appearing under the headline "Literature in the Battle for Truth."

What the Slovak writers had undertaken through their published speeches was to inform the reading public that they, the writers, were wiping their own slates clean. They also attempted to present to the nation the plight of the Slovak people by revealing the unjust and harsh methods employed against Slovak Communists by the regime in Prague. In short, they desired equal recognition for the Slovak minority within the Socialist state. This coincided with the general campaign of the Communist Party of Slovakia (KSS), in which the local Party press took part, over the unresolved issue of the Slovak question.

Thus, in his published address, Chorvath traced the history of *DAV*, an avant-garde literary movement of Slovak intellectuals active during the interwar period, whose foremost representatives were defendants at the trials of the so-called bourgeois nationalists in the early 1950's. Chorvath maintained that since the Kolder report had established the innocence of those tried, there never existed any truth to the charges brought against them. It is likely that Chorvath's contribution and other articles dealing with the same issue were attempts to force the Party leadership into fully rehabilitating the Slovak victims, something which the regime was still hestitant to do.(11)

During mid-June, for instance, Novotny used the occasion of an important speech before a Party *activ* (meeting) in Kosice to proclaim that criticism issued against bourgeois nationalism during the Ninth Congress of the Communist Party of Slovakia in 1950 "was in essence correct."(12) He further maintained that, in the eyes of the Party at least, men such as Gustav Husak and Novomesky remained guilty for disrupting the principles of Party unity and for failing to carry out the Party's program.

In his speech to the writers, Mnacko focused on an open letter he had written in 1956 to Deputy Premier Kopecky. The letter was to have been printed in *Kulturny zivot* but was arbitrarily withdrawn at the last moment, although most Czech and Slovak writers had favored its publication. In his preamble to the letter, finally published as part of the writers' conference proceedings, Mnacko referred to Kaplicky who, during the writers' Congress in 1956, had revived the principle of the writer as the nation's conscience. "Kaplicky is dead," wrote Mnacko, "but his name . . . can be considered as a symbol of those forces which unleashed the development and spirit within the Party and even in everyday life, and whose revival we are living through today."(13)

Mnacko, at the time completing his revealing anti-cult book *Delayed Reports,* portions of which began appearing in *Kulturny zivot* less than a month after the conference, had anticipated the year of ferment with his article "Conscience." Published in the Slovak writers' weekly, this forceful account, based on real events, revolved around man and his conscience during the Stalinist years. One episode, the trial and conviction of the chairman of a cooperative, ended with the trial judge calling the condemned man into his chamber and confessing: " 'I know that you are not guilty, but I had to do it.' "(14) The bold attack against the cult's "rape of legality," to use the writer's own words, renewed Mnacko's attempt of 1956 to revive the moral meaning of conscience not only among writers and journalists but within society at large.

The link between the Slovak writers and their Czech colleagues in forging a united front for reform was the presence of Hajek who appeared at the Slovak writers' conference as an official representative of the SCSS Central Committee. During his address, Hajek acknowledged the severe persecution of Slovak literature in the past, even after 1956, but noted that while the creative output of the younger generation of Czech writers had stagnated, Slovak literature was on the ascent. The present meeting and the fact that its major contributions would be published, he concluded, "signifies a new era in Czechoslovakia."(15)

While Slovak writers were making amends with the past and attempting to gain full recognition of not only their culture but also the injustices to which Slovaks had been subjected, their Czech counterparts also confronted the authorities on the path toward cultural reform. One of the first articles in this respect was printed in the December 1962 issue of *Plamen* (Flame), an SCSS monthly started three years earlier. The author, chief editor Hajek, used the recently completed Twelfth Congress of the KSC as an opportunity to hold Party leaders accountable for their words by asserting that while Czechoslovakia might well possess a world record for the number of proclamations made against dogmatism, the phenomenon nevertheless continued to exist. "This seemingly 'unseen' dogmatism continues to narrow the space of experimentation which is the first condition for any kind of development."(16)

A few days later, literary critic Milan Schultz joined the attack by predicting that during 1963 "everyone will have to express his own view" because "people won't be able to hide behind a 'collective' opinion. Newsmen will be bound to express their own (even the sharpest) judgments and those citizens or institutions criticized . . . will be bound to tell their standpoints, their own views."(17) It is interesting that Schultz's reference to newsmen and the response of those criticized, particularly institutions, was in principle at least similar to sections of the press law enacted a few years later.

The following month Eduard Goldstucker, while attempting to resurrect the works of Franz Kafka to their rightful place in Czech literature, outlined the writer's future role in his confrontation with the status quo:

> *The value of the critic's (and writer's) social involvement cannot be measured by the extent of his willingness to accept initiative from the outside. It must be measured by his ability to answer, on the basis of his own concept of social responsibility, the questions which occupy his mind and those of his readers. It seems that social responsibility will prove of extraordinary importance in the coming period. For it will determine the manner in which criticism (and creativity) will treat the expanding horizon of freedom whose contours are beginning to emerge from the mist.*

And, anticipating the coming era of humanist socialism, Goldstucker, a victim of the purge trials, concluded his article with a plea for the restoration of humanism in the practical application of theory to everyday life:

> *If history of our time has proved anything beyond a shadow of a doubt, it is that everyone was fatally wrong who believed that a new and higher social order could be created without the benefit of humanism and justice and that great human achievements in any field could be indefinitely loudly advocated in theory, while being trampled upon in fact. (18)*

The writers' demands for a more liberal course were immediately countered with words of caution and implied threats from the Party leadership. During a March speech before a Party *activ* in Ostrava, for example, Novotny warned against the infiltration of "bourgeois liberalism" into the nation's culture and sanctimoniously restated the principle of the Party's infallibility: "We need criticism like salt, like our daily food. But no one can touch our Communist Party, its program (and) our socialist system. That has to be and must remain for everyone holy." He then continued: "We don't want to oppress cultural life. But the Party reserves the right that as it directs the entire life of the nation, it similarly directs cultural activity."(19) Even earlier, during festivities marking the fifteenth anniversary of the 1948 putsch, the Party chief sarcastically referred to dissenting intellectuals as "clairvoyants" who claimed to have known "all the evils of the cult at the time of their commitment."(20)

Amidst this exchange of charges and criticism between Party leaders and the nation's reform-minded writers came the aforementioned Congress of Slovak writers and, within a month (May 22-24, 1963), the Third Congress of the SCSS. And while the atmosphere surrounding the latter was less electrifying and the speeches of its participants more realistic and less emotional than those of the former Congress, its general mood nevertheless did revive the spirit of 1956 and, in the end, proved to be more decisive and lasting. This was seen, for example, in concessions gained by the writers from the Party, particularly in the internal structure of their organization.

More than one half (24 out of 45) of the newly elected SCSS Central Committee members were newcomers to the body and many were backers of the liberal trend or at least moderates. Although the previous chairman, Ivan Skala, managed to retain his post, the three deputy secretaries, including the chief editor of *Literarni noviny,* Josef Rybak, were deposed. They were replaced in turn by Mnacko and Karel Ptacnik, both avowed adherents of liberalization, and Ivan Kriz, whose earlier orthodox views toward literature apparently had been modified.(21) Thus, the new deputies were able to counter-balance Skala's conservative position within the leadership.

The Congress' outcome, moreover, had a definite impact on the future course of literature. The meeting's general spirit again underscored the motto of the Second Congress (the writer is his nation's conscience), condemned once and for all dogmatism and conservatism in literature, and sought greater freedom for the nation's writers. This was succinctly stated in poet Jiri Sotola's summation of the Congress in *Nova mysl.* Maintaining that the speeches heard were not mere shallow manifestations of anti-dogmatism but constituted precise and penetrating analyses, Sotola declared that "it will be very difficult to turn back in literature, even if the will to do so were to still reveal itself somewhere."(22) He may well have subsumed in this reference to the "will" the chairman's speech which was intended to divert the writers from their desired purpose.

In his commentary, Sotola expressed the writers' feelings on the need for a more diverse and widely circulated cultural press, including new literary publications to replace those which no longer reflected the times. In addition, he outlined the writers' dissatisfaction with the direction of *Literarni noviny,* under the control of Party-installed editor Rybak since 1959. The Union's outgoing leadership was also chastised for having an undue concern with organizational and administrative matters rather than dealing with ideology and the arts. As an example, Sotola presented the suspension of *Kveten* which, he said, was the result of a superficial and unnecessarily hasty search for administrative solutions.(23) Finally, he emphasized the Congress' legacy as the writers' wish to pursue the stated mission of their organization: to strive for excellence in literary creation.

The writers' 1963 Congress thus upheld the nationalistic and reformist spirit revived during the previous Congress in 1956. The Third Congress also vigorously condemned the remnants of conservatism and dogmatism which continued to restrict the nation's cultural life. And while the writers retained a realistic outlook, by acknowledging the Party's primacy in society, they made it clear that literature could no longer be fashioned into a mere political tool under the Party's influence or exhortation, or that the writers alone could overcome negative aspects in the cultural sphere caused by deformities in the past. "Only the Communist party, truly the directive center of our public life, has sufficient authority to overcome conflicts and misunderstandings with the past."(24) The writers, therefore, held the Party leadership responsible for creating better conditions in which literature and other cultural fields could develop more freely.

Through their renewed activities, the liberal writers thus gave substance to the framework of reform which they had conceived in 1956. In their criticism of the regime and demands for change, they presented a generally united front which served as a focal center of dissent and an impetus for further liberalization.

Slovak Journalists Speak Out

The impact of the writers' Congress had hardly begun to reverberate throughout the nation when a forceful response came during a Congress of Slovak journalists held May 27-28 in Bratislava. More than forty participants ascended the speaker's rostrum to each in turn voice opinions and make demands, which together amounted to a unanimous and uncompromising stand against remnants of the personality cult. The most direct and incisive of the speeches came from a former editor of *Pravda* (Truth), Miro Hysko, who at the time was professor of journalism at the Philosophical Faculty of Comenius University.

Pursuing a theme touched upon by Slovak writer Zora Jesenska a few days earlier,(25) Hysko accused Prime Minister Vilem Siroky of having initiated the entire damaging campaign against bourgeois nationalism with his report to the Ninth Congress of the KSS in May 1950 whose conclusions could be regarded as *"the beginning of the familiar reprisals against prominent Communist workers in the entire republic."* Then, turning to the press, Hysko condemned what he termed the "anti-Leninist methods" and "administrative and even illegal intervention" which had been employed against intrinsic principles of the Socialist press, its partisanship and truthfulness. He further asserted:

> *It is our urgent task to reappraise the activity of Slovak journalism during the entire era that was affected by anti-Leninist norms in the life of our society, the era that lasted roughly from 1949 to 1962. For, and this is a well-known fact, the promisingly developing process of revival, begun by our country after the 20th Congress of the CPSU,* was impeded by authoritative intervention *from the end of 1956 onward and, instead of a real struggle against dogmatism, only the fight against revisionism as the main danger developed.*

Hysko concluded his address by maintaining that "as the soldier must obey only an order not in conflict with the law, similarly, the *socialist journalist should respect only those directives which are not in conflict with the fundamental principles of socialist morality."*(26)

Hysko's speech was unprecedented in the Communist regime's accepted procedure. For not only was it afforded added credence by being published in an official Party organ — *Pravda* — but, more specifically, it included a personal attack against a still active top Party functionary. (Siroky was both Prime Minister and a member of the Party's Presidium at the time.) Furthermore, Hysko explicitly called for a review of journalism in terms of Leninist norms for a period covering practically all the years of Communist rule, including those under Novotny.

Besides the critical speeches, the newsmen also staged what can be construed as an act defying the Prague regime by honoring, with a minute of silence, the memory of three victims of the Stalinist years — Vladimir Clementis, Andre Simone and Ivan Horvath. Although Clementis had been similarly acknowledged earlier by the Slovak writers, this marked the first time that Simone and Horvath had been publicly recognized as purge victims. Simone, executed along with Clementis and other members of the Slansky group, was not a Slovak but received recognition for his journalistic career which included a post on the editorial staff of *Rude pravo.* Horvath had died in prison while serving a twenty-two year sentence for bourgeois nationalist deviations.

The Slovak journalists, as the writers had done before them, also strove to make amends with the past. This took the form of letters sent by the Congress to both Novomesky and Husak, leading Slovak representatives of surviving victims of the purge trials, apologizing for the manner in which the Slovak press had vilified them. The participants moreover decided not to award any further state prizes bearing the name of Kopecky, the one-time Minister of Information and editor of *Rude pravo.* The action was undoubtedly prompted by Hysko's speech which heavily implicated Kopecky in the proceedings surrounding the purge trials. In essence, those present at the journalists' Congress desired to convince the public, as well as themselves perhaps, that they were done with the past at last.

The spirit displayed by the Slovak newsmen gained them support from *Kulturny zivot* which represented, at the time, the foremost voice of the reform movement. The weekly carried reports of the Congress and used the occasion to extend the journalists' discussion into the broader sphere of the future task of the nation's press. It was thus learned that, at the Bratislava Congress, Adolf Hradecky, a leading representative of the SCSN (and later its chairman), had criticized the nationwide journalists' Fourth Congress held in Prague a month earlier (April 22-23).

According to the *Kulturny zivot* article, Hradecky was especially critical of the Czech journalists for failing to discuss questions and solve existing problems which should have been considered. In an apparent effort to save face before the Slovak audience, however, he indicated that had the SCSN Congress been convened a month later, its general spirit would have approximated that of the current Bratislava meeting.(27) It is difficult to tell, though, whether or not a later Prague Congress would have reflected the true spirit of the moment since the overt fervor for reform during spring 1963 had been seized primarily by Slovak liberals. The SCSN Congress had generally adhered to the prescribed Party line as expressed by

Chairman Dolejsi with the only seeming ray of hope being the presence of Cestmir Cisar, a liberal-minded Party secretary and editor of *Nova mysl,* who nonetheless stuck to the old formula in his address — the model for the nation's print media was the press of the Soviet Union.(28)

In all fairness, however, it must be said that the SCSN leadership had debated certain issues at the time, but they were not resolved until the mid-1960's. This concerned the enactment of a new press law, creation of a news magazine and improvement of the journalist's performance and status. In 1963, however, Slovak journalists were far more vocal and active in demanding press reform than were their Czech counterparts.

Further reaction to the stand taken by journalists at the Bratislava Congress came from Pavol Stevcek, chief editor of *Kulturny zivot.* After referring to past travails and errors, Stevcek focused on the newly emerging era. "Newspapers cannot be merely a passive mirror of public opinion," he wrote, "they should be its formulator. They cannot merely speak about things, but are responsible for speaking to them." He contended that the spirit of the Twentieth Congress of the CPSU did not constitute a mere phrase but an act for all Party functionaries to follow, meaning the rehabilitation of such concepts as truth, legality, honor and morality. "The creation of our newspapers is nothing less than the creation of truth."(29)

It did not take long for the Party leadership to react by attempting to diminish the political significance of the journalists' and writers' actions and to discredit their evident leading role in the revival process. Thus, even *Pravda,* less than two weeks after publishing Hysko's speech, was forced to print a polemic which accused Hysko, as well as other liberal journalists and writers, of having "violated Party discipline" by publicly disclosing confidential Party information. This referred to the material discussed at the April 1963 plenum of the Party's Central Committee. "Such behavior has created the impression that it is the writers and journalists who are in the forefront of the struggle to eliminate the consequences and residue of the cult of personality," the article stated. "In actual fact, however, it is the Party that has been and still is the spearhead of the process of revival and . . . has settled and expressed what some comrades, like comrade Hysko, pass off before the public as their discoveries."(30) Hysko had obviously touched upon sensitive aspects of the established system.

Unlike 1956, however, Novotny's position had been weakened and, as a result, these initial warnings were not effective enough to either silence the dissenters or reverse the trend. The floodgates of criticism had finally been unsealed from their rusty hinges and could not be jammed back into place. The liberalization process had been allowed to proceed further than had been intended and the movement toward change continued while Party leaders vainly attempted to contain it within their control.

The Regime Reacts

Before exploring the leadership's reaction to the impact of de-Stalinization on the cultural press, it is important to note that following the Twelfth Congress of the KSC in December 1962, the Czech cultural weekly *Kultura* (Culture) and its Slovak counterpart *Predvoj* (Vanguard) were discontinued. They were replaced by *Kulturni tvorba* (Cultural Creation), a weekly devoted to culture and politics published by the Committee of Socialist Culture. *Kultura,* established in 1957, had been a constant irritant to the regime which frequently attacked its contents and contributors during the hunt for signs of revisionism. The change thus reflected the Party's implementation of certain safeguards to counterbalance de-Stalinization and also represented a step toward centralizing the cultural press.

One source of the conflict between *Kultura* and the Party leadership was that following the suspension of *Kveten,* a number of its staff members, including Josef Skvorecky and Arsen Pohribry, found refuge in the editorial offices of *Kultura.* Also, the weekly was the first publication during Communist rule which had not been specifically designated as an organ of an official organization or mass association. It was published by the Orbis publishing concern.

The intended tightening of the Party's reins over the cultural press backfired, however, since *Kulturni tvorba,* along with *Kulturny zivot* and *Literarni noviny,* became a vocal proponent of reform during the initial revival period. Indicative of *Kulturni tvorba's* liberal orientation was the removal of its chief editor, Miroslav Galuska, from his post in summer 1964 and the reassignment of the paper as an organ of the Party's Central Committee. Galuska, who had served as CTK's New York correspondent during 1951-52 and then as press chief at the Ministry of Foreign Affairs, later became Minister of Culture and Information in the Dubcek administration.

Repeated criticism of the nature of the cultural rebirth had been issued by regime spokesmen almost from the onset of de-Stalinization. The leadership's full indignation, however, culminated in a major document, "The Mission and Status of Cultural Periodicals," which appeared in Party publications during April 1964. It seemed evident that Novotny's patience had been exhausted by the writers' onslaught and, beginning to consolidate political strength once more after the Party reshuffle in 1963, he was bent on reasserting the Party's unquestioned supremacy in all major spheres of endeavor, including culture.(31)

The document, representing an official position paper of the KSC Central Committee, stemmed from debates during the Committee's December 1963 plenum, was discussed by its Ideological Commission the following February and was finally approved by the Presidium in March. Painstakingly enumerating the most serious errors committed and carefully delineating the correct procedures to be followed by the publications in question, their editors and respective sponsoring organizations, the document was intended as the ultimate directive for the cultural press. The Party chief's remarks soon after its release made this explicit: "We will judge comrades in the cultural periodicals according to the stand they adopt to this Party evaluation."(32)

Although the position paper was directed toward all cultural periodicals, those especially signaled out were *Kulturny zivot, Literarni noviny, Kulturni tvorba* and, to a lesser extent, *Plamen.* The first three mentioned represented a weekly press run of 284,500 copies out of a combined single press run, including all significant cultural periodic publications, of nearly one half million issues.(33) Other periodicals named in the indictment were *Host do domu* (Guest for the House), *Divadlo* (Theater) and *Vytvarna prace* (Graphic Work).

In no uncertain terms, the document condemned the liberalism displayed and condoned by the cultural press, going so far as to charge that some articles published could not be construed as anything else but "*a manifestation of opposition to the Party's policies.*"(34) It also referred to specific objectionable articles and cited by name those individuals considered the most serious offenders, thus marking them as persons whose future contributions required more careful screening or whose submitted manuscripts were to be confiscated and further publication prevented. The latter was the case with philosopher Ivan Svitak. Others mentioned besides Svitak were Stevcek, Evzen Loebl (one of the surviving victims of the Slansky trial), writers Ivan Klima and Antonin Liehm and poet Milan Hubl.

Employing such telling phrases as "snobbism of an intellectual," "the mobilizaton of negative elements," and "anarchistic tendencies," the document decried the periodicals' neglect to criticize specific published works from the accepted ideological standpoint, tendency to leave discussions open and thus allegedly confuse the reader, and failure to condemn kowtowing before the influence of bourgeois culture. The editorial offices, meanwhile, were held responsible for failing to examine rigorously enough questionable and immature materials and for keeping silent about expressed liberal tendencies, thus in essence tolerating them and providing them undue publicity.

But more important, the evaluation revealed that on several occasions articles containing "serious mistakes in content and ideology" were not published due to "intervention from outside editorial offices. These interventions . . . were subsequently discussed with editorial staffs, but seldom was a common agreement on views reached."(35) This was not only a clear admission of prior censorship but, moreover, an indication that editors were contesting such actions, even after they had been taken, thus opposing Party discipline and placing their positions and themselves in jeopardy. Accusations also arose over the matter of publicizing Western cultural trends at the expense of cultural activities in the Soviet Union and other Socialist states.

In outlining its demands, the Party laid the full responsibility for professional and ideological standards on the chief editors and, further, ordered the leaderships of the creative unions to take a more active and positive part in directing the orientation of their publications. "The Party's direction is based on mutual trust," which means, the document continued, "that editorial staffs and especially chief editors must fully realize that the trust of the Party's Central Committee in their ability and will to serve the Party carries with it the demand for greater responsibility and fastidiousness in employing the Party line in their periodicals." And, addressing itself to members of the KSC in the creative unions and editorial offices, the directive stressed the Party's right to demand from them, as Communists, "adherence to the Party's discipline, self-sacrifice and active participation in the struggle to fulfill the Party's decisions."(36)

The document's release was followed closely by Novotny's Banska Bystrica speech in which he left no doubt as to the consequences should the directive be disregarded: "There is only one party discipline and it is binding on everyone. And whoever thinks that he can interpret his party privileges and duties as he likes, we tell him beforehand to rather leave the party now before the party says good-by to him."(37) The gauntlet had been thrown and it was left up to the cultural press to respond to the challenge.

The Cultural Press Holds Firm

In its April 11 issue, *Literarni noviny* indicated general acceptance of the Party's evaluation and the criticism it entailed. The reply, however, reflected a commitment to change rather than the demanded uncompromising submission. Chief editor Sotola, author of the response, made this clear when he said that his comments did not mean a "desertion of the complexity of problems with which these periodicals have dealt . . . neither does it mean a return to the noncommital and passive attitude which fills the papers with materials that cause no criticism due to their uninteresting, toothless (and) empty character."(38) The Slovak writers followed much the same format, with their Union's Central Committee acknowledging that it had discussed the document.

The collective staff of *Kulturny zivot*, in a statement of defiance and independence which took almost a month before being released, held fast to its position by openly rejecting the document's criticism: "We are convinced that, basically, we have acted correctly. . . . Nothing could be more comfortable, but at the same time more irresponsible and immoral, than to accept this criticism repentantly and especially formally, as used to be the case in similar circumstances." Referring to the positive work of the cultural press, which the evaluation only cursorily mentioned, the weekly maintained it was solely from this standpoint that it accepted the document. To further emphasize its defiance, the staff promised not to abandon its contributors and underscored the pledge by including in the same issue works from some of the more outspoken and controversial figures of the period. Then, in conclusion, the staff declared:

> *The Leninist politics of our party, the tendencies of the development of our current life, provides us with great but by no means easy opportunities. We will avail ourselves of them with all the rights (and duties) afforded socialist citizen-journalists, writers (and) cultural workers, with the exception of one right which we voluntarily give up: the right to be indifferent. (39)*

It was apparent that the cultural press would no longer compliantly accept the total and arbitrary control of the Novotny regime. The thrust for change, initiated somewhat prematurely in Prague during 1956, had thus seven years later been seized upon by Slovak writers and journalists who set out to defy the established rulers by taking full advantage of de-Stalinization as an impetus for reform. And although administrative measures were directed against the writers (both editors of the writers' weeklies were removed, for instance), the full impact of liberalization could not be arrested. The decision to de-Stalinize had opened the gates of concrete and serious criticism and stimulated a powerful force of dissent from among the intellectuals, placing the regime on the defensive as all the major problems confronting the nation's leadership — economic, political, cultural, national, ideological — suddenly came to a head and began escaping the firm grasp of the regime's control.

Their denunciation of past deformities and forceful demand for change helped the Czech and Slovak writers to formalize a united stand against constraints in culture and arbitrariness of rule which, in effect, gave expression to the reform movement, an effort to create a freer existence not only in culture but in everyday life as well. In this respect, the cultural press, especially the writers' weeklies, served as the primary channel for the expression of criticism and exertion of pressures against the Party leadership.

Though the Novotny regime attempted to curb the dissent voiced by the cultural press, the silencing of criticism and suppression of opposition proved to be far more difficult in 1964 than it had been in 1956. The constant pressure of the regime on the writers and the cultural press only helped to strengthen their positions as oppositional forces which continued to defy the leadership and exert countering pressures against it. This continuous confrontation placed the writers and their press at the forefront of the reform movement.

The extensive and repeated criticism by the Party showed in effect that editorial staff collectives, especially those of cultural periodicals, formed what can be described as small interest groups which were crystallizing their dissenting views by means of repeatedly confronting the Novotny regime on issues dealing with cultural, economic and social problems. This, in essence, constituted political action, which must be viewed in light of the traditional role of culture and the writer in the nation's politics.

Thus, *Literarni noviny, Kulturny zivot* and *Kulturni tvorba* were fashioned by their respective staffs into what can be construed as opinion weeklies which frequently defied the regime on specific policy issues and, as a result, were regarded as the opposition by it. As Liehm so clearly stated:

> *Whenever people are deprived of political rights, whenever a society lacks a functioning political system commensurate with its level of development, then culture takes over the role normally played by politics. And culture continues to perform political tasks until normal political processes are restored. (40)*

This had been the case repeatedly in the past and came to the fore again during the 1960's. "The pen became the weapon and paper the battleground," a Czech journalist later observed of this period. "Writing became an act of confession and repentance, rebellion and pacification, exacerbation and purification. Here was the non-violent but deafening clash between ideals cherished and ideals betrayed, between fiction disguised as truth and truth concealed by fictitious lies."(41)

The writers were aided in their efforts by an awakening public opinion which was stimulated not only by events surrounding the de-Stalinization process but also by Western broadcasts. This increasing influence of Western transmissions and their effect on the press, radio and television in Czechoslovakia contributed to the varying degrees of dissent displayed by the mass media.

CHAPTER III

THE COMMUNICATIONS EXPLOSION AND ITS IMPACT

The communications boom emanating from the West during the latter part of the 1950's gained full force in the early years of the next decade. Marked by such characteristics as the transistor radio, rapidly expanding television transmission and global communication via satellite, this mounting flow of information knew no national boundaries or ideological demarcation lines. As a result, its impact was felt virtually throughout the world, including in Communist Czechoslovakia where it had a positive effect in gradually improving the information function of the mass media.

Meanwhile, the aforementioned economic doldrums induced the Party leadership to initiate friendlier relations with Western states in order to gain new technological and scientific information, stimulate tourism and improve trade. For the isolation to which the nation had been subjected had greatly hindered its progress, especially in terms of new production methods and technology. Other forms of exchange, primarily in the cultural field, soon followed.

Furthermore, the cessation of the jamming of Western radio broadcasts enhanced the freer flow of news inside the country. The news-hungry Czechoslovak public could not help but compare the type of reports provided by its own media with the scope of reporting evident in Western broadcasts. The obvious differences in quality and content between the foreign and domestic stations soon became a source of embarrassment for the Novotny regime, because often nonpolitical internal events (such as railway accidents) were not mentioned by the domestic media but were reported by foreign stations. Thus, the regime was finally forced to allow the nation's news media to become more information conscious and to diversify content in order to be more attractive to the public. This coincided closely with demands made by journalists for more responsible reporting and programing.

The new trends displayed by the mass media posed problems for the regime, however, because the media, with their newly gained incentive to be more creative and responsive, often exceeded prescribed bounds in their discussion of the negative aspects and shortcomings evident in Socialist society. The Party leadership, as a result, found itself in a somewhat difficult position. While it desired the media to be more informative and credible, the leadership nevertheless felt it was necessary, for reasons of self-preservation, to continue controlling media activities and regulating their content. This conflict of interest continued to be reflected in the ensuing phases of liberalization inside the country.

Increased Information from the West

In line with Khrushchev's emphasis on peaceful coexistence, the Czechoslovak regime stopped jamming Western radio broadcasts (with the noted exception of RFE) during fall 1963. Moreover, the increasing number of television sets being purchased by the onset of the 1960's allowed larger segments of the population — those in western, southern and southeastern regions of the country — to tune in programs enamating from either West Germany or Austria. This included such population centers as Karlovy Vary, Brno and Bratislava. Although special antennas and adapters were often required, and their purchase made difficult, the practice could not be deterred.(1) People in these regions, therefore, tended to purchase television sets in order to view German or Austrian programs, especially feature-length films, which served as windows to the West.

This represented an added impetus for the media's unrest and a dilemma for the Novotny regime since foreign broadcasts, especially radio programs geared toward East European audiences, often commented on both foreign and domestic events about which the Czech and Slovak news media had been forced to either keep silent or, at best, provide only a bare minimum of facts.(2) Increasingly, the practice of ignoring events or issues which soon became public knowledge proved awkward for the nation's leadership.

No less influenced by the increase of information from abroad were the intelligentsia and youth, both of whom desired to join the mainstream of prevailing trends in the Western world from which they had been forcibly excluded for more than a decade. While the former were primarily concerned with the freer exchange of cultural, scientific and technical information, young people, bored by the monotony of life produced by the dictates of Socialist morality, were being captivated by Western jazz, attracted to the blue jeans, long hair and beard fads, and inspired by President John F. Kennedy's challenge to youth.

Coinciding with this attraction to Western culture was a growing concern over the condition of the nation's economy, and the fact that the regime procrastinated in its willingness to seek economic and technological cooperation with the West added yet another pressure on the leadership to increase the flow of information. For it is apparent that if a state desires to improve economic conditions, it must increase the role of the intelligentsia in this area and acknowledge that significant progress in such an endeavor is inhibited without a relatively free exchange of pertinent information. Thus, Novotny eventually was induced to lower the barriers for economic, scientific and technical exchanges. Once this occurred, freer access to information in other areas, such as culture and the social sciences, soon followed.(3)

While a salient stimulus for improving internal communication was the issue of reviving the economy, since its decline prompted widespread discontent and malingering among the work force, inputs by foreign radio stations also caused the regime to reevaluate the performance of the nation's mass media and to permit them greater diversity and specialization. The leadership supported such diversification in order to raise the media's credibility among the public so as to enable the press, radio and television to counter more effectively what the Party called "Western bourgeois propaganda."

The influence of Western broadcasts was officially acknowledged in a 1965 *Nova mysl* article which contended that due to the increased output and overall improvement of Western broadcasting (meaning the replacement of hard-core propaganda by factual information and the soft sell approach), internal information had to be better, timelier and more convincing. The author, Kamil Horn, stressed that transmissions by stations such as the BBC, VOA and RFE (all broadcasting in both Czech and Slovak) represented a "thoroughly developed and modernized system" which confronted internal propaganda with a number of basic demands. "To begin with this means timely, concise and complete information about events both in the CSSR and abroad." Information lacking these qualities, Horn continued, "deprives our propaganda instruments of their monopoly in this field, causing political damage and forcing them into a defensive position which prompts their mistrust." He saw the task facing the media as not an easy one because their information had to be "reliable, precise and truthful." Horn also called for greater diversity in information because of the new social structure of society and the status of its various strata and groups as well as their varied interests, standards of education and life styles.(4)

The article thus implied that the regime was finally prepared to tolerate, and even support within limits, some of the contentions being made by journalists and writers, namely the need for timeliness and truthfulness in reporting, diversity in presentation and overall improvement in the field of journalism. This did not mean, of course, that the news media were unimpeded in their pursuits. Prior censorship and other restrictions remained and Party leaders continued to criticize the press, radio and television for failing to follow the Party line. In a lengthy 1964 *Nova mysl* editorial, for example, critical comments were aimed at not only the cultural press, the regime's usual target for such attacks, but also the electronic media.

After stating that "our ideological front, and even journalism, has accomplished a significant piece of work," the editorial noted that the achievement was being debased by certain journalists and articles "which are weakening the ideologically educational influence of the press, broadcasting and television." Such negative aspects had resulted in *"a distinctly incorrect tendency, departing from the Party line."* The editorial also expressed concern over discussions, within the context of the responsibilities of journalists and the press, which had touched upon such sensitive issues as the mass media's right to question Party decisions and a Communist's right to his own opinion. As expected, the Party leadership frowned upon this new practice of airing such internal matters in an open forum.(5)

Evidence of growing public support for the more outspoken publications, as well as the innovative radio and television programs being introduced, was contained in the same editorial which said that some journalists and chief editors used the display of agreement on the part of certain groups of readers and listeners to justify their actions. This use of what was termed "fortuitous and unrestrained" support was criticized as dangerous because it too closely approximated Capitalist press practices.(6)

During September 1964, the Party journal *Zivot strany* (Party Life), in its evaluation of media performance, raised similar complaints and was even more critical of individual journalists and editorial staffs for failing to display "political and ideological maturity." This euphemism meant, in essence, that those being criticized had failed to adhere unquestioningly to the Party line. The evaluation also reproved Party organizations within the mass media, as well as the writers' and journalists' Unions, for not devoting enough effort to the ideological education of their members.(7) This represented an admittance that the KSC was losing influence among media outlets other than those publications which it controlled directly through such bodies as its Central Committee.

Thus, the writers and journalists, both as individuals and as members of editorial collectives, continued in their efforts to be freed from the more stringent controls so as to better inform the reawakening public by discussing issues which generally were designated as taboo. Further, the atmosphere of competing with Western propaganda and the pressures being applied against the regime, even from among Party ranks, provided the journalists with less constricting limits within which to experiment and pursue their work in attempting to keep the nation informed. Initial inroads in this direction were made by the cultural press; however, radio, television and the daily press gradually followed the example, becoming increasingly affected by and involved in the process of reform.

The Electronic Media

Radio

In February 1965, the Central Committee of the KSC released major policy statements relating to the mission, responsibilities and problems of both radio and television. The directives, closely resembling the document on the cultural press issued in spring 1964, reflected not only the effects of the communications explosion being experienced in the West but also the fact that both media were undergoing changes to better correspond to new domestic realities, namely the realized need for less exhortation and propaganda and for more diversity in and greater access to information. This meant, in essence, departing from the Leninist dictum that a mass medium was a propagandist, agitator and organizer of society. (Although Lenin, in formulating his now famous principle, referred specifically to the press, Communist leaders soon adapted it to also include radio and, eventually, television.)

The general change in the mission of radio broadcasting was later underscored by the deputy chief of Czechoslovak Radio's literature and drama department during an interview published in *Kulturni tvorba.* Responding to a question specifically relating to Lenin's principle, he indicated that while it would continue to be followed, a new hierarchy of functions had been established for radio programing whose foremost task now was that of information and entertainment with such aspects as education, enlightenment and inspiration in a secondary role. Lenin's dictum, in other words, was by necessity being relegated to the background in practice if not in theory. The deputy further explained that not only the general scheme of broadcasting but the principle as well had been altered in order "to conform to changes in the rhythm of life, mentality of listeners, living atmosphere . . . and the development of television."(8)

The initiated changes, therefore, represented a more realistic approach to broadcasting than the earlier attitude which was dominated by the concept of the "universal listener," meaning that it was considered sufficient to offer a similar programing diet to everyone alike. There finally appeared to be an acceptance of the fact that different audiences possessed different needs, tastes and interests which had to be considered if the medium was to be at all effective and have any kind of desired impact on a given group. It should be kept in mind that, as opposed to the press, Czechoslovak Radio had to contend with direct competition from the West.

To better understand the situation existing at the time, it must be realized that as of September 1964 the saturation ratio of radio receivers was 4 to 1, or practically one receiver in every household. The figures are based on 3,106,703 radio concessions for a population totaling some 14 million. This does not include 1,060,684 cable concessions or the countless transistor radios.(9) Also, a 1963 audience survey conducted by Czechoslovak Radio's research department indicated that the most listened to programs were news or reportorial type broadcasts.(10)

Already during summer 1960, the Party Central Committee, apparently alarmed over the ineffectiveness of its broadcast media in mobilizing the masses and the inroads being made by Western transmissions, issued a directive aimed at remedying the situation. In terms of radio operations, the document stressed the need to raise technical and program content standards and to diversify programing by providing the public with a greater choice in network outlets. The proposed scheme, to be fully implemented by 1963, included four central programs (stations) within a national network providing both statewide and local transmissions.

The two main domestic stations of the newly devised system, which approximated somewhat the BBC's network structure, were Radio Prague and Radio Bratislava, broadcasting in Czech and Slovak, respectively. Their prime output was official news broadcasts; political, economic and cultural commentaries; and other informational and propaganda-related programs. Czechoslovakia I, a statewide hookup, incorporated programs in both languages. Its diversified offerings included news reports, music, and original literary and musical productions which, according to the 1960 directive, would permit the station to achieve greater appeal and influence."(11) The fourth central outlet was Czechoslovakia II (VHF) which fashioned its programing for the more discriminating listener by presenting higher quality programs in music, drama and topical discussions, as well as other special features. These central stations were in turn aided by eleven regional and district outlets whose responsibilities were to supplement the four main programs with transmissions reflecting the needs of the geographic areas they served.

Due primarily to technical difficulties, however, the new network scheme was not realized until 1966.(12) Even at that time, certain parts of central and eastern Slovakia were still not receiving VHF broadcasts. Nevertheless, the more diversified broadcasting network did provide most of the country with a wider choice in programing which tended to emphasize more timely news information and appealing entertainment during morning, afternoon and late evening hours. Prime evening time by then was generally devoted to television viewing.

The new approach and diversification added a new dimension to broadcasting and provided radio personnel with a greater degree of freedom than in the past, a factor generated by the overall liberalizing trend and, also, by the need to counter the output of foreign broadcasts. An example of the latter aspect was a comment by a girl listener cited in an article discussing the listening habits of adolescents. At issue was a new program, "Microforum," initiated during 1965 and consisting of popular music as well as interviews with song writers and performers.

> *When we heard about the (newly) prepared program for youth, we began to laugh. We did so because we didn't . . . trust the so-called programs for youth. We told ourselves, 'New competition for*

> *(Radio) Free Europe, and Czech competition at that,' and we could imagine what it would be like. After listening to 'Microforum' for the first few hours, we happily discovered that we had been wrong at the time.(13)*

Aside from RFE programs featuring popular music, young listeners were attracted to English language Radio Luxembourg broadcasts due to their emphasis on contemporary music and the opportunity of picking up the latest English and American youth culture terminology.

As opposed to Czechoslovak television which had only one main channel at the time, the diversified radio network was afforded the opportunity to be more flexible in live coverage of special or important events, a versatility which also stimulated more impromptu programing. This aspect became especially important during democratization and later during the invasion when, despite a general news blackout, radio became the primary mass medium in providing direction to the nation by instructing the population and keeping it abreast of the latest developments.

Television

While Czechoslovak television was to become probably the single most influential mass medium in unfolding on a day-to-day basis the events of the Prague Spring, it was the last of the media to join the trend of reform during the mid-1960's. This was due in part to its technical limitations but, in no small way, also to the rigid controls imposed on its operations, especially programing. But once television did join the press and radio in more critically examining and discussing some of the pressing problems facing Socialist society, it did so with a determination and continuity which was virtually uninterrupted until after the invasion, thus helping to expand the swell of public opinion and the people's democratic consciousness. "The more the pressures of unsolved political and social problems shifted to the center, the more Prague Television became the main outlet for controversial writing."(14)

Television broadcasting on a regular basis began in 1954, but it was not until the end of the decade that television became a mass medium in the true sense and was regarded as such by the leadership. The main programing centers were Prague, Brno and Ostrava in the Czech lands and Bratislava and Kosice in Slovakia. Utilized by the regime primarily as a cultural-political outlet, a segment of its cultural front, television programing was divided about equally into three categories: news, political information and propaganda; culture and entertainment; and sports.

Until after de-Stalinization, the overall quality of programing was poor in content as well as in its technical aspects. Such shortcomings were underscored in the Party Central Committee's evaluation of the medium whose programs were criticized for "responding feebly to current problems of society" and for "vacillating" and being "unbalanced" in their composite structure.(15) Furthermore, television programing was described as lacking coherency and a sense of planning, and the general work of its personnel was seen as being deficient and not in the proper direction.

By 1966, regular daily news broadcasts were being aired morning, noon and twice in the evening hours. They were supplemented by more penetrating commentaries which soon gained popularity among viewers since general news reports followed the prescribed line and failed to fully reflect the true picture of daily life. Commentators frequently utilized international events as stepping stones to focus attention on domestic issues.

One program which drew attention to problems on the home front was "Face to Face." The series soon was regarded as the "combat unit" of the news department, because it frequently tended to touch off confrontations between television personnel and the censor or Party spokesman.(16) Personalities from such fields as economics, journalism, philosophy and sociology took part in this regularly scheduled discussion program. Heightened interest in these opinion broadcasts soon prompted the replacement of the late evening news with a commentary during which a staff editor voiced his or her views (within self-imposed limits, of course) on the day's events, ignoring for the most part press releases and news handouts.

Actually, the first public interest programs were made by regional stations such as Ostrava and Brno with their features "Ostrava Seconds" and "May I Interrupt?" Even the Party Central Committee acknowledged the importance of these programs by saying that they had "awakened an active interest among viewers."(17) While the regularly scheduled program "Seconds" was one of the first to explore problems involved in human relations and to point out specific incongruities existing in the nation's economy, the Brno originated series encouraged viewer participation, thereby stimulating expressed public opinion. One of the central reasons regional stations, as opposed to Prague Television, were able to make the initial breakthrough was the more rigorous control of the latter. This was in line with the Novotny regime's basic policy on censorship — the larger the potential audience, whether readers, listeners or viewers, the stricter the control.

Gradually, Prague Television also adopted an innovative and inquisitive approach in its programs. Among these was "Gong," a live presentation focusing on problems of day-to-day living. It was this series, for instance, which during spring 1966 acquainted viewers with the fundamental points in economist Ota Sik's proposal for economic reform.(18) Another significant contribution was "The Czechoslovak Expedition" series which, by means of eyewitness reports, dealt with such provocative topics as the Jachimov concentration camp for political prisoners operated during the early 1950's and the difficulties involved in the postwar settlement of regions bordering West Germany.

As a means of improving television's entertainment output, while at the same time competing more effectively with Western programing, the state-operated Telexport was created at the end of 1964. Within its initial months of existence, the agency arranged contracts for the coproduction of four films with television studios in West Germany and one with Austrian television.(19) Exchanges among experts and artists for purposes of discussion programs also were arranged with Austria.

The appeal of foreign films prodded the regime to allow the importation of a greater number of full-length features and television series, especially from the West, so that Czech and Slovak audiences became familiar with such American personalities as Jackie Gleason, Dinah Shore and Dick Powell and such series as "87th Precinct," "Wild Kingdom" and "Dr. Kildare."(20) These foreign features were supplemented by various news programs and documentaries through Intervision and Eurovision exchanges. Representatives of the two cooperative systems met in Prague during January 1966. Although the meeting tended to stress obstacles which persisted between them, *Mlada fronta,* in its January 21 issue, reported that regular exchanges of news and features would continue and "should avoid all remnants of the cold war."(21)

Since television displayed a certain boldness in programing, there were numerous occasions when programs were brazenly cut by the censor or withheld entirely from being shown. This caused repeated confrontations between the more liberal staff members and Party representatives, prompting Party leaders to include television in its critiques and evaluations, usually negative in tone, of the mass media. The aforementioned February 1965 official policy statements in which the Central Committee denounced certain aspects of both radio and television production serve as an example.

While unnamed artists and cultural workers connected with television were criticized in the document for their "ideological shakiness" and others were chastised for using the medium as an instrument for "expressing their own subjective views," specific programs were accused of possessing "ideological weaknesses" and failing "to strengthen the ideological and political unity of the Party." Among those named was a segment of "May I Interrupt?" Also cited was the disproportionate number of reports about Capitalist countries. "The leadership of Czechoslovak television must make greater efforts," the document stressed, "to gain timely reports about socialist countries, especially the USSR." An additional aspect regarded as negative was the voicing of "individualistic views on some problems," which was seen as distracting attention from the specific needs emphasized by the Party in the development of society.(22)

In the accompanying statement on radio broadcasting, its staff members were told that, as an active Party instrument, the medium had no place for views which did not correspond to Party policies. Staff members, therefore, were urged to help uncover those individuals among them who desired to proclaim their own "egotistic interests" above those of society as a whole, meaning those of the Party. "Broadcasting cannot casually adopt the same method in publicizing such views, for instance, as are discussed in cultural periodicals."(23) The document also urged Party organizations to be more mindful of the ideological education of its members. This was necessary, it was explained, since Czechoslovak Radio's administration had been confronted by Party groups in the political and foreign broadcasting departments (probably the two most important sections) on the issue of actualizing the correct Party line in their respective program transmissions.

The tone of such criticism and urging, then, represented a clear indication of the conflict existing between staff collectives and Party representatives in the higher administrative echelons, a dissension which repeatedly strained the relationship between electronic media personnel and the regime throughout the liberalization process.

The Print Media

Cultural Press

The general upsurge during the 1960's in the more timely dissemination of information was no less evident in the print media which by then had divested itself of much of the drabness and sameness prevalent during preceding years and had become more interesting as well as diverse in content and number. The basic characteristic of this period, however, was that while the ongoing conflict between Party conservatives and liberals did surface on occasion in the press, most of the day-to-day confrontations were hidden from public view, being submerged within the confines of editorial departments, censorship bureaus, conference rooms and private offices.

The growth and expansion of mass communication was accompanied by a reluctance on the part of the regime which, on the one hand, purported to support liberalization while, on the other, attempted to circumvent it by utilizing devious methods and conflicting arguments to keep the media in check. A typical example of the latter was the editorial statement of *Zivot strany* on "The Significance of Information." After maintaining that "(t)he Party supports the position that *open, complete and objective information is an indispensable component* in the evolvement of a socialist democracy," (emphasis added) the same editorial, four paragraphs later, stated that in the interest of society certain matters had to be kept secret. "The expanse of information, therefore, has its limits which are determined by the Party and responsible organs as presented by the need to defend the interests of the state."(24) Besides national defense, examples given of cogent categories involving questions of state interests included production advances, scientific discoveries and trade relations.

Another example of the regime's tactics was the practice of suppressing outright or initiating staff changes in the more outspoken publications, especially those in the realm of the cultural press, while at the same time allowing new periodicals to be launched. A case in point was the suppression, during winter 1965-66, of two liberal monthlies — *Tvar* (Visage), started in 1959 by the SCSS as an outlet for younger writers, and *Knizni kultura* (Book Culture), published since 1964 as an organ of the Center for Book Culture. Their demise came amidst another barrage of accusations and complaints issued by the Party against the cultural press, especially *Literarni noviny* and *Kulturny zivot,* as typified by a 1966 article published in *Zivot strany* under the heading "Disquieting Tendencies."(25)

Of the two closures, the suppression of *Tvar* was by far the more controversial since it involved not only the Union of Writers' Central Committee but the Union membership as well. The central issue in the controversy was the staff's desire "to cross every barrier, respect of which at the time was considered necessary and polite."(26) Initially, attempts were made to curb *Tvar's* outspoken and independent tendencies by altering its editorial board to better reflect the Party's wishes and limiting its monthly press run to 4,000 issues.(27) However, during a meeting of the SCSS Central Committee held in December 1965, the monthly's chief editor, Jan Nedved, speaking on his own and the editorial board's behalf, refused to comply with these prescribed conditions. Thus, *Tvar* was suspended as of January 1966, and, soon thereafter, Nedved was expelled from the KSC.

The announcement of the editor's expulsion was accompanied by a severe attack against him in Party organs, including *Zivot strany* which said that while Nedved desired to remain a Party member, "he wanted to retain his absolute 'freedom' to deal with and decide for himself against the political line of the Party."(28) His actions, quite understandably, were in direct conflict with the Party's demand for "strict and conscious discipline."

During the same time, however, new cultural periodocials appeared. These included *Sesity pro mladou literaturu* (Notebooks for Young Literature), to replace *Tvar,* and *Impuls* (Impluse), to take the place of *Knizni kultura.* In March 1966, the journal *Orientace* (Orientation), published by the SCSS, also made its debut. Both *Impuls* and *Orientace* dealt primarily with literature and criticism, with an emphasis on contemporary themes. And while *Impuls* was fashioned into a conservative mouthpiece in the cultural field, *Sesity* followed the tradition of its predecessor.

In the first issue of *Orientace,* the editorial board outlined its policy by stating that selection of articles would not be based on narrow group interests or the question of generations but on "the necessity for a confrontation between the various viewpoints as a premise of natural literary development."(29) Materials would be judged "above all as works of art," which implied that board members rejected such concepts as propagandistic value or ideological purity in the evaluation of prospective articles.

The activity surrounding the cultural press during the 1965-66 period was part of a continuing campaign by the regime to assert itself in the field of culture. Thus, virtually all periodocials, in the Czech lands at least, were affected to some degree, especially *Literarni noviny.* Following a prolonged process lasting from March to October 1966, during which various organizational and personnel changes were initiated and then again altered, the writers' weekly was ultimately placed under the close supervision of its editorial board headed by a new chairman, Jan Ocenasek. The chief editor, Milan Jungmann, retained his post but was given the title of "responsible editor."(30) Ocenasek, who in 1959 was most critical of the writers' Second Congress, held the Gottwald State Award and in March 1966 received the title of Meritorious Artist. Thus, he was considered trustworthy by the Party. It was evident by the actions taken that the Novotny regime desired to keep the influential voice of reform in line, especially during the months prior to the writers' next congress scheduled for spring 1967.

Daily Press

Meanwhile, the nation's daily press had also undergone considerable changes which became discernible in the more timely presentation of a greater variety of domestic and, especially, foreign reports. TASS no longer served as the primary source of news from abroad. Since the last part of the 1950's, the CTK had been provided a freer hand in selecting news from other major wire services with which it had working agreements — Associated Press, Agence France-Presse, Deutsche Presse Agentur and Reuters among them. By 1958, the national news agency's foreign news output contained only some thirty percent of translated or rewritten TASS reports.(31) Prior to 1956, use of the Soviet agency's materials, which even included news about Czechoslovakia's Socialist neighbors, amounted to eighty percent of the CTK output.

As part of the overall effort by the Socialist bloc to gain greater influence among developing countries, the CTK displayed considerable interest in securing news exchange agreements with African and Asian countries. This interest was extended to the creation of the International School of News Agency Journalism and Technology which by completion of its fifth six-month course in May 1965 had graduated some 100 students, mostly Africans, either as news agency correspondents or technicians. (32) In addition, teachers were sent to various African states, such as Mali and Algeria, for the purpose of conducting short courses in journalism.

Providing a still greater and regular input of foreign news for domestic consumption was the network of CTK correspondents stationed abroad. By the end of 1962, no less than twenty-eight newsmen were in the field, sending dispatches from major world news centers such as New York, London, Paris, Rome, Bonn, Vienna, Stockholm, Geneva, Peking and Hanoi.(33) In several countries, primarily those of Eastern Europe, the agency maintained joint correspondents with *Rude pravo,* the only newspaper to have its own correspondents abroad on a permanent basis.

At the same time, the communication field became increasingly concerned with certain concepts which until then had been kept in the background or were totally absent. This involved such practices and techniques as advertising, public relations, audience research studies and related public opinion surveys. More important, traditional journalistic forms and literary genres adopted for journalistic use again came into prominence and with them the personality of the individual reporter and commentator. Readers again were able to recognize bylines and associate the names with specific journalistic forms or special areas of international and domestic reporting.

The public, which for a decade had been deprived of any substantive press news from abroad, was eager to follow international developments more closely. During 1963, for instance, *Kulturni tvorba* published an extensive account by two Czechoslovak traveling writers describing the economic miracle of postwar Japan. The article caused somewhat of a sensation among the public which, having had little information about the country's recent development, was interested in learning all it could. As a result, the issue containing the account was sold for fifty crowns on the black market, more than forty times its actual price.(34) Another indication of the new approach in foreign reporting was the name change for the international relations section of the Union of Journalists which became the Club of Foreign Affairs Reporters.

The daily press also grew more introspective in terms of domestic issues so that the economy and other pressing socio-political problems were more frequently discussed. Good examples of this were several articles published by *Pravda* during fall 1966 which dealt with sensitive topics and contained what might well be called unorthodox views. In one such article, a university professor expressed skepticism about the often stated prediction that the nation would soon enter the final stage of socialism — communism — and he further proposed that Capitalist countries were a prototype of socialism due to their high per capita incomes.(35) Then, less than a month later, writer Miroslav Kusy probed the problem of "The Social Roots of Dogmatism."

Utilizing the Chinese Cultural Revolution as a relevant peg (a favorite device for discussing foreign events in such a manner as to make them applicable to the domestic situation), Kusy examined the consequences of the personality cult. Dogmatic Marxism was not in the interest of the working class, he contended, "but only in the interest of a ruling group which has taken a stand outside this class . . . and which claims to be above it and to have the right to make decisions independent of it." He went on to characterize such a leadership as having to "protect its position through a dictatorship of dogmatized ideology which is to sanction every step, justify every action and uncritically approve the given state of affairs as the best of all alternatives."(36) The reader was not required to possess an above average insight to determine for himself what ruling group Kusy really had in mind.

Although often miniscule and seemingly insignificant to the uninitiated observer, innovations in the communication media evident during this liberalization period of "repressive tolerance"(37) proved nonetheless to be psychological victories for the reformers and stimulated further efforts toward change. This tedius struggle presented a process whereby a new wave of reporters, broadcasters and other media personnel attempted to divest themselves and the communication media of outmoded Party dicta. They endeavored instead to incorporate in their work a sense of reality which was more in step with the times and reflected more accurately the anticipated rejuvenation of their society than the worn-out pronouncements of the Party leadership.

Thus, the global communications boom, coinciding with de-Stalinization inside the country, provided an added forceful pressure on the Novotny regime to tolerate demands for a more responsive media. Moreover, due to the prevailing apathy and stagnant economy, the Party leadership needed more credibility in order to mobilize public support for the Party's programs. It had become evident that propaganda, exhortations and repeated urgings, as well as distorted reports about conditions existing in Capitalist countries, had not achieved the desired effect and, in fact, were for the most part resented by the public.

The changes initiated as a result of such pressures represented another important step in gradually transforming the mass media into more information oriented communication channels which contributed to stimulating public opinion and increasing the flow of news and ideas inside the country. This overall activity was also significant in preparing the media for their future function in the democratization process.

The movement toward increased professionalism in the journalistic field in turn brought new pressures to bear on the regime. For, once given the signal to become more professional and individualistic in their work, reform-minded journalists became increasingly difficult to contain within the ideological confines prescribed by the Party leadership. The repeated criticisms and warnings issued by regime spokesmen against the media attest to this fact. And so the press continued to test the limits of established authority and to gradually reclaim its traditional function in society, thus becoming ever more deeply involved in the liberalization process.

CHAPTER IV
PROFESSIONALISM AND THE PRESS LAW

The official sanctioning of liberalization during 1963 stimulated a desire for the implementation of modern methods and practices in various fields of endeavor. The intelligentsia especially attempted to overcome persisting and cumbersome restrictions and to abandon ineffective practices in an effort to keep abreast of new trends in other developed countries. Liberal-minded journalists were no exception. For the reevaluation of the function of the press in modern society, undertaken once de-Stalinization had been initiated and further stimulated by the impact of the communications boom, readily revealed that the mass media, especially the press, had to initiate changes and innovative practices if they were to become more credible and, thus, more responsive to the public.

This meant, for instance, the use of public opinion surveys and audience research studies, and also the revival of traditional journalistic forms to which the public could more readily relate. Above all, however, there existed a need to keep society informed by means of competent reporting which, for all practical purposes, had been grossly neglected during past years when the emphasis was on propaganda and exhortation in an effort to reeducate the masses. In brief, the field of journalism found itself confronted with the need to professionalize and, within the shortest possible time, bridge the gap created by some fifteen years of repression, stagnancy and inertia. This was no easy task. Despite the repeated demands by the regime for increased effectiveness on the part of the mass media, Party bureaucrats, in the name of the same regime, hampered progress toward this end by controlling media performance through censorship and various conforming restrictions.

In their attempt to diversify and upgrade media content, the journalists intensified their efforts to obtain greater access to pertinent sources of information. This increasing activism by the media and their tendency to overstep the established Party line became a major concern to the regime as reflected in the "Theses" prepared for the Thirteenth Congress of the KSC scheduled for May 31 - June 4, 1966. The document dealt at some length with the mass media's role in the future development of Socialist society.

Although the "Theses" seemed to suggest that the Party leadership intended to adopt a more liberal attitude toward the media and cultural pursuits, actual practice soon revealed that this seemingly changed position was merely a new means to the same end — that of control. The new approach in guiding the press and cultural activities was to be realized through a self-policing policy, incumbent on all creative artists, writers and journalists, to be implemented through the mechanism of the creative unions and social organizations involved.(1) Such a method, according to the regime's reasoning, would avoid further use of the more blatant, and largely discredited, administrative methods associated with the past, while ensuring the Party's continued direct influence in matters of culture and the press.

Closely aligned with and adding emphasis to this ongoing concern for the communication media was the preparation of a press law. The liberals were well aware of the precarious status of the progress made since the advent of de-Stalinization and desired some form of legal safeguards to protect their gains. They sought a press law which would define the rights of editors and the specific duties of censors so as to diminish the arbitrary use of censorship and, further, to improve conditions for access to information. Thus, the journalists continued to articulate professional concerns.

Professional Interests Stressed

In connection with the Thirteenth Party Congress, and as a result of several meetings on various levels within the journalistic field, the Central Committee of the SCSN issued two basic documents preceding the national gathering of the KSC representatives. The first of these documents, released in January 1966, was aimed specifically at the aforementioned "Theses" being prepared for the Congress. The second, issued in May, consisted of a detailed evaluation of the press, radio and television between the Twelfth and Thirteenth Party Congresses, representing a span of some three and one half years.

Both documents emphasized the importance of the mass media's informing function and stressed above all that the prerequisite for effectively executing this function was access to information. The January resolution, therefore, called for the removal of "incorrect practices by certain individuals and institutions which attempt to withhold from them (media representatives) unpleasant realities and the true picture of things." It also underscored the need for expressed criticism by the media, more research in the communication field, and modernization of technical and production aspects in both the print and electronic media. Furthermore, the resolution held that greater differentiation would create the possibility "for good competition among the individual organs of the press, broadcasting and television."(2) Quite obviously, this represented a departure from the Communist concept of press competition as an undesirable evil associated with capitalistic press practices.

The supplemental evaluation that followed in May was prepared by a special commission created for the task. And while its contents did not radically depart from the usual and accepted form of criticism, the statement nevertheless expressed a certain candor and, by defending the news media, brought professional interests to the fore. Moreover, it later stood in contrast to the damaging critique of the press, radio and television which was issued in August by the Party Central Committee.(3)

After noting the importance of the act of informing, the SCSN evaluation urged editorial offices to develop and use their own sources of information instead of seeking the most convenient and easiest way of obtaining news material. It pointed out that this also meant the elimination of barriers which prevented journalists from gaining access to information. "Little initiative and a dependence on information provided by the wire service, together with the effort on the part of the CTK to monopolize the coverage of some organizations and institutions, leads in both instances to stereotyping and uniformity in reporting."(4) Thus, the SCSN criticized the continuing practice of limiting access to information and the tendency of its centralized dissemination through the state-controlled news agency.

Most of the remainder of the evaluation was devoted to problems related to core areas of news content, namely economics and technology, domestic politics, foreign affairs and culture. In this respect, the SCSN Central Committee saw the need to upgrade the content of political commentaries and improve and extend the coverage of Socialist bloc countries. Among other recommendations, it urged the creation of a research institute for public opinion.

It should be pointed out that criticism aimed at domestic reporting and the lack of coverage given to Socialist bloc countries was generally justified. This stemmed from the fact that by the end of 1965, the main news interest of the public and journalists alike tended to focus on international affairs. For the public, which previously had been deprived of substantive information about foreign events, especially those concerning the West, it represented a novelty. For the journalist, reporting foreign affairs proved more interesting and productive than covering the domestic scene and, besides, the field offered an opportunity to travel abroad, including in the West, which in itself presented an appealing incentive.(5) Many of the best journalists, therefore, turned to foreign reporting which resulted in better coverage of the West and other parts of the world at the expense of that provided domestic and East European affairs.

For understandable reasons, this proved to be a constant source of criticism by the Party leadership. In one of its frequent attacks against the nature and content of articles published in the cultural press, for instance, the Party journal *Zivot strany* contended that such " 'tirades evoke the effect of well-paid advertisements propagating the western style of life.' "(6)

By this time, it had become evident to many of those involved in the communication field that in order for the mass media to be effective in mobilizing society it would take more than repeated urgings in the name of Socialist construction or the continued clumsy use of propaganda. The public by now had become immune to such tactics. Most journalists and writers were well aware that members of a developed society wanted and needed to be adequately informed and provided with factual explanations as to why things, especially the truths of everyday life, were as they were.

As Vladislav Jisl put it in his argument on the issue: "The weight of public opinion demands that matters be explained properly — for instance, what is the actual situation in the maintenance of houses in Prague. Falling plaster and cornices are impossible to be concealed by a terse administrative statement which says nothing." He warned that if the public fails to receive frank answers, "it will then seek its own explanations elsewhere, and find causes even where none exist."(7) This, of course, had been understood and advocated much earlier by various individuals; however, their contentions had then fallen on deaf ears among those who were in a position to affect the necessary changes. But as pressure from the liberal forces became more pronounced and articulate, conditions for reform improved.

Revival of Traditional Forms

Among the indices of change evident in the press during the mid-1960's was the reappearance of many traditional journalistic forms which had long been in use by the Czechoslovak press prior to its Russificiation following the coup of 1948. This included such basic genres as the reportage, in-depth interview, personal commentary, feuilleton, vignette, sketch and travel report. More important, perhaps, was the individual character and unique flavor brought to each form by the journalist or writer who developed a certain proficiency in utilizing it for his specific purpose. It should also be emphasized that, as opposed to the American or British journalistic style, forms employed by Czechoslovak journalists are by tradition closely tied to literary writing. This is reflected to an extent even in the most common of news reports.

Attempts at reviving traditional forms had been made since the mid-1950's, but the process was slow and erratic. In 1958, for example, the then new weekly *Kultura* started publishing interviews with popular personalities as a regular feature in an effort to revive the use of this form. Symbolically, the first of these was conducted with Adolf Hoffmeister who during the First Republic had gained prominence as a master of the art of interviewing.(8) In 1931 he had published a book, *Pis jak slisis* (Write as You Hear It), which included penetrating interviews with some of Europe's most notable personalities of the period. Hoffmeister's book was reissued in a new edition during the 1960's.

The real departure in the *Kultura* series was an attempt at publicizing an individual's views and opinions on topics related to his or her profession or field of expertise. Other newspapers soon followed the weekly's example but with much less effect since their reporters tended to confront lesser officials with mundane questions. Contributing to their vapidness was the general inaccessibility of leading officials, especially top Party functionaries, and also the limits imposed on reporters' questions in the event an interview was granted.

As stated in a 1965 article dealing with the development of this journalistic form, interviews published in the daily press at the onset of the 1960's tended to focus on factual material (as opposed to personal views) which could as well have been treated in a basic news format. As an example, the author cited an interview in *Vecerni Praha* (Evening Prague) with an actor following a premier performance, a review of which appeared in the same issue.(9) Both the interview and review contained virtually the same information since the interviewer failed to discriminate between the actor's personal viewpoint and the play itself which, naturally, was covered by the drama critic.

The author concluded, however, that subsequent use of the form had been extended from merely reproducing factual data to recording personal opinions and thoughts. This had heightened and expanded the societal function of the genre. "In my opinion," she wrote, "the interview, which brings forth subjective views of notable personalities, reflects to a certain degree the level of commitment of individual papers to the revival process and struggle against dogmatism. For, the absence of opinion is one of its (dogmatism's) trademarks." The author also suggested that more interviews be conducted with leading Party functionaries "who have not expressed themselves" through the use of this genre. (10)

Among the journalists of this period who were closely associated with the interview was Liehm whose effective use of the technique can be seen in the dialogue "Two Days with Novomesky," published in both *Kulturny zivot* and *Literarni noviny* in April 1966. (11) Focusing on the theme of culture, Novomesky made some rather frank remarks about the problems existing between Czech and Slovak literature and the writer's future role in the struggle for freedom of expression.

In a majority of cases, an in-depth interview included both the question and response, thus providing readers with the opportunity to determine for themselves how well the respondent confronted a given issue. The method proved most effective and revealing when sensitive topics were discussed, a trend which after 1965 proved more frequently to be the case.

The popular weekly *Kultura,* prior to its suspension by the regime in 1962, was also instrumental in helping to revive the feuilleton, long an integral part of Czech journalism but much neglected after its Russification. In July 1958, the weekly launched a regular series in this genre under the heading "Dopis v lahvy" (Note in a Bottle). The general idea, as conceived by the series' creators, was to single out some absurd and vexing aspect of everyday life in the hope that, like the letter in a bottle thrown wistfully out to sea by one shipwrecked on an island, it would summon help — in this case, rectify or eliminate the situation discussed. The feuilleton was written alternately by one of the three originators who remained anonymous to everyone except the chief editor. They were Alexej Kusak, staff member; Jaroslav Bocek, film critic; and Josef Brukner, contributor. The article usually consisted of a dialogue among the three, designated only as First, Second and Third Man.

One such typical episode concerned service policy in railway dining cars. It was pointed out that while beer was sold on trains, it could initially be obtained only with the purchase of a meal. If one did order beer, it would be served after he had finished eating his soup. After a specific stop along the line, however, beer could be purchased without food if the established norm for food sold on the train had been fulfilled. In the event that it had not, beer could be bought only if the customer also paid for at least one cup of coffee.(12) Understandably, satirical treatment of such common farcical realities proved popular with readers and helped to relieve the monotony of the otherwise generally drab newspaper fare which marked the period.

By the mid-1960's, considerable strides had also been made in the general area of reporting. It should be kept in mind, however, that in Czechoslovak journalistic tradition, the reportage form subsumes not only the recording of basic facts but also the reporter's personal observations, evaluations and views. In terms of Western practices, it can perhaps best be compared to the news commentary or opinion column.

According to journalism professor Karel Storkan, noticeable changes in the style of reporting first became apparent at the beginning of the 1960's. Among the more important factors contributing to this internal revival of the traditional use of the reportage was a weakening in the regime's antagonism toward innovative or experimental work by journalists and writers. "The author's subjective view was frequently underrated and creative thought was regarded as bourgeois individualism," Storkan wrote of this previous attitude. "Only toward the beginning of the 1960's (were) more systematic and often even successful attempts made to be liberated from the conventions which had marked the Czech reportage." The new approach in reporting was achieved, he added, because "the period of radical economic changes in the 1960's, a period . . . which began to stir people, even their way of thinking, was seeking its own expression, its own style. It opened the way for new themes and new directions."(13)

The significance of the reportage, especially during the liberalization period, was perhaps best stated by Goldstucker:

> *The importance of the reportage . . . lies in the fact that during periods of rapid social and historical change, it is the first (genre) which explores the field, states the new elements and brings . . . by live and absorbing means the inventory of the occasion. Therefore, reporting has tremendous significance during turning points in history, during periods of transition from one era to another, when*

it can capture, by means of its method and fashion, the new visage of reality.(14)

There is another important observation in Storkan's article which should be noted. In his initial remarks on the subject, Storkan made the point that changes in the handling of reporting by the Czechoslovak press became evident about the same time that journalists in the West had abandoned their "apathetic manner" of the 1950's and started to "wander the back streets and alleys" in search of realism.(15) The implication is interesting, for he evidently seemed to link the internal improvement in reporting to innovative developments in the West.

This coincides with the view expressed by Kusak, for example, who maintained that Czech journalists as a rule did not lack information about trends in the West. Each major editorial office was allowed to subscribe to at least one, in some cases more, prominent Western daily newspaper or news magazine besides the daily digest of international news compiled by the CTK. Although their availability was restricted to the main editors, the foreign papers nevertheless did manage to find their way into the hands of interested staff members. Daily newspapers and sometimes weekly or monthly journals from Britain, West Germany, Switzerland and other countries were read thoroughly and the information traded and discussed with colleagues from other papers who had access to different publications from the West.(16) And while the information gained in most cases could not be included in their articles, journalists at least attempted to adopt some of the methods used by their Western counterparts. Another indicator of this trend was the increased references to English language texts in articles dealing with journalistic practices and published in journals such as *Novinarsky sbornik.*

The tendency to turn to the Western press as an example can be explained in two ways. First, the basic practices involved were closely related to the Czech journalistic and literary traditions which evolved during the nineteenth and first part of the twentieth centuries, traditions which also were a part of the Czechoslovak Communist press until its Bolshevization during the 1930's. Thus, turning to Western concepts, specifically those related to traditional Czech journalistic forms, seemed only natural during the revival process, as the liberalization phase was often called.

Second, the new approach presented the best method for communicators to fulfill the realized need that the public, if it was to fully support the movement for reform, must read, hear and see the truth and be provided with realistic explanations about the existing situation and the many pressing problems facing the nation. The imposed practices and principles regulating the mass media after 1948 had by and large been discredited and proven inadequate to meet the task at hand.

Thus, journalists and writers turned their attention to existing conflicts in society and became concerned with the very content of life, primarily the people's longings and desires and their attempts to attain them. They searched for these goals within the context of the existing actuality which up to then reporting had not fully revealed or portrayed. As Jean-Paul Sartre wrote: "It was not a question for them of calling for the return of bourgeois liberalism but, since truth is revolutionary, of claiming the revolutionary right to tell the truth."(17)

Among the new politically oriented publications which helped to upgrade professional standards in journalism and frequently managed to pierce the armor of the Novotny regime was *Reporter*, initially a bimonthly magazine of the journalists' Union first published in April 1966. The idea for publishing a news magazine originated within the organization in 1962 as an outgrowth of the need for the SCSN to publish more than a trade organ, as was their monthly *Novinar* (Journalist), and to gain additional revenue in order to be less dependent on the government.

The idea was revived in 1965 and ultimately proved fruitful. But due to various technical difficulties, such as the time required to produce a two-tone front cover, printing delays and problems encountered in delivery (all frequently referred to in the initial issues), *Reporter* became primarily a magazine of commentaries, interviews and round-table discussions rather than of actual news as originally intended. Not until January 1968 did the periodocial, dubbed "The Red Spiegel" by the staff of the Hamburg-based *Der Spiegel*, became a weekly publication.

Preceding the appearance of *Reporter* by about six months was *Student*, a weekly organ of the Czechoslovak Union of Youth (CSM), whose audience consisted primarily of university students. Although less conventional than most papers in its class, it did not gain any real notoriety throughout the remainder of the Novotny era. During the first half of 1968, however, after officially breaking with the CSM, the weekly became the radical voice of the young intelligentsia and was at times criticized for its fervor. Along with the writers' weeklies and a few other newspapers, *Reporter* and *Student* helped considerably in upgrading journalistic standards and eventually were among the most prominent voices of democratization in 1968.

The new approach which took root in journalism during liberalization, and came to fruition in spring 1968, must also be seen in light of the journalists' desire to improve their accessibility to information so as to carry out their intention of fully informing the people by telling them the truth, and thus also expurgating their field of the rancidness which journalism had absorbed during the most oppressive years of Communist rule. (A desire for confessing past mistakes due to naivete and blind idealistic fervor became almost an obsession on the part of some journalists once all obstructions disappeared during the early months of 1968.)

The reformers tried, under the then existing circumstances, to again enter the main current of thought, creativity and development from which they had been isolated, reviving meanwhile old practices and absorbing innovative trends from wherever they could. Simply, they were motivated by a desire for change — a process based not on violence but on rationality, common sense and legality stemming from a long tradition in the nation's nonviolent approach to reform. It was this general spirit which, in part, also provided the impetus for the drafting of a press law.

Enactment of the Press Law

Despite its overall limitations and inadequacies, the press law of 1967 was in some respects both enterprising and unusual when considering the political milieu which then prevailed inside the country. It was, for example, the first statute since the Communist takeover enacted by the National Assembly at the initiative and recommendation of two of its own bodies — the Cultural and Constitutional Commissions. This is significant when realizing that the common practice was for the Assembly to serve merely as a rubber stamp for motions presented by the Party leadership.

During discussions on the measure, moreover, members of the SCSN were present as "expert consultants" in the respective committees involved.(18) Even the initiative for a press law came largely as an outgrowth of discussions on relevant problems (i.e., the relationship between information and society, access to and dissemination of information, raising journalistic standards and upgrading media performance) conducted during and after the SCSN Congress in 1963 with preliminary work on drafting its basic provisions beginning the following summer. This initial task was undertaken by a subcommission established for the purpose within the framework of the Commission on the Press and Journalists of the SCSN. After being discussed by the Central Committees of both the SCSN and SSN, the suggestions were reviewed by appropriate Party bodies and finally drafted into a bill in the National Assembly which approved the measure on October 25, 1966. Thus, the process followed in formulating and enacting the press law can justifiably be compared to the mechanism generally employed by interest or pressure groups in pluralistic societies.

After some thirteen years, then, pre-publication censorship was legally defined and officially acknowledged. The task of censoring materials was entrusted to the Central Publication Authority (UPS) — the new name assigned to the censorship agency — whose mission was that of "safeguarding the interests of society." Specifically, its responsibilities were outlined in Part V, Section 17:

> *(2) The Central Publication Authority assures that no information which contains facts considered to be governmental, economic or official secrets will be publicized in the mass information media. Should information contain such facts, the Central Publication Authority will prevent its publication, or eventual dissemination.*
>
> *(4) Should the content of information be in variance* with other interests of society, *the Central Publication Authority will draw the publisher's and chief editor's attention to it. (19) (emphasis added)*

Clarification as to the specific meaning of "other interests of society" was not provided in the law.

Some of the innovative aspects of the press law stemmed directly from the newly outlined missions of the mass media as stated in the law itself. That is, the media were to provide "timely, truthful, comprehensive and as complete information as possible about events from every aspect of life in the Czechoslovak Socialist Republic and from abroad."(20) The law in essence furnished the news media, within the scope of the 1960 constitution, with a legal base from which to pursue their task of gaining access to information and reporting it. Realistically speaking, the base proved to be a rather weak one as the nation's press corps soon discovered, but it nonetheless did impose (within the letter of the law at least) certain limits on censorship and provided courts with the power to examine specific acts of prior restraint if contested by the publishing body involved. This was stated in the following paragraph:

> *(3) A decision by the Central Publication Authority to prevent (publication) shall be reviewed, upon the request of the publisher, by a district court. The procedure used to hear the request shall be the civil-legal regulations. (21)*

Another provision in the law granted chief editors greater authority. A chief editor was: 1) responsible solely to the publisher or publishing body, 2) provided the right of access to information and 3) able to keep his sources secret, if requested by them to do so. The second point mentioned was specified in Part IV, Section 13:

> *(2) State organs and organizations, scientific and cultural institutions and economic organizations are bound to provide chief editors and other editors on the same level of authority information which is essential to truthfully, timely and comprehensively informing the public, or to provide them with the means of gaining information of this type. (22)*

And while exceptions to the above were outlined in the very next paragraph, pertaining again to state, economic and official secrets, the proviso nevertheless represented a significant change in attitude on the function of the press in Communist society, since the section constituted a legal basis for editors to seek information on their own initiative.

Additionally, two legal concepts existing in Czechoslovak law prior to February 1948, but expunged soon thereafter, were reinstituted in the new statute. This concerned the responsibility of chief editors for libelous material and the mandatory retraction of published information proven to be false. Part VIII, meanwhile, concerned the foreign press and news agencies, emphasizing the free exchange of information between the CSSR and other states. The law made it possible for foreign publications to be printed and distributed and news agency bureaus to be established inside the country, so long as the distribution of such papers or information did not contradict the interests of Socialist society. (23) Similar provisions had been abolished during the early 1950's. Such was the letter of the press law which went into effect on January 1, 1967.

The Regime and the Press Law

In order to place the new statute regulating the press and the role of the UPS in proper perspective, one must consider the intent of an official policy statement approved by the Party Presidium on August 30, 1966, several months before the press law became effective. The document, "On Actual Questions Pertaining to the Party's

Direction of the Press and Other Mass Media of Ideological Influence," in essence subordinated the UPS to the central *apparat* of the Communist Party.(24) As a result, the censorship agency, despite the press law which defined its activities and limitations, continued serving as the Party's instrument, arbitrarily concealing the latter's secret rulings from the public. "Censorship in fact restrained everything which it considered restrainable, relying meanwhile not on the law but on internal Party decisions."(25) Such decisions were generally issued via telephone or memoranda to censors in editorial offices who in turn advised the editors.

Examples of this type of concealed directives were revealed by *Reporter* which, in 1968, published texts of several of the many memoranda issued by the HSTD between 1964 and 1966. Although the following examples from the *Reporter* article occurred while the press law was being drafted, such practices continued after the law was enacted.

> *15. April 1964: deputy chief Lt. Col. Kovar issues the following directive — probably valid for two years:*
> *It is forbidden to publicize, by the entire publishing sector, any articles or other materials whose author is Ivan Svitak. All prohibited materials by the author should immediately be surrendered to the HSTD leadership.*
>
> *30. March 1966: chief of the HSTD, Lt. Col. E. Kovarik, issues, in accordance with an appeal, the following directive:*
> *It is forbidden to publicize, without consulting the HSTD leadership, reviews or commentaries on the film "THE GUESTS" whose director is Jan NEMEC.*
>
> *6. September 1966: chief of the HSTD, Lt. Col. E. Kovarik, issues the following directive for a duration of three months:*
> *It is forbidden to publicize the death of an industrial school student . . . caused while servicing a hops combine on a state farm in Libesice near Zatec. (26)*

Further illustrating the Party's use of the censorship agency are the 141 recorded instances of prior restraint initiated by the UPS against *Literarni noviny* between January 1 and September 23, 1967, the time when the weekly was unceremoniously wrenched from the Union of Writers' control. As the weekly's editor later noted, all the cases concerned the abstruse and undefined provision that the material in question was in conflict with other interests of society.(27)

It should be clear by now that the press law was intended as a compromise by the regime, but one weighted decisively in its favor.

On the one hand, Party leaders desired to placate liberal forces and public opinion by providing evidence of seemingly furthering the guarded liberalization policy which the regime professed to follow. On the other, Novotny and his associates saw the need for tighter control of the information media due to the belief, as expressed in the August 1966 document, that the mass media were being used for the "subjective distortion" and "nonhistorical evaluation" of past developments, and even for the "negative distortion of the overall politics of the state and Party."(28) They evidently believed that by legalizing censorship and including enough safeguards in the press law both their desired goals would be achieved.

Another significant step in this respect was the decision to reinstitute the Ministry of Culture and Information which had been abolished at the onset of 1953. Speaking at the December 1966 Party Central Committee plenum considering the matter, Novotny justified the action by maintaining that the mass media's constant expansion and increased influence had created the need for a "qualified, competent and all-powerful governmental unit for the spheres of culture and information which would provide them with day-to-day direction." He added: "At the same time, it is understandable that the Party retain full ideological direction of the instruments of mass influence — the press, radio and television — and even the direct supervision of Communists in the creative unions."(29) The reinstitution of the Ministry, then, must be seen as an effort by the regime to create yet another regulatory body for these troublesome areas.

An added unwritten Party policy concerned censorship and publishers, a majority of whom were KSC members. By an internal Party decision, and bound by Party discipline, publishers were directed not to seek court settlements (although specifically permitted to do so under the law) in instances of prior restraint but to arbitrate the decision with the appropriate Party department which, in most instances, proved to be the defendant in the case.(30) The regime, therefore, was prepared to employ every means at its disposal in order to keep the most bothersome elements within the mass media in check. And indeed, the leadership felt that it had found in the press law the necessary method to accomplish this goal. Such was not to be the case, however.

As one critic later summarized: "The press law was supposed to be a whip against newsmen. . . . But the fact remains that in this (the bureaucracy's use of the statute for its own aims) the press law could not be relied upon." He went on to explain: "As it continued to be used according to the old practices, prior censorship constituted illegal action."(31) And while the trend to illegally censor material continued virtually unabated, it no longer went unanswered. Individual journalists and writers spoke out, citing specific instances of illegality(32) while calling for amendments to the press law and, later, even total abolition of prior restraint.

Actually, recommendations for the suspension of censorship, to be replaced by a form of post-publication supervision, were included in the initial proposal of the SCSN subcommission in 1965. The proposal said in part: " 'In the current epoch . . . the existing form of press censorship is an anachronism, consisting of an unnecessary, illegal and undignified character of preventive control by a socialist state of its socialist press.' "(33) Similar views were expressed at the time by the dean of Charles University's Law Faculty and even a staff member of the Party Central Committee's Legal Commission.

It is not surprising that the recommendations were disregarded in the final drafting of the statute. The appropriate Party departments made certain of that. What is significant, however, is that such proposals were actually made, reflecting opinions toward press control held at the time by individuals in responsible positions. Further, it helps to highlight another important reason for the growing unification of opposition against the Novotny regime and the emergence of the political crisis toward the end of 1967. For the press law, and specifically its disregard by the Party *apparat,* actually helped precipitate the crisis within the Party rather than allay it.

In effect, the press law represented a compromise measure on the part of the regime which felt the need to ease the mounting pressures being applied against it by liberal forces in their continued drive to broaden liberalization through reform. But instead of providing a solution to the problems created by a more activist press, the Novotny leadership's use of the law for its own ends only contributed to accentuating the arbitrary and repressive nature of the regime.

This, in essence, constituted the crux of the conflict between the Party leadership and activist journalists and writers. For how could the regime's policies and actions be supported when they not only often conflicted with public interests, but also restricted the press in its attempt to become more responsive to society. The inherent contradiction in this situation contributed to solidifying opposition to the regime among the intelligentsia.

Such, then, was the prevailing political undercurrent in the cultural sphere at the onset of 1967, a period when preparations for congresses of both the writers and journalists were in progress. It was the beginning of what journalist Dusan Hamsik has referred to as the "entrenched war of nerves"(34) between the liberals and those in power.

Up to this point, the Novotny regime had been able to avert, by means of various tactics and methods, a major confrontation with the liberals. The closest it had come to such an open clash, perhaps, was during the 1963-64 period. But the unresolved problems — continued arbitrary rule and censorship among them — began to reach a boiling point. The crisis finally manifested itself in 1967, especially during the writers' Fourth Congress, and eventually led to a decisive confrontation within the highest reaches of the Party hierarchy.

PART II

DENOUEMENT: THE CRISES OF FREEDOM

Among the noteworthy and consequential events of 1967 affecting Czechoslovakia's future course was the rebellious June Congress of the Union of Writers and the regime's subsequent retaliatory actions against some of the more outspoken participants. No less meaningful in this respect was the writers' loss of control over their official voice, *Literarni noviny,* which, as punishment for their defiant stand at the Congress, the Party leadership placed under the supervision of the Ministry of Culture and Information. Together with the suppression by police of a peaceful student protest march in Prague and Novotny's expressed anti-Slovak bias, as well as his unwillingness to wholeheartedly support a much needed overhaul of the nation's economy, the unresolved pressures which had accumulated over the years led to a confrontation between liberal forces and the old guard. In the end, Novotny was unable to fend off the damaging charges brought against him. His disregard for the basic needs of the country and its people had continued for so long and been carried to such an extent that some of his closest associates were moved to turn against him.

The political struggle which took place within the confines of the Party Central Committee and its Presidium between October 1967 and the first days of January 1968 resulted in a change of the KSC's leadership and paved the way for a major reorientation in policies. This was reflected in the extent and scope of the liberal program proposed by the newly formed Dubcek government.

As indicated in the preceding section, changes had been occurring inside the nation since the initiation of de-Stalinization at the end of 1962. Some were significant innovations, others merely minor ones. But together they amounted to an overall transformation which served to alter the thinking of the people, especially the intellectuals, reactivate public opinion and prepare the nation for its new course. Thus, once the last major remaining obstacle to the movement for reform had been eliminated and Novotny removed from power, the reformers undertook to implement the Czechoslovak road to socalism. The relative speed with which the process evolved was indicative of not only how much the nation desired change, but also how well some of the main sectors involved were prepared to cope with such a major task. The preparedness of the mass media is a case in point.

The press, radio and television became an integral part of the reorientation process. Once freed from the constraints of censorship and arbitrary control, they intensified their condemnation of the past and undertook to explain and support the newly adopted course. How well they succeeded represents, no doubt, one of the crucial aspects of the Czechoslovak experiment as well as an important key to understanding the military intervention that followed. For more than any other reform, the abolition of censorship initially reflected the meaning and significance of the Dubcek administration's proposed course. The freed media allowed the public to comprehend what their country had become, and why, and how the new leadership would change the negative results of past years if given the opportunity and support to implement its policies.

"The free press," to borrow Karl Marx's words, "is a spiritual mirror in which a nation is able to see itself." The idea was very much applicable to Czechoslovakia between the beginning of March and August 21, 1968. During this brief span of some six months the free press exposed much of the pent-up antagonism of the past twenty years, while expressing the nation's hopes and plans for the future.

CHAPTER V

PRELUDE TO CHANGE

One of the immediate consequences of the new press law, which became effective January 1, 1967, was a general review of the nation's press. This resulted in the abolition of many factory organs and small papers of limited circulation and an increase in the size of daily newspapers. An additional factor in these changes was the Party's desire to place added emphasis on the central mass media. Besides, the smaller publications, which had been used primarily for propaganda purposes, had become ineffective and obsolete.

Another prominent issue was the increased demand for information, including access to Western publications, stimulated by a more activist media. As a result of a provision in the press law, the government began importing a limited number of Western papers to be sold for public consumption. Initially, only a few West German and Austrian dailies were imported, but later newspapers and journals from other Western states were added.

While the journalists continued their demands for freer access to information and the reorganization of their Union, the writers focused attention on creative freedom as part of their pre-Congress discussions. They were concerned over the intensification of repressive measures being employed against dissident writers in the Soviet Union and were fearful that a similar wave of suppression would be initiated in Czechoslovakia. Signs of such a trend had already been evident the previous year when *Literarni noviny,* the writers' weekly, had come under frequent attack and its editorial department successively reorganized.(1) Generally, the regime had adopted a tougher policy toward the mass media during fall 1966.(2)

All these factors combined, plus Novotny's fierce condemnation of Israel during the Middle East war which preceded the writers' June Congress by a few days, turned the Congress into a rebellious session, punctuated by passionate speeches condemning censorship and the regime's cultural policy. The result was a break between the Party leadership and the SCSS. In retrospect, it can be said that the Congress, especially the regime's strong reaction to it, signified the beginning of the end of the Novotny era. For the punitive measures taken against the writers and their organization during the months following the stormy session served to further unify the intellectual community against Novotny. Most important, this opposition was felt even among liberal members of the Party's leading bodies.

In marked contrast to the writers' meeting was the Congress of the SCSN which followed in October, a month after the regime had announced its actions against the writers' Union. The carefully staged journalists' Congress voiced support for Novotny's policies and, moreover, criticized the writers' activities and those of its weekly. This ignominious act later greatly affected the journalists and contributed to the eventual reorganization of their Union.

With the ascendancy of Dubcek to the post of Party First Secretary in January 1968, the journalists and writers intensified their demands for the abolition of censorship and freer access to information. They were soon joined by an increasingly aware public which also sought the restoration of freedom of expression. This intensified activism provided substance to the democratization process.

Central Press Emphasized

The beginning of 1967 witnessed several developments concerning the nation's press, stemming not only from the press law but also from a new economic program initiated at the time. The economic reform measures, designed and proposed by economist Sik, affected both prices and wages. In January, for instance, the price of newsprint rose as much as 100 percent above the normal world level while printing costs, due to new wage agreements, increased by 30 percent.(3) Such factors, combined with relevant provisions in the press law, contributed to a consolidation of the press system.

The new economic measures did not greatly affect the nation's major newspapers or viable journals despite the fact that most increased their sale price to reflect the overall increase in material and production costs. They did have a considerable impact on smaller publications, however, especially district and factory newspapers which, during the initial years of Communist rule, the Party had particularly emphasized as propaganda outlets. The number of district papers declined from 95 at the end of 1966 to 61 a year later, while the number of factory publications fell from 373 to

96 during the same period.(4) The main reasons given for the decline of such publications were their "absolute ineffectiveness" and high production costs.(5)

Coinciding with this change was the increase in the average number of pages per week for the major daily newspapers which, as of January 1967, rose by 10 percent from approximately 40 pages to a maximum of 44. As would be expected, the greatest increase was realized by *Rude pravo* whose weekly average rose to 56 pages. According to an official report, the increase in space was aimed at "improving and broadening the papers' content and ensuring their diversified orientation."(6) The perpetual lack of space in the dailies, due primarily to a purported shortage of newsprint, had been a source of constant complaint by journalists. The abolition of smaller papers and increase in space provided the daily press proved to be a positive step since the former publications had displayed low professional standards, both in terms of content and typography. It also was an indicator of the public's growing attraction to the central communication channels, i.e., national papers, radio and television, which increasingly had become more informative and interesting.

Once the press law became effective, all of the nation's periodic publications came under review and were reregistered according to two categories or systems. This review proved to be an additional process for eliminating obsolete, mostly small, publications. The primary category, under which most of the newspapers and periodicals were registered, was the so-called "basic system."(7) This meant that they were considered significant enough to warrant state subsidy, the extent of which generally was determined by their importance. *Rude pravo,* for example, had its own allocation of newsprint, enabling it to have the largest press run of all dailies.

All other publications were registered outside this system and were not subsidized by the state. They had to secure their own financial support from their sponsoring organizations, such as industrial concerns or major factories. These publications were closely controlled and regulated by the ideological and material provisions outlined in Part II (paragraphs 4 and 7) of the press law:

> *Periodicals may be published by political parties, voluntary social organizations, state organs, scientific and cultural institutions, and economic and other organizations in fulfilling their social assignments.*
>
> *(2) Registration cannot be completed if the publication of a periodical is not assured according to planned material-technical,*

> *financial and economic provisions or if, in the application, other provisions are not included to guarantee that the periodical will fulfill its social mission.(8)*

The task of classifying and reregistering the nation's press, in which the SCSN took an active part, was not completed until the final weeks of 1967. Compared to the beginning of the year when a total of 1,247 periodic publications were in existence, the end of 1967 saw the number decline to 1,160, including 931 in the Czech lands and 229 in Slovakia.(9) Of the total, 805 publications were registered under the first category and received some form of state subsidy. The consolidation which occurred in the press was due in part to the shift in the economy but also to the expanding role played by radio and television as well as major newspapers and periodicals.

By the beginning of 1967, no less than 27 daily newspapers were being published, while the number of television sets was quickly reaching the saturation point as 2,328,680 licenses had been issued by December 1, 1966. An additional indicator was that the purchase of television sets had declined from 400,000 in 1965 to 250,000 the following year.(10) It also should be recalled that radio had reached its saturation level several years earlier.

It was evident, therefore, that many of the smaller local publications, originally intended for primarily propagandistic and exhortative purposes, had become obsolete and uneconomical. The main emphasis thus turned to those central mass communication channels which were more attractive to the public, influential and economically efficient.

Access to Information

Another significant development which marked the early months of 1967 was the gradual influx of Western, non-Communist periodic publications which, on a limited scale, were offered for sale to the public. Initially, upon the initiative of the Czechoslovak government, agreements were reached with West Germany and Austria for the importation of four major newspapers from each country. The German papers were *Frankfurter Allgemeine Zeitung, Frankfurter Rundschau, Die Welt* and *Suddeutsche Zeitung,* while from Austria came *Die Presse, Kurier, Arbeiter Zeitung* and *Express.* They were sold primarily for foreign currency at major hotels and spas, but for the first time a limited number of issues were publicly sold for Czech crowns at special newsstands in Prague. Provisions were also made for the public to subscribe to some West German periodicals.

By May, newspapers and magazines from other countries were sold at hotels and other facilities which had provisions for the exchange of foreign currency. Among the forty publications made available were leading newspapers and journals from Austria, France, Great Britain, Italy, West Germany and the United States.(11) And while most of these periodicals could be purchased only for foreign currency and were imported primarily for tourists, a few did reach the special newsstands for local sale.

Although inroads were being made in terms of public access to information, including Western newspapers, the regime continued to maintain control over all incoming publications. The government reserved the right to withhold any foreign papers or magazines which contained information considered detrimental to the state. At times this practice was inconsistent with official statements, as noted in a *Literarni noviny* article. The author pointed out that while the magazine *Der Spiegel* was often held up as an example to Czechoslovak journalists and referred to as "one of the most prominent journals with progressive tendencies" published in West Germany, copies of this magazine mailed to him were confiscated.(12)

The concern regarding access to information and the public's right to know, which first found expression in the press a few years earlier, was intensified with the passage of the press law. One of the main articles pursuing the general topic of how well the nation was informed appeared in *Kulturni tvorba* during December 1966. It was written by Galuska, chief editor of the weekly before it was taken over by the Party Central Committee.

Maintaining that the quantity and saturation of the mass media did not automatically correlate with how well a society was informed, Galuska stated that the public's democratic control remained "an empty word as long as serious social questions are examined behind its back." He then cited specific problem areas where the public was deprived of information, giving special emphasis to the economy. Turning to censorship, Galuska noted that the self-censorship which each journalist found necessary to practice, lest he inadvertently disturb national interests or relations with other states, prevented him from openly expressing what he believed to be the truth regarding certain events and actualities, truth which the public expected from him. Such a situation, Galuska contended, led to "conformity in reporting as well as in commentaries."(13)

Closely related to the question of information access was the frequent attack on the ineffectiveness of the press law and infringements made upon its provisions by various organizations and industrial firms. This continued criticism of censorship and the existing barriers to obtaining information voiced by many major papers, including the Party press in Slovakia,(14) proved to be the main issue pervading the persistent confrontation between the regime and liberal forces in the media. Amidst this tense atmosphere came the six-day Arab-Israeli war, followed within a few days by the writers' Fourth Congress. But before considering this meeting, it is necessary to compare the writers' and journalists' organizations.

Unions and Congresses

Differences Between the Unions

Ever since 1956, following the denunciation of Stalinism and revival of the writer's traditional role as the "nation's conscience," Czechoslovakia's men of letters strove to assert themselves and to liberate literature from the constraints of Socialist realism to which culture was being subjected by the regime. Initially, this was undertaken by, among others, such individuals as Seifert, Mnacko, Hrubin and Skvorecky. The Third Congress in 1963, the Kafka Conference of the same year and the defiant stand taken by the cultural press against increasing Party pressures together served to unify the writers into a center of dissent so that by the onset of 1967 their oppositional role had been crystallized. The writers' organization, therefore, developed into a political force within the cultural field and, as was the case during the nineteenth century, the writers became the opposition to established power and spokesmen of the people.

But how did this come about? Why was the writer's organization, as opposed to that of the journalists, in the forefront of the struggle for national reform? A comparison of the organizational structure of the two groups will point up the basic differences existing between them, differences which in large measure determined the positions they took during their respective Congresses in 1967. It should also provide a better understanding of their actions, especially those of the journalists, once a new leadership took over the reins of government in January 1968.

The Union of Writers was comprised of two basic groups divided along Czech and Slovak lines. The Slovaks, however, were formally organized as the Union of Slovak Writers, considered a subunit of the SCSS, while the Czech writers were identified solely with the national Union. (The two groups did not gain equal status until federalization in 1969.) Thus, the Slovak writers, as a group, were subordinate to the Czech writers who, in essence, dominated the SCSS. This basic structure was of concern to many Slovak writers who, along with reform-minded liberals within the Party in Slovakia, sought more autonomy and an equal footing with their Czech colleagues. This was expressed, for instance, in an interview with the head of the Party section of the SSS which appeared in *Nova mysl.* (15) Translators, meanwhile, comprised a separate part of both sections of the Union.

By 1967 the national Union had 835 members, candidates and translators, broken down as follows: the Czech section — 299 members, 87 candidates and 158 translators; the Union of Slovak Writers — 169 members, 55 candidates and 67 translators. Union headquarters were located in both Bratislava and Prague, while branch organizations existed in Brno, Ostrava, Banska Bystrica and Presov. Further, the SCSS had two publishing houses (in Prague and Bratislava) plus a number of facilities where members could go to pursue their creative literary interests in leisure.

Most important, however, the Union published eleven newspapers and journals and administered its own Literary Fund, monies for which came from voluntary payments in addition to the taxes paid on published books and articles. The fund was used primarily to support writers in their travels or while they were engaged in working on major literary projects. According to one source, between 1961 and 1967 the SCSS registered a profit of some 16.5 million crowns. (16) Thus, the writers possessed their own well-established publications through which they could voice their views, whether on culture, the economy or politics, and were self-sufficient so that they did not have to depend on state subsidies.

On the other hand, the journalists' organization managed to secure a national voice, *Reporter,* only in April 1966 and its own fund, the so-called *Zurfond* (an offshoot of the Literary Fund), the same year. The main purpose of the fund was to support activities leading to the further development of journalism. This included travel grants as well as support for individual journalists engaged in major projects. The SCSN did have some established sources of income, such as money received from the International Organization of Journalists (IOJ) headquartered in Prague, but it was far more dependent on the state for support than was the writers' Union. (17) These two aspects, publications and financial self-sufficiency, represented perhaps the most important differences between the writers' and journalists' organizations. In the end, the SCSS was a smaller but more viable and closely knit organization which was better equipped to counter the regime on major issues than was the Union of Journalists.

Writers' Fourth Congress

In light of events preceding the writers' Fourth Congress, it seems apparent that a confrontation between the regime and writers was inevitable. The date of the Congress was rescheduled numerous times, and the critical nature of articles which appeared as part of the pre-Congress discussion was intense on both sides. Articles published in the cultural press focused on clearly defined demands for more opportunity in the advancement of creative freedom, rehabilitation of still-silenced writers and restoration of literary trends which continued to be held in disrepute by the regime. Such demands carried the implicit requisite of increased liberalization. The Party leadership, meanwhile, intensified its opposition to liberal trends and through Party publications frequently criticized the writers' views and their press, especially *Literarni noviny.* On one occasion, *Rude pravo* even accused the weekly of expressing "anarchic moods."(18) A further harassment was the sharp increase in instances of censorship against materials planned for publication by the weekly's staff.

Between the Union of Writers' Third and Fourth Congresses, the censors intervened a total of 381 times against *Literarni noviny.* With the exception of one case, concerning a reference to the sale of arms by the Czechoslovak government to Nigeria,(19) all such acts of censorship were undertaken with the vague and undefined explanation that the material in question (often a mere phrase or only a word) was in conflict with the best interests of society. The following is an annual breakdown of interventions:

Year	*Number of Interventions* (20)
1963	25
1964	124
1965	85
1966	57
1967 (to September 23)	141

This graphic portrayal of censorship also serves as an added and interesting indicator of the wave-like pattern which liberalization followed.

In preparation for the Fourth Congress, the Slovak writers met on May 11 to elect a new Central Committee and to outline the future tasks and goals of the Union. The leading Party functionary present was Vasil Bil'ak, First Secretary of the KSS, but neither his presence nor his dry speech deterred the writers from demanding increased freedom in the cultural field. The resolution which they issued, therefore, urged "continued and uninterrupted broadening of the scope for the free exchange of views, realization of diverse creative methods and comprehensive democratization of the Union's life." It also expressed full support for all creative work "engaged in criticizing violations or distortions of the humanistic ideals of man."(21) This pronouncement was reflected in the measures taken during the meeting to rehabilitate more writers of the *DAV* group who had been purged in the early 1950's.

During the proceedings, Vojtech Mihalik announced his resignation as the Union's chairman and Miroslav Valek, a non-Party member, was elected to take his place. In his farewell address, Mihalik touched upon several sensitive points along the liberal line, but the remark which stimulated most reaction was his declaration that the writers' Union should establish contact with Czech and Slovak writers in exile. The suggestion was a daring one because the regime regarded any such contact as a treacherous act, subject to severe penalty.(22)

Parenthetically, it should be noted that reaction to the trial and sentencing of Soviet writers Yuli Daniel and Andrei Sinyavsky was deeply felt by the liberal writers in Czechoslovakia, so much so in fact that a delegation of three was sent to Moscow in March 1966 with a protest issued by the SCSS leadership. The delegation's true mission was not revealed publicly, of course, although news of it was carried in the March 15 issue of the Italian Communist paper *L'Unita.*(23) Concern over the fact that Stalinism was returning became even more intense when the conservatives plainly took charge of the proceedings at the Soviet Writers' Congress in May 1967. It was at this meeting that Solzhenitsyn's famous letter urging Union members to safeguard the freedom and rights of all Soviet writers was suppressed. (Later, Solzhenitsyn's letter was read at the Czechoslovak writers' Congress, causing the leading Party representative to storm out of the meeting hall.)

These telling developments were followed by the Middle East crisis and the outbreak of war between the United Arab Republic and Israel, resulting in the break of diplomatic relations between the Soviet Union and the latter state. The Novotny regime was the first in Eastern Europe to imitate the act, at the same time launching a rather vicious propaganda campaign against Israel which was branded the aggressor.

This campaign, waged through the mass media, went to such lengths as to be painfully reminiscent of the anti-Semitic atmosphere surrounding the show trials of the 1950's in which many of the defendants were Jews. Thus, people began to wonder whether the condemnation of Israel was justified and they asked themselves, as did playwright Pavel Kohout during his Congress address later,(24) whether Czechoslovakia could justly have been termed an aggressor in 1938 had their country fired the first shot against Hitler's forces instead of humbly submitting to the dictates of the Munich Agreement. The conservative nature of the Soviet Writers' Congress in May 1967 and Novotny's condemnation of Israel were of great concern to the Czechoslovak writers who feared such actions might be a prelude to a more repressive climate within their country.

This, then, constituted the politically turbulent atmosphere in which the Fourth Congress of the SCSS took place in Prague on June 27-29. The actual events of this now famous defiant stand against the regime's policies are too well known to repeat here. Numerous sources have since appeared which describe the proceedings and summarize the speeches quite adequately.(25) It need only be said that virtually all the writers who addressed the Congress spoke as the nation's social and political conscience, confronting meanwhile the very essence of the Novotny regime's moral and political corruptness — its disregard for basic human values and personal and arbitrary use of raw power.

It must be explained, however, that some writers present were less intense than others in their desire for change and maintained a more sober approach to political reform. Such individuals, for instance, regarded the speeches of their colleagues with a certain amount of apprehension. An example of this concern was expressed in a letter, issued during the course of the Congress, which characterized the proceedings as having adopted excessive political and emotional overtones.(26) Known as the Slovak letter, because it was initiated by some of the Slovak participants, the document was signed by nineteen Czech and Slovak writers.

But this action in no way detracted from the total impact of the

Congress. The message issued by the writers was clear: abolition of censorship, cessation of state interference in the creative process and restoration of humanism in guiding the country.

Journalists' Fifth Congress

In stark contrast to the rebellious proceedings of the writers' meeting was the Fifth Congress of the Union of Journalists which followed in Prague on October 19-20. It can rightly be said that its organizers stage-managed the meeting to perfection; the agenda was followed as outlined and no one spoke out of turn. What is more, the Congress condemned the writers' actions, including the past activities of *Literarni noviny.*

In a prepared letter sent to the Party Central Committee, the Congress delegates, after profusely thanking the Committee for its understanding and support, turned to the matter of the writers' weekly.

> *The positive efforts and purposeful activities of an absolute majority of journalists were disrupted by serious inadequacies, namely in Literarni noviny, which went so far as to attempt to formulate its own oppositional platform. We do not agree with this negative aspect, for it harmed our nation's journalism and depreciated the positive efforts of a large segment of socialist journalists. (27)*

This undignified act on the part of the SCSN represented an added blow to the writers' Union which only a month earlier had been severely disciplined by the regime.

And while the action was officially rescinded in June 1968, it nevertheless proved embarrassing to many journalists, especially to those who sympathized with the writers. It also reflected some of the differences existing between the two organizations. Among the most basic in this respect was the attitude with which the liberals in each group approached reform. As has already been said, the writers generally regarded their mission to function as spokesmen of the people and, consequently, viewed the reform movement on a broader plane than tended to be the case among journalists who focused their attention on reforms within the mass media or areas specifically related to their field, i.e., professionalism, access to information and an improved status in society.

The journalists' approach to internal or professional reform stemmed from a number of realities, primarily the heavy constraints placed on their field and the propagandistic role played by the media during the 1950's, the poor journalistic standards that resulted and, consequently, the low status journalists had reached in society.(28) After de-Stalinization had been initiated, therefore, these internal shortcomings became the focus of attention of liberal-minded journalists who worked toward improving conditions within their profession. And by 1967 the journalistic field had made considerable strides in this respect as delineated in the foregoing chapters. Also, the criticism against infringements in access to information and violations of the press law continued to be voiced in the press throughout the remainder of the year.

Contemporaneous observations made in the West are another source for evaluating the Czechoslovak press of this period. At the onset of 1967, for example, even the conservative *Economist* said that *Rude pravo* was "probably the least unreadable (paper) of its kind in the Communist world," while a former CTK London correspondent, Antony Buzek, noted that after 1965 the daily press in Czechoslovakia was much improved, well informed and performed a good job of reporting.(29) Such remarks, plus the fact that the regime continued in its criticism of liberal journalists, further indicate that the press had indeed changed considerably for the better from its drabness and complete subservience of the 1950's.

What many journalists (especially professionals as opposed to Party hacks) were attempting to do during the latter phase of liberalization was, in essence, to bridge the gap between theory and actual practice. This meant divesting themselves of doublethink phraseology and worn-out Communist cliches. The plain and direct use of the Czech and Slovak languages once again came through quite clearly in the press, as can readily be seen on the pages of *Reporter.* Articles and commentaries by individuals such as Stanislav Budin, Jiri Ruml and Milan Weiner are good examples of the new trend in journalism of this period.

Meanwhile, the journalists' organization itself became an overriding issue to those concerned with reform. During 1967 it consisted of 4,332 members(30) who accrued virtually no social or material benefits from their obligatory membership. This was in marked contrast to the immediate post-World War II period and initial days of Communist rule when organization members had a privileged status and obtained definite material advantages. But during the ensuing years, especially in the 1950's, the SCSN had been increasingly subordinated to the dictates of the Party so that it failed to serve in the capacity of a professional interest group.

As a direct result of this subservience, the SCSN leadership was composed of individuals who for the most part were not involved in practical journalism but served as mere bureaucratic *apparatchiki* carrying out the dictates of the Party leadership. Thus, a definite conflict as to purpose and professional objectives existed between the Union's membership and its ruling body. Due to this situation, most practicing journalists worked outside the organization toward reform, either individually or through their respective editorial departments or collectives with colleagues of similar political beliefs. Such an approach was further necessary because the SCSN, in order to neutralize the influence of the core membership — practicing and in the main reform-oriented newsmen — was artificially inflated with a large number of individuals who had little to do with everyday journalism. This was achieved by including as members many editors of house organs and factory papers, who were subordinate to their respective enterprises, as well as worker-correspondents and 'editors' of bulletin board type newspapers.(31)

Since the Union utilized the principle of regional and district representation, many delegates to the congresses were national committee functionaries who posed as journalists. Their sole claim to this status was that they were responsible for the press in their respective local areas. This regional and district make-up of congress delegates prevailed despite the fact that most practicing and influential journalists (one source has placed it as high as ninety percent)(32) were centered in Prague and Bratislava, the nation's two most important news centers. Yet, they were not allowed to have their own organizations or official groups and, therefore, were not proportionately represented at the congresses. This was the case during the Fifth Congress and provides a partial explanation for the body's willing compliance to Party dictates.

But lest this represent too bleak a picture of the SCSN, one should keep in mind that it did play a prominent role in initiating the press law and, as discussions prior to the Fifth Congress indicated, pressures were being applied by some members for substantial organizational changes. An article of this nature appearing in *Novinar* clearly stated that the SCSN could no longer remain only an ideological and professional organization but, simultaneously, had also to become an "interest" organization. This meant, the author said, that the organization would have to delineate common professional interests "which must be upheld and defended in order that journalistic work be advanced and further development of the mass media assured." He went on to say that it was over precisely this point, what each journalist desired from the organization, that most of the conflict arose among members who frequently asked: "Why do we need a journalists' organization anyway?"(33)

This increased tendency to question, combined with overt confrontations with the regime on specific issues of policy, as was the case during the writers' Congress, was indicative of the tense atmosphere which pervaded the remainder of 1967. And while the Party leadership attempted to reverse the trend, threats alone proved insufficient. Novotny had to resort to actual punishment and repression, which only intensified the display of overt dissent and opposition to his policies.

Novotny's Final Struggle

On September 26 and 27, the Party Central Committee held a plenary session at which time a whole series of repressive steps and reprimands were issued against the SCSS, its publishing house and a number of its members. The stringent measures were a reaction to the writers' Fourth Congress and related activities. *Literarni noviny* was placed under the direct control of the Ministry of Culture and Information with members of the editorial staff either being dismissed or resigning. Three writers lost Party membership, two were severaly reprimanded and dramatist Jan Prochazka was dropped from candidate status of the Party Central Committee for "political mistakes," a euphemism for having expressed pro-Israeli sentiments.(34) Even the chief editor of the Central Committee's *Kulturni tvorba* was replaced to provide the weekly with a more conservative outlook.

The intellectual community's reaction to the regime's repressive stand against the writers was immediate and forceful. A readers' boycott of the reorganized *Literarni noviny* quickly materialized while the Novotny-installed editor, Jan Zelenka, initially found it difficult to obtain credible copy even though he offered larger sums for articles than had been the practice before. Later it was revealed that the paper's operations were funded through the Czechoslovak Center for Book Culture and, subsequently, from a private fund of the Minister of Culture and Information.(35) A tongue in cheek review of the weekly's maiden issue under the Ministry's direction, published in the writers' monthly *Host do domu,* said the paper represented something truly new which everyone could recognize at a glance. "It's almost pathetic how quickly one can recognize it."(36)

Coinciding with the evident opposition to Novotny's handling of the writers' affair was the surfacing of other pressures on the regime. Among them was dissatisfaction on the part of the country's youth whose national congress in June had been pervaded by a political undercurrent and a rather discordant atmosphere. On another front, opposition was voiced by Slovak liberals within the Party. Although the main focus of their concern centered on the ineffectiveness of the new economic reforms and the related economic plight of Slovakia, it encompassed other areas as well. Thus, disagreement also arose over Novotny's policy toward dissident writers. As a result, the Party press in Prague and Bratislava adopted differing viewpoints in articles and commentaries published in recognition of Press Day, celebrated each September 21 in commemoration of the founding of *Rude pravo.*

While *Rude pravo,* in its main commentary of the day, generally backed the regime's policies pertaining to the mass media and spoke in favor of maintaining the status quo in the political situation,(37) the Slovak dailies *Pravda* and *Praca* (Work) took a more realistic and critical view of conditions surrounding the press. A week prior to Press Day, Julius Pal'o, writing in *Pravda,* pursued a nationalistic tone (which the Slovaks' confrontation with Novotny had adopted) by stressing that the nation's press had democratic tradition which had to be continued and even extended. To further emphasize his point, he was openly critical of Lenin's reference to the press as a propagandist, agitator and organizer because, Pal'o contended, these attributes did not provide for the exchange of views and opinions among individuals.(38)

Juray Chorvat, in a *Praca* article published on Press Day, observed that newspaper circulation had not followed dictates "from above," referring to the regime's creation of press run quotas. Praising the diversification of press content, he said that because of it readers were beginning to select papers according to their own preferences and tastes. "We have come to terms with the fact that readers no longer buy their papers according to who publishes them, but according to the type of content and whether or not a paper agrees with the individual's personal or group interests."(39) This underscores the point made earlier concerning public support of those papers which satisfied the demand for current information as opposed to publications, primarily local in nature, which continued to pay lipservice to Party propaganda. Chorvat criticized the persisting interference experienced by newsmen seeking information and also attacked censorship, contending that despite the press law it continued to be used by "central organizations" in order to withhold unpleasant information.

This contrast between the Czech and Slovak Party press on not only matters pertaining to the mass media but other salient questions as well continued and, in part, signified the split within the Party hierarchy, specifically between the regime in Prague and the leadership in Bratislava. Amidst this tension came the Party Central Committee plenum at the end of October which, unbeknownst to anyone at the time, proved to be the beginning of the end of Novotny's political career.

While the meeting was in progress, an incident occurred which intensified the situation and greatly heightened anti-Novotny sentiments. This was the suppression by club-swinging police of a spontaneous and peaceful candlelight march held in Prague by students from the Technical College of Strahov who were protesting the repeated breakdown of the electrical and heating systems in their dormatories. News of the incident quickly circulated throughout Prague, reinforcing opposition to the Novotny regime.

Although the confrontation took place on the evening of October 31, it was not referred to in the press until November 2, and then it was only briefly mentioned.(40) The first comprehensive account of events surrounding the demonstration and methods used to suppress it was published by *Reporter* almost two months later. The article cited the fact that students who had remained in their rooms during the march were later dragged from the dormatories and beaten by police. A dozen students required hospitalization, including a few foreign students from African states, while one participant was critically injured during the melee.(41) Ruml, author of the report, later received a national journalism award for this and a follow-up article on the affair.

Prior to its full disclosure, however, the incident was escalated into a major national issue by students and young professors at the Philosophy Faculty of Charles University. Throughout November they held a number of meetings and sit-ins during which they protested the cruel treatment displayed by police and accused the press of misrepresenting the students' position in the matter. The latter accusation stemmed primarily from an article written by Frantisek Kolar, the new chief editor of the Party weekly *Kulturni tvorba*.

Kolar, formerly of the *Rude pravo* staff, charged student leaders with voicing sentiments similar to those expressed by dissidents at the writers' Congress in June and, further, argued that statements used by some demonstrators indicated a thorough knowledge of Western anti-Communist propaganda such as that disseminated by Radio Free Europe. He added: "The kind of journalism presented by *Literarni noviny* for the past ten years also had its influence."(42) In the end, however, the government submitted to student protests and demands. The special commission established earlier to investigate the incident issued its findings in mid-December with the result that several individuals lost their positions and others were reprimanded.

While the public and press were thus involved in following developments relating to the student demonstration, Novotny found himself struggling for his political life within the confines of closed meetings of the Party Central Committee and its Presidium. During the October 30 plenary session, a confrontation took place between Dubcek and the Presidium's faction of Novotny supporters. In his twenty-minute speech, the future Party First Secretary went from the general to the specific by initially mentioning the perennial issue of Slovakia's development and then launching into a sober but direct attack against Novotny's leadership, although not referring to the Party chief by name. Dubcek concluded his address by demanding the creation of a constructive program aimed at, among other points, resolving the national (Slovak) question.

What ensued was an open debate with the Central Committee resembling, as one observer described, "a bourgeois parliament in a period of crisis."(43) Unbeknownst to the general public or the mass media, the meeting had developed into what was to be the third immediate reason for Novotny's descent from political power (the other two being the June writers' Congress, along with the Party's dramatic reaction to it, and events surrounding the Strahov student demonstration). For Dubcek's attack prompted others to come forward and make their personal views known on the issue of Novotny's power and policies. This, in essence, "mobilized the only body that could alter the leadership of the Party and so created conditions at the top favourable for new policies, new methods of managing the Party itself, and far-reaching social reforms."(44)

The unstable political situation was still unresolved toward the end of December, despite a 48-hour visit to Prague by Leonid Brezhnev in response to Novotny's invitation. Nevertheless, an outward appearance of harmony was projected when the Central Committee session was recessed for a two-week holiday break on

December 21, prompting the *Christian Science Monitor's* East European correspondent to report: "The inference is that compromise — for the sake of unity — gained the day. Apparently once again that master of the Communist 'old guard,' President Antonin Novotny, has proved his skill in weathering criticism. For the time being at least, he is carrying on as party chief as well as head of state."(45) A few days later, *The New York Times* expressed its editorial opinion on the situation in Prague: "Novotny would never have survived this long were he not a skilled politician and intriguer. But every sign suggests that he now faces the sternest test ever, one whose results could have consequences far beyond Czechoslovakia's borders."(46) And although the aging Party chief resorted to various maneuvers and tactics to meet the test and maintain his posts, the situation had gone too far for Novotny to retain control.

Following the holiday recess, the sessions of the Central Committee and Presidium resumed with a committee, appointed in December, submitting a recommendation that the top Party post and presidency be divided and a new Party First Secretary be nominated. The Presidium, however, remained deadlocked as to the nomination of Novotny or Dubcek. Ironically, it was the former's right-hand man and the writers' greatest antagonist, Jiri Hendrych, who, while attempting to save his political existence, managed to dislodge the Novotny faction.(47) Thus, on the morning of January 5, 1968, Dubcek's unanimous nomination was presented to the Central Committee which, in turn, unanimously elected the Slovak functionary as the KSC leader. The action marked the beginning of a new era, for it represented the first major step on the nation's own path toward a more responsive and humane form of socialism.

The Emerging Spring

Although the change in Party leadership was duly reported by the news media, the reports were general and brief so that, initially, the nation seemed suspended in a kind of limbo, waiting for some concrete indication from Dubcek as to the future course. But he remained silent for several weeks. As a result, rumors and speculations ran high throughout the country. The people, who as yet had not been fully informed about events preceding the change, initially displayed some apprehension. But when no major pronouncements were forthcoming, they tended to adopt the attitude that it was simply an internal Party matter — a palace coup — and life would proceed as before.

Even the press provided no clear indication at first as to what the future would bring. The mass media were still operating under the old system of self-censorship and, besides, it was not until well into January that Presidium member Hendrych, still functioning as the Party's chief ideological spokesman, explained what had transpired during the past months at a two-day gathering of editors from all media summoned for that purpose.(48) But even then the entire story was not told. Thus, after the first shock of the news wore off, day-to-day life continued as before.

The initial signs of change which eventually did begin to appear were barely discernible ones, intended not to alarm the public but to prepare it for future developments. This provided Dubcek and those around him with time to consolidate their positions. These initial indicators, appearing in the press as well as on radio and television, were the focus of articles or interviews by such men as Goldstucker, Husak and Josef Smrkovsky, all purge victims who later became prominent spokesmen for the new political course. The first overt sign of a shift in policy, meanwhile, occurred in the cultural field and centered on actions of the writers' Union. This helped stimulate activism among other groups, including Prague journalists. In essence, it was not Dubcek who paved the way but others who spoke for him.

During the second week in January, *Kulturny zivot* published an article by Husak in which he reviewed the successes, shortcomings and deformations of the past while providing a glimpse of what was to come. Emphasizing the negative aspects of previous years, he stated that past policies had led to the bureaucratization of social institutions which contributed to a violation of the relationship between the leadership and the citizenry. This had resulted in complications within the spheres of economics, culture and Czech-Slovak relations.(49) These, it should be recalled, had been the three most pressing problem areas confronting Novotny.

Husak then turned to the future. "Today's European man wants to know what is happening in his state. He wants to understand it, to say something about it, to help decide about his nation's fate and living conditions, to elect its leadership and, then, according to its actions, wants to laud, criticize or recall it." In such a state, he continued, this man "wants to change into everyday concrete practices the constitutional principle that the people are the source of power."(50) Husak further maintained that the citizen desired to have guarantees whereby he could freely apply his right of selection, control and responsibility. Although few at first, similar articles, devoid of the usual monotonous cliches associated with Communist pronouncements, contributed to creating a rejuvenating atmosphere.

Two days following Husak's article, an editorial in *Rude pravo* gave the first indication that Party leaders wished to improve conditions in culture and make amends with the writers. In addition to warning the Ministry of Culture and Information that irregular administrative sanctions would not be tolerated in the future, the editorial also hinted that past cultural policy was being reviewed by the new leadership.(51) Thus, almost seven months after the writers' June Congress and four months after the Union's new Presidium had been constituted, the SCSS, at a meeting of the organization's Central Committee, finally chose its own top leadership. Goldstucker became the new chairman while Valek and Prochazka were elected to serve as vice-chairmen.

The most significant action taken during the meeting, however, was the decision to again publish a weekly newspaper. The publication, named *Literarni listy* (Literary Pages), was to be staffed by the same individuals who had worked on the writers' former newspaper prior to its loss to the government, including chief editor Hamsik and three writers (Klima, Liehm and Ludvik Vaculik) who had been expelled from the KSC following the June Congress. There was no question as to the viewpoint the new weekly would follow. As stated by Goldstrucker, the main purpose of the weekly was "to aid everything that is progressive, cultural and enlightening in the life of our society. It is self-evident that it will not concentrate merely on questions of literature." Then, quoting Bertolt Brecht, he added that "the arts without politics is unthinkable. Therefore, any effort which desires to separate these two spheres is useless."(52)

Indicative of the still unstable situation which existed at the end of January was the fact that the SCSS met with some resistance in its plans for the new publication. This came primarily from the Ministry of Culture and Information which desired to restrict the weekly to 10 pages and a press run of only 50,000.(53) However, after appealing to the Cultural Commissions of the Party Central Committee and the National Assembly, the SCSS reached a compromise with the Ministry of 12 pages and a 120,000 press run. Initially, the writers had requested that their new weekly have 16 pages and a press run of 150,000 in order to be on equal footing with their previous paper, now published under the auspices of the Ministry. The registry permit for *Literarni listy* was issued on February 20.

While the writers were thus engaged in readying the first issue of their new publication, the journalists also moved into action. On February 23, Radio Prague announced that members of several editorial offices in Prague were demanding the convocation of a general meeting of journalists, an *aktiv*, in order to reconsider the results of the Fifth Congress. They were concerned above all with that part of the resolution issued following the Congress which was critical of the writers and their weekly.(54) According to the report, the journalists also demanded discussions on the ineffectiveness of the press law and reasons why some of its provisions were being violated. Besides Radio Prague staffers, the call for such a meeting was supported by the editorial offices of *Zemedelske noviny, Prace, Mlada fronta* and the SCSN publication *Svet v obrazech* (The World in Pictures).

Three days later, upon the initiative of the Agricultural Journalists Club of the SCSN, 380 journalists met in Prague on the occasion of the twentieth anniversary of the Communist takeover in 1948. Following the main address by Professor Sik, who commented on the general political and economic situation, the meeting turned into a stormy session during which the journalists' Fifth Congress, especially its final resolution, was repeatedly condemned. As a result, a call was issued for an irregular congress to be held as soon as possible. In addition, the meeting sent letters to the Central Committee of the SCSN and to Dubcek.

In their letter to the new Party chief, the journalists present gave full support to his part in the revival process of the Party and the democratization of national life. "We want to assure you that the Central Committee (of the Party) can count on us to uphold the progressive thought of the Party's January plenum."(55) Actually, this was the second such communication forwarded to Dubcek by the journalists. In mid-January, a meeting of the SCSN Central Committee unanimously approved a letter to him pledging, on behalf of the nation's newsmen, to stand actively behind decisions reached during both the October and January plena of the Party's Central Committee.(56)

In line with this growing activism on the part of writers and journalists articles continued to appear which helped to further explain the position of the new leadership. Among the more important during the first month of 1968 was one by Smrkovsky, one of the most vocal supporters of the Dubcek administration. A victim of the purges, Smrkovsky nonetheless had gained membership on the Party's Central Committee and was Minister of Forestry and Water Conservation by 1967. His article, published in the January 21 issue of *Prace,* was followed by a political commentary in *Reporter* where he touched upon similar points. This commentary, as well as those by other liberal politicians, journalists, and radio and television broadcasters, brought to public attention the essence of Dubcek's proposed policies. After pointing to the open and responsible actions which a majority of Central Committee members took during the political crisis of 1967-68, Smrkovsky said:

> *If we want the largest number of people to take part in this revival process, we must above all cease to conceal that about which we deliberated. This has nothing whatever to do with sensationalism. What we want and will do is to tell the people the truth, even if it is difficult and unpleasant.*
>
> *This is nothing new; for according to positive traditions of the Party and our nation, no secrecy should exist between the central committee and the people. The more members of society taking part in the political process, the better it can develop. This is why we have to listen to the voices of citizens and provide an avenue for their thoughts. Only in this way are new actions born. (57)*

It is quite clear that what spokesmen such as Smrkovsky attempted to do through these initial articles was not only to inform the public but, above all, to regain the public's trust and reestablish credibility for the Party and its leadership. The reformers well realized that without full public support they could not execute their intended programs completely and effectively. In their endeavor to obtain such support, the new leaders were willingly aided by all the influential mass media, which also sought to regain the full trust of society. And the media were most successful in achieving this end. As a Western journalist visiting Prague later in the spring described it:

> *When the papers came out, crowds stampeded the kiosks. Those gazettes, four small pages of badly printed grayish paper, poor but written with feverish joy by journalists rediscovering freedom of expression, were devoured. The Rude Pravo itself became readable; good Czech replaced its dreary Marxist cliches. When people were not pouring over newspapers, they were avidly listening to the radio or watching television. Tape recorders disappeared from the market; the insatiable ones would record radio programs at the same time they were watching TV. (58)*

It was this initial united effort between the reformers and the press, radio and television which ultimately created the national spirit that permeated the Dubcek era.

On February 29 the first issue of *Literarni listy* was published. In Prague the newsstands which sold the issue were virtually stormed by anxious readers so that the entire edition was sold out by 7 o'clock in the morning.(59) The leading editorial came from the pen of Union of Writers Chairman Goldstucker who eloquently expressed the spirit of the times:

> *Since January 5, I have had the feeling that all of us in this statistically small but in experience and mission large country long for the realization of the ideals of socialism; that is, brotherly love and freedom. We are filled with well being in knowing that from a lost path we have returned to the correct road.(60)*

It soon became apparent that a spontaneous disintegration of the political system established in Czechoslovakia during 1949-52 was occurring. This breakup of Czechoslovakia's closed society, theoretically conceived in 1956 and tentatively initiated in 1962-63, had finally reached its most critical stage toward the end of 1967 when it became evident to most reformers, especially those in the Party, that if their aims were to be achieved it was essential to remove from power the embodiment of the old order, Novotny, and decentralize the closely interwoven Party and state bureaucracy created during his fifteen-year reign.

The spirit of reform with which the opposition was able in the end to remove the old order gradually filtered throughout the nation, helping to unite all the dissenting groups which had worked independently for reform. Thus, there was increased activism among journalists to reorganize their Union so that it would be more responsive to the needs of its members as well as to society in general and more involved in the democratization process which characterized the nation's new political life.

This growing political activism which developed during the first two months of 1968 set in motion conditions for the joining of purpose between the mass media and the new leadership. Both hoped for the establishment of a Socialist democracy, one based on the principles inherent in the nation's pluralistic and humanitarian traditions.

CHAPTER VI

DEMOCRATIZATION AND A FREE PRESS

While January 1968 was a month of some uncertainty and anticipation, followed by a time of power consolidation for the new leadership, the end of February and beginning of March represented a period during which the Prague Spring began to unfold and blossom. This was amplified by the fact that constraints of censorship were gradually waning. During the first two months of 1968, then, journalists in all media proceeded cautiously in their work. But finding increasingly less resistance from the censors, they became bolder in reiterating their earlier demands (i.e., need for more information and ready access to the Western press(1)) and began to respond more fully to the actions taken by the Party Central Committee at the beginning of January.

Meanwhile, press articles, as well as discussions broadcast on radio and television, focused on the need for a freer exchange of views and opinions. The frequency with which this demand was heard soon made freedom of expression a paramount issue not only among the intelligensia but also with the general public which, by this time, was greatly attracted to and involved in the new developments taking form.

Thus, the initial days of March represented the demarcation line after which, for all practical purposes, prior censorship ceased to exist in Czechoslovakia, allowing the nation's communication media to become (until August 21) "among the freest in the world."(2) Instead of directives and Party discipline, the criteria guiding journalists and writers at the time were professional ethics, political maturity and, above all, their own conscience.

The independence gained by the press allowed it to participate fully in discussions concerning democratization and the nation's future course. In so doing, the press not only reflected public opinion but also influenced it and, thus, became a viable political force. During this period of the Prague Spring, the media were supported in their endeavors by the journalists' Union which was reorganized and, under new leadership, reoriented into a true interest group serving both its members and the mass communication field at large.

The activism displayed by the media exceeded the expectations of some members of the leadership and, as a result, attempts were made to curb press freedom as early as April 1968. But because freedom of expression represented a core issue of democratization, the press was able to defend itself effectively against such efforts.

Primarily because of their independence, outspokenness and criticism, the mass media soon came under attack from the Soviet Union and other Communist bloc nations. This later developed into a full-fledged propaganda campaign against Czechoslovakia's leaders and their program as well as the nation's mass media. For the merger of socialism and democracy which socialism with a human face implied and which was fully supported by the Czechoslovak press was seen by Soviet and other Warsaw Pact leaders as a direct threat to the status quo in their own countries and to the maintenance of an already precarious Soviet hegemony in Eastern Europe.

Abolition of Censorship

The need for freedom of expression became a major issue frequently raised in the press and during public discussions once the political situation finally began to stabilize after the initial uncertainty following the Party's January plenum. This was due to two main factors. First, the struggle for a free press had been a continuing and popular issue, so that it presented a familiar rather than a new topic. Second, and most important, the freedom of expression concept was intrinsically connected with the movement for reform because, as one close observer later noted, free speech initially represented "the only guarantee of democratization."(3)

In addition, because of past experiences, most writers and journalists, as well as much of the general public, were distrustful of Party rhetoric. They desired proof in the form of concrete action. For, as playwright Vaclav Havel later noted, "democracy is a matter not of faith but of *guarantees.*"(4) It should be added, however, that from the KSC leadership's viewpoint, press freedom was not so much "a *guarantee* of democratization . . . as a necessary *means* toward it."(5) Dubcek, after all, needed public support against the entrenched Novotnyite bureaucrats and for his Action Program; he required public opinion on his side. What better way to gain it than through a favorably inclined mass media? Thus, pressures from below and needs from above worked hand in hand, placing the mass media in an advantageous position.

As early as January 30, a letter demanding that people be allowed to express themselves freely and voice their opinions openly was signed by 175 prominent individuals from all fields and sent to Dubcek. This was followed during ensuing weeks by declarations from editorial offices, concerned organizations and spontaneously assembled ad hoc groups calling for free speech and abolition of censorship. Even *Rude pravo* became involved in this general concern, first cautiously but later more forcefully. An article published under the heading of "Concerning Tolerance," for instance, was critical of the daily's own past coverage of cultural affairs. The author noted that instead of talking about the content of certain books and articles, or the free flow of ideas, "we quite often only discussed the right of their existence."(6) He also urged a freer atmosphere in the exchange of differing opinions.

The first issue of *Literarni listy* included a feature in which prominent figures in the creative field were requested to comment on the future role of the writers' weekly in the democratization process by responding to the question "From where, with whom and where to?" In the light vein which was his style, but which did not detract from his meaning, novelist Skvorecky said: "From the spot in the ring where you were downed by a blow below the belt (the writers' loss of their weekly in 1967), with your readers who are your fans and until victory with a K.O. over strongmen for whom tomorrow represents yesterday." In a more serious tone and perhaps best summing up the essence of all other responses, Svitak answered: "From a totalitarian dictatorship toward an open society, toward the liquidation of power monopoly and active control of the power elite by a free press and public opinion."(7)

Typical of the many published declarations demanding a free press was the statement issued in early March by the Faculty of Enlightenment and Journalism of Charles University. Stressing that the mass media "must play a vital role in the revival process," the statement called for a return to earlier conditions "when no prior censorship existed."(8) It further urged that the National Assembly, i.e., the government, publish its own daily newspaper and that the deprecatory attitude toward journalists be altered.

In mid-March, Communist members of the UPS also issued a public statement in which they indicated full support for the initiation of democratization and, surprisingly, recommended that preliminary political censorship be abolished.(9) The statement followed a February meeting during which the censors had critically evaluated the UPS and its activities. They also expressed concern over the fact that their superiors, including Interior Minister Josef Kudrna, had remained silent despite the public outcry against censorship. (Shortly thereafter Kudrna was dismissed from his post.)

As a result of the urgency and frequency with which the issue of press freedom was raised both publicly and within the Party, the new leadership was forced to respond. The first positive action taken in this respect was by the Party Presidium which, on March 4, rescinded its August 1966 decision regarding control of the censorship board, thus removing the UPS from the jurisdiction of the Ministry of the Interior and concomitantly from the arbitrary control of the Party *apparat.* (10) After more than fifteen years, then, for all intents and purposes, prior censorship ceased to exist in Czechoslovakia.

At the same time, steps were initiated to amend the press law in order to legalize the Presidium's action. During March, the Ministry of Culture and Information requested the SCSN, the SCSS and the two National Assembly committees which had assisted in drafting the press law to reevaluate it and submit those recommendations they deemed necessary. Deliberations on the proposed amendment, however, proved to be strained because when it came to the final question, complete abolition of censorship, not all those concerned were willing to go to such lengths. Besides, the leadership itself was divided on the question.

This was made clear in a *Reporter* article which pointed out that opposition to unlimited press freedom existed within various sectors, including the Party Central Committee. It further stated that as a result of the evident procrastination and indecisiveness in amending the press law, writers, journalists, scientists and others in various sectors of society were growing impatient. The article concluded with a strong argument in favor of a free and politically uninhibited press, stating in effect that promises and claims should be supported by action:

> *If it is contended that socialism will go beyond capitalism, even in regards to such questions as democracy and liberty, this means that we have to proceed along the following premise, that is, from assuring formal and political freedom of the press to the developing of a true and positive liberation of man from various economic, political and social pressures. (11)*

Similar arguments continued to be voiced in the mass media and during public discussions so that, after nearly four months of hesitation, the amendment to the press law was finally passed by the National Assembly on June 26. Thus, a practice which had been in effect since early March was formally and legally confirmed.

The Assembly vote on the measure was 197 for, 30 against and 17 abstentions.(12) The briefly worded amendment said in part:

> *(1) Censorship is inadmissible.*
>
> *(2) Censorship is understood to be any infringement whatsoever by state organs against freedom of the word and picture and their dissemination by the mass information media. This does not affect the authority of the public prosecutor or the courts.(13)*

The law did hold chief editors or their deputies responsible for not allowing any information to be published which concerned state, economic or military secrets. But this was to be primarily a matter of editorial judgment with the editors guided by a list of topics covering the above categories. The list, to be compiled by the government, was still in the process of being completed at the time of the August invasion. It must be made clear, however, that with the passage of the amendment to the press law the mechanism of censorship was disbanded. The censors, who since March had been merely biding their time, vacated their desks in the editorial offices. Prior restraint ceased to exist.

As expected, the abolition of censorship was favorably received by the public as revealed in a survey conducted by the Czechoslovak Institute of Public Opinion which, during the period between January 1968 and March 1969, recorded trends in public opinion on various events and situations. Of the quota sample (N = 1772) used in the survey on the press law, 86 percent approved its passage while only 5 percent did not approve and 9 percent had no opinion.(14)

Passage of the amendment was essentially an action after the fact and, as such, represented another peculiarity of the democratization process. This was the revolutionary fervor which permeated the initial phase of the Dubcek era, best reflected in that reforms were often adopted and put into practice by resolution or political decision. Only later were they legalized by the passage of formal legislation. This also characterized the speed with which democratization took hold in the country.

The restoration of a free press must be viewed from two perspectives. First, it was the only method whereby the mass media could regain its credibility and achieve those ends for which it had struggled, under the leadership of the cultural press, following de-Stalinization. Equally important, the reformers considered a free press a primary guarantee that democratization would be carried to its conclusion and the proposed Socialist democracy established.

It must be rememberd also that at the time Dubcek replaced Novotny, the Party's credibility among the public was extremely low. It became essential, therefore, that the people's trust in the Party be restored. Clearly, this could no longer be achieved through halfway measures. It had to be accomplished through the adoption of such radical and wide-ranging provisions as were contained in the Action Program.

This document represented the blueprint for a new model of Socialist society which incorporated democratic concepts, including freedom of expression and other basic human rights, and conformed to the traditions, needs and existing realities of the Czechoslovak nation.(15) In brief, the Program, approved April 5, represented the vehicle through which socialism with a human face was to be initiated and the public provided with the means whereby it could participate to a degree in the decision-making process.

As naive as it may now seem, the public's participation in helping to determine the nation's course was nevertheless the essence of democratization and the spirit of the Czechoslovak experiment. At the heart of it was a free press. Ironically, press freedom was also a major issue contributing to the deterioration of the Dubcek era. For almost as soon as it was realized, press freedom became a primary target of criticism launched against Czechoslovakia by Soviet and other East European leaders. To them, the functioning of a free press represented a definite threat which had to be nullified.

The elimination of censorship, the first main public issue considered following the January change in Party leadership, thus enabled democratization to unfold inside the country as rapidly and as extensively as it did. It also transformed the press into a more independent and generally united political force which influenced as well as reflected public opinion and provided a cohesive base for the nation's unification of purpose. One cannot help but be reminded that 120 years earlier the imperial decree of March 15, 1848, also abolished censorship and established a new era in Czech and Slovak journalism.

Political Metamorphosis of the Press

Soon after the Party's January plenum, definite changes began to be reflected in the nation's print media. This was seen not only in press content and a greater diversification among the individual publications, but also in staff changes, redefinitation of editorial policy and, especially, increased media independence. The general transformation became most evident in Prague's major dailies, although it quickly permeated the entire mass communication field, including radio and television.

This change can be interpreted as a natural reaction to the tight controls which had been imposed on the press during the past two decades. But it also must be seen as an effort on the part of journalists to vindicate themselves and cast off the image of their being spokesmen for the Novotny regime. Wanting to be free, to act independently and to fully support democratization, therefore, was a logical outgrowth of the journalists' desire to regain credibility and public trust, and to cleanse themselves of the lackey image which they had acquired under the previous political regime.

It also must be realized, however, that freedom of action was in effect thrust upon them. Once censorship was abolished and provisions of the Action Program initiated, there were no directives or instructions to the press forthcoming from above. No longer were journalists told what was right or wrong in either domestic or foreign affairs, what resolution would be approved unanimously and with great enthusiasm at one meeting or another, or generally what to write about and how. No longer were editors instructed on what page to publish an article by some Party functionary. "The question of 'how to do it' had to be answered by the individual editorial offices and their staff members themselves."(16) Or, as the former editor-in-chief of *Literarni listy* later wrote: "For the first time in our lives we were producing a paper with no censorship and no outside dictation of ideas; nothing but our own conscience and sense of responsibility."(17)

Another policy change was the discontinuation of the nomenclature rule, meaning that no longer was it mandatory for only Party members to fill responsible positions in the mass media. Thus, persons who had been previously deprived of gaining such positions were provided the opportunity to do so. This also meant that individuals recognized as opponents of the status quo under Novotny, as well as those who supported democratization generally, gained prominent positions in editorial offices. Such editorial staff changes were conducted in a democratic manner, by consent of editorial councils and approval of the editorial staffs involved. A case in point was the situation of *Reporter*.

Although in March Hradecky was reaffirmed to continue as chief editor of the magazine by the Central Committee of the SCSN, the editorial collective of *Reporter* opposed the decision and forced him to resign. In an open editorial, the staff explained that because Hradecky had been hesitant in fully supporting the new course and continued to follow a compromising policy after January, he had progressively lost the confidence of journalists, including those working in the editorial office of *Reporter.* "We therefore cannot agree that comrade Hradecky remain at the head of the magazine."(18) He was replaced by Budin, a former editor of *Rude pravo* who had been expelled from the KSC in 1936. Hradecky, however, was allowed to remain as Budin's deputy. It is important to note that Hradecky had been chairman of the journalists' organization during its Fifth Congress in 1967 when it denounced the writers and their weekly. This no doubt contributed to the action taken against him by his staff.

Similar decisions were reached in other editorial offices. In late March, for instance, *Vecerni Praha* announced the dismissal of its chief editor, while a few days later a new editor-in-chief was named to head *Prace* which, along with *Zemedelske noviny* and *Mlada fronta,* initially stood at the forefront of this internal transformation and liberation of the press. By such actions, the journalists let it be known they were done with the past while making certain that their freedom would continue.

This was indicated, for example, in a statement by a member of the editorial council of *Prace* to a meeting of the Party members of the Revolutionary Trade Union Movement (ROH). Contending that the direction of the daily must change, he declared: "In order to prevent any deformations from taking place in the direction of the paper, so that in the movement's interest Prace is able to express itself basically and critically about this or that organization or functionary, even if he stands on the top rung of the ladder, we request that Prace be directed not by a single ROH secretary or a single department or even by a functionary of the apparat, but by an elected body."(19) The staff demanded, in effect, that the relationship between it and the ROH leadership be changed in order to prevent any future arbitrary control as had occurred in the past.

A similar situation developed within the staff of *Student* which, in an editorial stance on March 6, 1968, took steps to become an independent publication. Since its founding in 1965, the weekly had been an organ of the Central Committee of the Czechoslovak Union of Youth and its Council of Higher Education. Its main audience, therefore, was university students. In a lengthy editorial, the staff noted that due to the conflict which had arisen between the CSM and the organization's university student members, *Student* could no longer serve both.(20) The conflict referred to, whose roots were in CSM activities under Novotny and its pro-regime stance in the Strahov affair, had intensified by the end of January to the point of a break between the two groups. A month after publication of the editorial, *Student* ceased to be a CSM organ and became, until its demise following the invasion, a weekly journal of the young intelligentsia. Its staff, meanwhile, was altered with the new staff, headed by Kusak, comprised of graduates of the Journalism Faculty in Prague. The paper soon developed into one of the most radical publications and spokesmen of the Prague Spring.

The changes which took place in the press had a profound effect on the democratization process. The influence of the press, as well as radio and television, was reflected in the fact that it fought for and achieved the abolition of censorship and was the prime mover in the March 22, 1968, resignation of Novotny from the post of President. Toward the end of this campaign against Novotny, even *Rude pravo* joined the cause when, on March 18, the paper 'invited' Novotny to step down from his office. Geoffrey Moorhouse, in the next day's issue of *The Guardian,* explained the Communist daily's action to his English readers in this way: "It is as though in two days flat the 'Daily Express' had invited the Queen to abdicate and vowed to go pro-German from now on."(21)

In fact, two days following its stance on Novotny, the editorial collective of *Rude pravo* issued a self-criticism of its past activities, citing the errors which it had committed. It also expressed full support for the actions taken by the Party Central Committee in January and the democratization process.(22) Although attempts were also made to unseat the daily's chief editor, Oldrich Svestka, these efforts failed. However, three of his conservative deputies were replaced by two more liberal-minded journalists who served as a check on the editor.(23) In the end, even the most conservative of the Party papers joined the cause of the revival process.

Perhaps the best indicator of the success of the press in improving its image and regaining public trust was the increased demand for practically every issue of the leading dailies, weeklies and magazines. Some editions in Prague were sold out within an hour of reaching newsstands. Press runs had to be rapidly increased to meet this demand. In January, for instance, *Prace* had a circulation of some 70,000, while by March the number had increased to 114,000.(24) This represented an increase in excess of sixty-two percent within three months. The only major daily which dropped in circulation and sales during this period was *Rude pravo.* (For circulation figures of other dailies at this time, see Appendix II.)

It must be added, however, that the independence gained by the press was not, in all instances, utilized for unselfish purposes. Some sensationalism, opportunism and irresponsible reporting on the part of individual journalists and publicists did occur. According to a former Czech journalist, there were cases when newsmen wrote contrary to instructions given them by their editors. In most of these cases, the article in question was not editorially revised because "any tampering with the author's text would be considered a violation of the proclaimed freedom of the press." Hence, he concluded, "there is no doubt that there existed the conditions for a kind of anarchy; but it should be noted that actual anarchy was only a marginal phenomenon in the reform media at the time, although the Warsaw Pact critics were of course making a great deal of it."(25) This example shows to what lengths editors went in safeguarding freedom of expression. But it also exemplifies prevailing conditions which lent themselves to negative interpretations by those who opposed a free press and the nation's new course.

Despite such individual cases, the press on the whole acted responsibly and accepted its role in society with a great deal of seriousness. If it had not done so, it is difficult to believe that the press would have gained the support and influence it did achieve in the end. It spoke out openly and kept the nation informed. As a result, the press, together with the electronic media, constituted a political force — a supporter of democratization and fierce critic of those who would stand in the way of the reform process.

The journalists' organization, meanwhile, was restructured into a more responsive and active body. As such, it was able to assist the media in fulfilling their new role.

Activity Within the SCSN

Efforts to revitalize the Union of Journalists and improve conditions for the press, as noted in the previous chapter, were begun in February at the initiative of the editorial departments of Radio Prague and several publications based in the city. The spontaneous action was unexpected by the SCSN leadership, still under the direction of chairman Hradecky, whose initial response on February 29 was merely to take the issued demands under advisement. But the leadership failed to formulate any concrete action based on or in response to the demands. Instead, it called for a joint meeting, to be convened within two weeks, of the Central Committees of the Union's Czech and Slovak sections.(26) Other pressures, however, were soon brought to bear on the SCSN Presidium.

These came in the form of official statements by the Slovak journalists, whose Central Committee met on March 8, and the newly founded Club of Independent Journalists, composed of free-lancers, whose organizational meeting was held three days later. Both groups expressed full support for the Party's post-January course. They also took up the call for rescinding all negative actions taken by the SCSN Fifth Congress against the writers, abolishing censorship, and rehabilitating those journalists who had been illegally prosecuted or purged during past years.(27) While the free-lance journalists also demanded that an irregular congress be held as soon as possible, the Slovaks sought to recall all documents and official references which had condemned their actions during the 1963 Bratislava conference.

A joint meeting of the Central Committees of both the Czech and Slovak journalists' organizations was held in Brno, but not until March 19-20. And although the convocation of an irregular congress was recommended at the meeting, no definite date was specified other than it should be held before the end of the year. Hradecky resigned as SCSN chairman but retained his seat, along with twelve other incumbent members, on the new seventeen-member Presidium that was chosen. It seemed evident that the conservative leadership was not prepared to give much ground to demands for organizational reform.

As a final gesture, the Presidium attempted to explain the circumstances behind the critical references to the writers and their weekly which had been incorporated in the SCSN Fifth Congress documents issued the previous fall, including a letter from the delegates to the Party Central Committee. The leaders maintained that a member of the Party *apparat* had insisted that criticism of the writers be included in the letter without providing delegates a text prior to its approval.(28) At best this was a weak attempt at shifting the blame for its own irresponsible action to someone else. This was underscored in a critical declaration published by the

Reporter staff a few days later. "In place of sincere criticism, the Presidium is seeking excuses for its actions of the past."(29) The staff further declared that because it could not agree with any of the Presidium's decisions made during the meeting, it was disassociating itself from them.

Due to such evident stalling and hesitation on the part of the SCSN leadership, a need arose for more forceful action from the membership. The most significant event in this respect came on April 1 when 870 Prague journalists representing all media, including the CTK, founded the Prague Branch of the Union of Journalists (POSN).(30) The Prague journalists adopted a wide-ranging ten-point program which sought better conditions in the communication field, including press freedom, reorganization of the SCSN, and improvement in relations between the government and the press, especially in the area of freedom of information.

These and other requests pertaining to furthering democratization in mass communication were contained in a letter addressed to the Party Central Committee and personally delivered to Cisar, one of several Party secretaries, who assured the delegation that the Central Committee "does not intend to renew any form of direct management of the press."(31) The Prague Branch in essence took over the leadership of the Union, helping to accelerate and finalize plans for the Irregular Congress and, thus, stablilize the situation within the organization. Instrumental in creating conditions favorable to a more independent press, the POSN served as an interest group in both helping to formulate the amendment to the press law and seeing to its approval by the government. Separate commissions were created to coordinate these activities as well as to consider the rehabilitation of journalists, draft new SCSN statutes and review the status of Prague journalists serving as members of the SCSN Central Committee. The liberal attitudes of its members were not only reflected in the Branch's policies but also carried over to Prague editorial offices, influencing the type of reports and commentaries published in the press and broadcast over radio and television.

The June 21-23 Irregular Congress, legally convened after more than one-third of the SCSN membership signed a petition as provided by statute, can be seen as both an end and a beginning. It ended an era during which the nation's "information system was deeply deformed" and the uncontrolled force of power that created it "led to the disruption of democratic and national traditions, expressed itself in bullying directive methods, and reached its height in a system of political censorship."(32) It also signified, however, the beginning of a period which saw the nation's press traditions restored — the functioning of an outspoken, critical and well-informed press that took an active part in the nation's political direction.

The Congress adopted new statutes in which the Union was no longer an ideological organization but a voluntary, social, creative and interest or unionist organization. This was significant because the SCSN could again safeguard not only professional standards but also its members' material requirements and other needs of a unionist character which had been much neglected in the past. As part of its actions, the Congress renounced once and for all the 1967 resolution criticizing the writers and the activities of *Literarni noviny.*

In regard to organizational matters, the SCSN was restructured so that its two sections, the Union of Czech Journalists and the Union of Slovak Journalists, were made autonomous, united through their respective Central Committees under the Center of Journalists of the Czechoslovak Socialist Republic (UNCSSR). The two groups met in separate sessions on the third day of the Congress. Thus, the journalists were the first formal group to take positive steps toward federalization, a provision included in the Action Program, which actually went into effect January 1969. (Unlike most provisions contained in the Action Program, the proposal to federalize Czechoslovakia was implemented after the Warsaw Pact invasion.)

On the second day of the proceedings, Dubcek addressed the Congress. It was a low-keyed, realistic speech in which he thanked the journalists for their support and urged them to continue their work in keeping the public aware of and active in national affairs:

> *It is impossible to imagine the public's participation in politics without your active work. And without the participation of the public, without the activity of the people regardless of their party affiliation, the approach to the new politics would be impossible. There would be no renaissance of political life.(33)*

He also cautioned his listeners to be aware of the dangers emanating from the left (the ultra reformers) and, especially, from the conservative elements within the Party.

Two resolutions were approved by the Congress. One was politically oriented while the other dealt with legal matters pertaining to the press law. The latter cited the following as the most important points in guaranteeing the unabridged dissemination of word and picture:

> *I. inadmissibility of any censorship whatsoever,*
>
> *II. abolition of administrative permission for the founding of newspapers and periodicals,*
>
> *III. safeguard of the broadest law possible concerning sources of information,*
>
> *IV. realization of legal protection for the professional status of newsmen and adjustment of their right-to-work conditions. (34)*

The political resolution, meanwhile, represented a declaration of freedom, calling for the unabridged pursuit of democratization to its ultimate end. The concluding portion of the document said:

> *The nation's press, radio and television after January gained a historic opportunity to work under conditions of freedom, which the dogmatic revision of principles of socialist journalism disclaimed both in theory and practice. But actual practice has proven that free journalism is not only possible under socialism, but also that it is a necessary condition of socialism's democratic development and the instrument of the public's self-realization. (35)*

The Irregular Congress was a culmination of steps taken toward revitalizing the SCSN and, thus, rehabilitating Czechoslovak journalism from its enforced subordinate role. Such steps, begun during liberalization following the December 1962 decision to de-Stalinize but greatly intensified after the events of January 1968, were undertaken by rank and file members and later spearheaded by the organization's newly formed Prague Branch. The Congress, as a result, was primarily political in nature. Aside from signifying a clear break with the past, it openly confirmed what had already become evident — the mass media's entry into the nation's new political life. This was made explicit by Vlado Kaspar, the Union's newly elected chairman, who explained the significance of press activism since March: "The intense discussions, and in the end even the voices of the fiercest critics, substantiate the fact that the nation's journalism has entered the public arena as a co-creator of politics."(36)

The cords of structure, deeds, practices and personalities which had bound the SCSN to an ignoble past were thus visibly cut. A new era began, marked by new press principles and practices as well as new relations between the media and society. At the same time, however, the campaign against such developments was being intensified in the press of the Warsaw Pact countries.

In Defense of Freedom

Throughout most of the first three months of the Dubcek era, the press of the Warsaw Pact countries refrained from commenting on Czechoslovakia's internal situation after having officially acknowledged the change in Party leadership. And, likewise, it can be said that Czechoslovakia's press soon became engrossed in its own country's affairs so that, with the exception of the Polish student demonstrations during March 1968, it took little notice of its Socialist neighbors. Even those journalists who under Novotny had preferred reporting international affairs turned their attention to covering and commenting on developments at home.

In March, however, this seemingly quiet atmosphere in the neighboring Socialist countries began to change. And soon a full-fledged propaganda campaign against Czechoslovakia developed in the press of the Warsaw Pact nations, with the noted exception of Rumania.

The initial charges raised came from East German leaders who said, in essence, that events taking place in Czechoslovakia were affecting the relations of the two countries. The accusation was made by Politburo member Kurt Hager who, a few days later, criticized Smrkovsky in particular. This was significant because not only was Smrkovsky one of the leading exponents of democratization, but he was also soon to become a member of the KSC Presidium and chairman of the National Assembly.(37) Hager's speech, published in *Neues Deutschland,* followed a meeting in Dresden at which Dubcek was called on to explain the situation in Czechoslovakia to leaders of the Warsaw Pact countries. At about the same time, Czechoslovak publications ceased to be distributed in East Germany.

Although East Germany's accusations were officially protested by the Czechoslovak government, the nation's press initially did not become involved in such exchanges. Only later, when the campaign against the nation's new liberal course, press freedom and specific individuals became explicit and intensified, did journalists feel they could no longer remain silent.

Among the first press reactions to Soviet articles commenting on developments inside Czechoslovakia was that of *Zemedelske noviny.* This was in regard to a TASS statement and a lengthy article by the daily *Sovetskaya Rossia* (Soviet Russia) concerning the investigation being conducted into the death of former Foreign Affairs Minister Jan Masaryk, son of the nation's first president. Articles had appeared in the Czechoslovak press which linked Soviet agents to his alleged suicide in February 1948. While TASS merely labeled such accusations as "attempts to stir up anti-Soviet sentiments among politically unstable people," the Moscow daily actually accused President Tomas Masaryk of having financed a plot to kill Lenin in 1918.(38) The unsubstantiated charge carried added impact since President Masaryk was in the process of being fully rehabilitated and restored to his rightful place in the nation's history.

The Czech daily characterized the Soviet statement as so lacking in objectivity and disrespectful of Czechoslovakia's first president that it was unworthy of comment.(39) Several subsequent Soviet articles which were critical of developments or individuals inside Czechoslovakia were reprinted in the nation's newspapers, enabling people to read what was being written about their country in the Soviet press.

By this time (early April), some opposition to the press was being voiced inside the country as well, even by several leading proponents of the revival process. Such criticism was, in large measure, a response to articles which dwelt on the theme of the deformation of socialism by describing the mistakes and illegalities committed under Communist rule in the past. In part, however, it was also a reaction to the journalists' and writers' campaign seeking the abolition of censorship. As noted earlier, not all leaders were prepared to proceed quite so far as to allow complete press freedom. As a result of the anti-press sentiment expressed in some quarters of the country, worker organizations were established in defense of a free press.

The first such Workers' Committee for the Defense of Press Freedom was formed as early as the end of April in an Ostrava chemical plant, although it was not acknowledged until a month later. When reporting the creation of this Committee, *Literarni listy* pointed out that, shortly before its formation, top Party functionaries were criticizing the press in the area.(40) On the same day, Radio Prague also reported the emergence of such groups, which by then had been organized in five other plants in the Ostrava region. Quoting from their programs, the report said that the Committees would exist "as long as censorship is not abandoned and as long as freedom of the press is not guaranteed by unequivocally clear laws."(41) While there is no real evidence to suggest that such Committees were overly active, their existence nonetheless does show that there was support among the workers for the cause of the writers and journalists.

Despite such support, the press soon found that it had to defend itself against a two-front attack. By May, it was facing criticism both from within the country and from abroad. The Soviets kept a close eye on the Czechoslovak media, critically commenting on any article which seemed to be outside the proper conduct of a Socialist press. A good example was the censure of Havel by *Literaturnaya gazeta* (Literary Gazette) in response to an article by the playwright published in the April 4 issue of *Literarni listy.* Havel had expressed the belief that the true guarantee of a Socialist democracy was not only a free press but a "Socialist social structure patterned on the *two-party model."*(42) In other words, he was speaking in favor of creating an opposition party.

The Soviet literary weekly attempted to tie Havel's views to those expressed by VOA and, concerning an interview Havel had given, maintained that he had "overjoyed *The New York Times* with a whole series of confidences."(43) The Soviet publication viewed such activities as an attack on the Socialist system in Czechoslovakia.

On the domestic front, the critical nature of the press and its influence on the public was also viewed with some alarm by the Party leadership. This concern could be seen, for instance, in Dubcek's speech to the Party Central Committee plenum held May 29 - June 1, 1968, in which he was clearly critical of the excesses of the press and its disregard for the possible consequences of its actions. Expressing hope that the press would continue to support the policy of democratization, he nevertheless charged that journalists "did not see the objective consequences of their influence upon society. The one-sided underlining of mistakes and shortcomings influenced public opinion to the effect that there arose a feeling of uncertainty and mistrust among part of the people toward our policy." He then continued:

> *If communists and socialist-minded journalists want to support the regeneration of socialist democracy, they must take into consideration the real political situation, which changes quickly, and the objective influence of their activity. They cannot proceed only from their subjective wishes. Unconsidered, even though well-meant appearances harm it objectively and play into the hands of both rightist opposition elements and dogmatic forces.(44)*

Such words of warning were an attempt at restraining the mass media from excesses in criticizing too severaly the shortcomings of Communist rule, because the Party leadership was only too well aware of the nervousness displayed by the leaders of the Warsaw Pact countries over Czechoslovakia's process of democratization and what to them were anti-Socialist manifestations. Some journalists and writers also attempted to serve as a restraining force on their more impatient colleagues who were quick to condemn the past. As Budin wrote in one of his commentaries: "The press and mass media must courageously expose all the evil and rottenness that has accumulated in our society — but they should not take on the task of judges."(45) These realists in essence attempted to maintain a perspective and balance in the press, reminding eager and radical co-workers of their social responsibility as journalists during the rapidly changing and often chaotic times.

Meanwhile, during a June visit to Moscow at the head of a parliamentary delegation, Smrkovsky assured his Soviet questioners that press freedom in Czechoslovakia was only temporary and that after the journalists had had an opportunity to expend themselves they would be curbed.(46) It is difficult to assess whether or not Smrkovsky really envisioned his prediction, but it certaintly was intended as an assurance to the Soviets that the KSC was in control of the situation.

Smrkovsky's remarks soon became known to Czechoslovak journalists, however, and caused them not only to criticize him for the comment but also to intensify their drive to have specific statements pertaining to the press clarified and to ensure the passage of the amendment to the press law. At this stage, because of such remarks and the anti-press feeling being voiced, most journalists were actually more fearful of internal suppression of their rights than intervention from abroad.(47) Thus, the relationship between the mass media and the Party leadership was somewhat strained during the months of May and June.

This critical mistrust, however, soon changed into cooperation when during July and August the leaders of the Warsaw Pact countries, through the press and a series of meetings, intensified their criticism of the Czechoslovak path to socialism and its principle of press freedom.

The Final Phase

The relative calm and rejuvenating spirit which had pervaded the spring months in Czechoslovakia was abruptly halted on June 27 with the simultaneous publication by *Literarni listy* and three Prague dailies of the now famous manifesto called "2,000 Words." Its publication marked the beginning, although not necessarily was it the cause, of the final two anxious months of the Czechoslovak experiment of 1968. Penned largely by Vaculik, an editor of the writers' weekly, the manifesto was signed by some seventy persons from all walks of life.

The document was not anti-Communist. In fact, it expressed support for the Action Program and for the liberal wing of the KSC and urged the people to back their government, even with weapons, "so long as it does what we give it the mandate to do." What the manifesto did criticize was the nation's misdirection by the previous Party leadership and, as a result, it requested the resignation of discredited leaders "who had misused their power." To achieve this end, it called for, if necessary, "public criticism, resolutions, demonstrations, . . . strikes, and boycotts."(48) The primary reason for the document was to express dissatisfaction with the slowness with which the Party leadership was initiating its liberal program. It demanded that this process be speeded up and carried to fruition as soon as possible.

The manifesto's most prophetic words, as it turned out, were those at the end: "This spring, as after the war, a great opportunity was returned to us. Again we have the possibility of taking into our own hands a common cause, . . . The spring has just ended and will never return. During the winter we will know everything."(49)

It was evident that the manifesto had caught the Party leadership off guard. The Party Presidium, hurriedly convened into an extraordinary session, condemned the "2,000 Words" manifesto, as did the National Front Central Committee. Even Dubcek inserted an extemporaneous remark of "great concern" into a prepared speech, (50) disassociating himself and the Party leadership from the views expressed in the manifesto. A number of leaders, not all conservatives, issued statements criticizing the document.

The sharpest public response, however, came in an article published in *Pravda* (Moscow), the official Soviet Party voice, which called the manifesto an oppositional platform that would "pave the way for counterrevolution." It also took Czechoslovakia's mass media to task for openly conducting "subversive" activities, adding that some press and information organs had taken an affirmative position on the manifesto:

The newspapers Prace, Zemedelske Noviny and Mlada Fronta and Prague radio and television are endeavoring to influence public opinion toward supporting "The 2,000 Words." In doing this they attempt to make it seem as if they speak on behalf of the people. Judging from the Czechoslovak press, some reactionary journalists and writers have been expressing support for this position. These are the same people who have more than once called for putting an end to the C.C.P.'s (KSC) guiding role and for returning to a "democracy" that would in fact mean the restoration of capitalism.(51)

Furthermore, the Soviet response compared the events in Czechoslovakia with those in Hungary during 1956, contending that the same tactics had been used by the counterrevolutionary elements in Hungary. This was supported by a quote from Hungary's leading Party daily which said, in essence, that the Hungarian people had lived through a similar period and understood the true thoughts and intentions expressed in the manifesto.(52) This comparison, as it turned out, was not insignificant.

The lengthy and detailed Soviet response was followed on July 15 by what has since become known as the Warsaw letter. It was issued as a stern warning to the KSC leadership by representatives of five Warsaw Pact countries, excluding Rumania which, along with Yugoslavia (not a Pact member), sided with Czechoslovakia in the controversy. And while the content of the letter has since become well known, it is important to note that its stated requirements as to measures to be adopted in defending Socialist gains in Czechoslovakia included the following point:

the party's assumption of control over the mass media — the press, radio, and television — and utilization of them in the interests of the working class, all the working people and socialism.(53)

The meaning of the letter was clear: reinstitution of censorship and complete control over the mass media along the line previously practiced, including the elimination of independent-minded journalists and writers.

It was to the Dubcek leadership's credit that in its answer to the Warsaw letter it fully defended a free press and adopted a firm stand in this respect. What is more, the position taken again emphasized the critical part a free press played in the new leadership's program for the future and in its relationship with the people:

There is also another, in our opinion, decisive aspect to this situation: the rise of the authority of the new democratic policy of the party in the eyes of the broadest masses of workers, the growth of

> *the activity of the overwhelming majority of the people.* The overwhelming majority of the people of all classes and sectors of our society favor the abolition of censorship and are for freedom of expression.(54) (emphasis added)

The continuation of press freedom in Czechoslovakia after issuance of the Warsaw letter ultimatum represents one of the most decisive steps in the nation's confrontation with the Soviet Union and, therefore, must be included among the most crucial determinants which led to the invasion. The decision to take such a stand, no doubt, was a difficult one to make. But had Dubcek adopted a more conciliatory position and curbed press freedom by reinstituting prior censorship and forcing the most outspoken journalists and writers, those who had come under attack in the Soviet press for instance, from their editorial posts, he would have greatly undercut the chances of fulfilling his domestic program. Such regressive actions would have cost him the spontaneous and active support of the "overwhelming majority" of the people not only for his leadership but, what seemed most crucial, for the Communist Party as well. Further, any such compromising actions would have emasculated the Action Program by negating its essential principle and, thus, the intended and anticipated completion of the nation's political life would have dissipated. It was essential, therefore, that freedom of expression be upheld and defended as it was.

Due to the threatening nature of the Warsaw letter, the mass media even more than before supported Dubcek and his program and a certain bond of cooperation was established between the media and the administration, reinforced by the seriousness of the situation. It should be recalled that the threat was not merely verbal but quite tangible in the form of Warsaw Pact troops which were participating in training maneuvers on Czechoslovak soil during the summer months.

The press expressed its loyalty to the Party leadership as exemplified in the response to the Warsaw communique issued by *Student.* After rejecting the contention that Party leaders were pursuing an oppositional path, the editorial said: "We are convinced that no leadership of our Communist Party during the past 20 years has done as much for socialism as the current leadership has during the past six months." The weekly went on to say that the process initiated by the new leaders in January "has opened the path for the liquidation of the bureaucratic-political system in our country and the construction of a democratically socialist and economically developed state."(55)

Further active cooperation followed, resulting in the creation of an *activ* of Communist journalists, representing nearly all major newspapers and organizations, which was attached to the Party Central Committee as a consulting body. The group considered all matters pertaining to political decisions and proposals dealing with the mass media as well as problems connected with day-to-day journalistic activity.(56) It represented a liaison whereby many of the delicate issues in the relationship between the media and the administration could be solved.

And while the press did not lose its critical sharpness and outspoken tone, it pursued a course of self-discipline. This was evident in the criticism *Literarni listy* and some Prague dailies voiced against *Student* for its publication of the first article in an intended series about Radio Free Europe. The article was harmless enough, dealing primarily with RFE's history and including interviews with some of the station's Czech and Slovak personnel. But it appeared at an inopportune moment and, besides, *Student* had come under sharp attack in the Soviet press for being an anti-Socialist voice.(57) As a result, the weekly's staff was severaly criticized in articles published in several newspapers and the rest of the series never appeared. The same fate befell a similar series on RFE planned by *Obrana lidu.*

Despite the discipline imposed upon themselves during this tense period, there existed no doubt as to where the journalists and their organization stood in their support for the new Party leadership's program, especially freedom of expression and unabridged access to information. Two days following the conclusion of talks between Czechoslovak and Soviet Party leaders at Cierna nad Tisou (July 29 - August 1), the Center of Journalists of the CSSR met in Bratislava. Although commending those Czechoslovak leaders who had confirmed that press freedom would be preserved, the UNCSSR was most critical of what it called the "terse and general" communique which was issued after the Cierna meeting but did not satisfy the anxious public. The leaders of the organization maintained that press freedom was meaningful and could be guaranteed only as long as all journalists were kept immediately and fully informed. They then declared:

> *During this situation, Czech and Slovak journalists wish to help the Communist Party of Czechoslovakia and the government in overcoming differences among socialist states. This does not mean, however, that they are willing to be silent in cases when, in whatever country, attacks are continued against principles of our*

nation's new politics or when its new standardbearers are defamed. We believe, therefore, that it would be unhealthy, and in terms of socialism detrimental, if all criticism of our domestic or even foreign politics were to disappear from Czechoslovakia's mass information media.(58)

It was a forthright, courageous and defiant statement, but unfortunately it only served to support the Soviet leadership's misguided and prejudiced view of developments in Czechoslovakia.

It should be noted that the concrete points raised at the Cierna talks, aside from personnel changes within the Central Committee of the KSC, were: 1) disallowing the rebirth of the Social Democratic Party; 2) abolishing the Club of Committed Non-Party People (KAN); 3) abolishing Club 231 (K-231), an organization of former political prisoners; and 4) controlling the mass media. The last point subsumed a provision whereby the Party leadership would take the necessary steps to discipline the most outspoken journalists. Smrkovsky, a member of the Czechoslovak delegation, subsequently indicated that the delegation believed the point regarding media control would be most difficult to adhere to because they did not wish to reimpose censorship which only recently had been lawfully abolished. Following the meeting, Brezhnev called Dubcek daily, asking why the agreement reached at Cierna had not been carried out. And although Dubcek attempted to explain, the Soviets eventually accused the KSC leadership of failing to fulfill the agreement decided upon at the tense meeting.(59)

Thus, for all practical purposes, the fate of the nation's half-realized desire for self-determination was already sealed by early August. A decisive step had been taken by the KSC leaders in their answer to the Warsaw letter, an answer which strongly defended the principle of freedom of expression. The importance of the issue was further emphasized by the Soviet response, published in *Pravda* (Moscow), to this KSC stand. The Soviets reiterated the charges against Czechoslovakia's mass media, including the belief that "rightist, antisocialist forces" were "bringing matters to the point of eliminating the Communist Party's guiding role in society" and had "taken over the mass media — press, radio and television — and are using them for antisocialist propaganda, trying to inflame hostility to the Soviet Union and other socialist countries." Then, after restating the demand that the KSC must take control of the mass media, the response concluded with a direct quote from the Warsaw letter, a point later expanded in the Brezhnev Doctrine which served as justification for the invasion:

> *'each of our parties bears a responsibility not only to its own working class and its own people, but also to the international working class and the world Communist movement, and cannot evade the obligations deriving from this. Therefore, we must have solidarity and unity in defense of the gains of socialism, our security and the international positions of the entire socialist commonwealth.'(60)*

The spring had truly ended for Czechoslovakia and, as predicted in the "2,000 Words" manifesto, the answer was delivered before winter by the combined military forces of five Warsaw Pact nations which invaded the country during the night of August 20-21, 1968. And the end of the Prague Spring also meant the end for the newly gained freedom of the Czechoslovak press.

The abolition of censorship had been the first major reform for which the nation's press and public actively campaigned during the post-January period. The introduction of de facto freedom of expression during March, therefore, served as the act which gave substance to the democratization process. It also enabled the previously controlled press to become a generally independent and united socio-political force and to perform again its traditional role in society — informing the public and, thus, influencing as well as reflecting public opinion.

Once the constraints of prior censorship were eliminated, it was as though a massive logjam had been loosened which unleashed a powerful stream of grievances accompanied by demands for their rectification. Many individuals who had occupied top positions in the media under the old regime were replaced, bringing into a more prominent role journalists who were, on the whole, staunch supporters of the ongoing revival process. Such journalists, along with other activists in the print and electronic media, became intricately involved in their nation's political life.

Under the pressure of criticism from the Warsaw Pact nations, the Dubcek leadership and the mass media formed a close union of cooperation in defending the freedoms gained during democratization including, most importantly, freedom of expression. For it was well realized that without the guarantee of a free press, the phenomenon which was the Prague Spring would never have materialized. It was the irony of the Czechoslovak experience in 1968, however, that the very condition which was at the heart of the democratization process — an independent and vigorously active press — also represented a major factor in its demise.

CHAPTER VII

FINAL OBSERVATIONS

This study has examined and hopefully brought into meaningful perspective the changing status of the Czechoslovak press under Communist rule and its role in the national reform movement of the 1960's. Although initially fashioned into a rigidly controlled instrument of propaganda after the Communists gained power in 1948, the press eventually became a prominent channel of dissent and, in the case of the cultural press, one of several oppositional forces which developed during the liberalization process. Culmination of this metamorphosis on the part of the print media came during spring 1968 with the emergence of an uncensored, political, informative, critical and popular press.

The overall change in the print and broadcast media coincided with the general movement against the oppressive policies of the Novotny regime and toward reform which initially became apparent in the nation's cultural sphere but soon encompassed its economic and political life as well. This national revival progressed through two distinct phases generally referred to as liberalization and democratization. While the former was initiated from above, by the Party leadership's decision to de-Stalinize at the end of 1962, it nonetheless was prompted by both external and internal pressures, including demands from the intelligentsia. As early as 1956, segments of this societal strata, gravitating around the liberal writers, constituted the nucleus of dissent which set out to formulate a framework for reform.

Once initiated, the liberalization process was gradually extended under the repeated pressures exerted against the regime. Such pressures were channeled primarily through the cultural press and, by the mid-1960's, through other mass media as well, until a reorientation occurred in the political system itself. This regeneration of Czechoslovak society, however, was not intended as a break with socialism. Rather, it was an attempt to implement a new model of socialism which the reformist Party leadership believed would better serve the nation's needs and reflect its dominant traditions.

This was the democratization process of 1968. The second phase of the national revival, it represented "the merging of a reform movement inside the existing political structure with another reformist tendency which emanated from the nation's traditions, from its spiritual disposition and intellectual potential."(1) Or, as one Czech economist-journalist succinctly stated: *"To improve the destiny of individuals* — that was the supreme goal of our 'socialism with a human face.' For the first time in history we wanted to make the humanist creed an everyday reality."(2) This prevailing inclination, a reflection of the nation's political culture, was nothing more than man's enduring quest for liberty, humanism and basic civil rights, above all freedom of expression. And it soon became evident that none of these could be realized unless a free press existed. As the liberal writer Klima phrased it: "Without freedom of the press, an absolute frank exchange of views and ideas taking place, not just within a limited circle of those directly concerned but in public, is unthinkable. Without the broadest public participation, democracy cannot be achieved."(3)

Thus, freedom of expression stood at the very center of the democratization process. The new leadership well realized that without a freer exchange of ideas and increased participation in the decision-making process by a larger segment of society — especially interest groups — the new path toward socialism could not be achieved. The Czechoslovak experiment of the Dubcek era was in essence an attempt to make one-party rule more responsive to and, therefore, accepted and supported by the people.

The initial impetus for this phenomenal transformation of not only the press but virtually all facets of society was, more than anything else perhaps, the aberrations of the early 1950's. The political show trials especially demanded the catharsis of 1968. The ever-widening gap between theory and practice had a profound effect on the intelligentsia, especially on those who had actually participated in spawning the oppressive regime.

One of the many ironies evident throughout Czechoslovakia's experience under communism was the reality that many of the same idealists who had helped bring into being the dogmatic and bureaucratic system embodied in the Novotny regime were among its most vocal adversaries, devoting their energies to the reform movement. In the end, such individuals — writers and journalists primary among them — became disillusioned and turned against the system they initially had so willingly supported, because it had corrupted the very ideals in which they believed. They felt betrayed and at the same time guilty for having contributed to the creation of a demagogic regime whose practices and methods were contrary to the Socialist ideals it was to uphold. One is reminded of Mnacko's statement, referred to earlier, that although at first he supported the nation's post-1948 political order through his journalistic activities, the show trails of the early 1950's made Mnacko realize that the Party leadership had gone awry of its professed goals, causing him to oppose the regime. He was not alone in this volte-face.

As close observers of everday life, the writers and journalists especially were able to perceive that the tenets which they were forced to uphold through their writings and journalistic endeavors no longer resembled that which was being practiced. The promised equality and freedom from exploitation that life under socialism was supposed to bring had turned instead into an existence of terror, hatred and fear. This continued incongruity between ideology and the facts of everyday life, also apparent in the disparity between the purported function and actual performance of the press, led to the alienation of not only the idealists but the general public as well.

Due to its increasing unresponsiveness and disregard of basic humanitarian principles, the Party leadership lost contact with the masses and, thus, any popular support it had once enjoyed, necessitating repressive measures in its single-minded effort to reshape society. This included an intensification of police terror and political censorship, causing the suppression of information and ideas deemed a threat to the regime. The press, therefore, became a tool of mass political indoctrination and propaganda, while the journalist was reduced to the level of a clerk and forced to adopt the Soviet press as his model. In the Russification of the nation's press that ensued, the press lost touch with its traditional national character. One Czech journalist has described this period as a time when "special features of the Soviet press were sometimes mechanically transferred into our press without taking into consideration the different conditions, our national traditions, genre forms which had deep roots (such as (Jan) Neruda's feuilleton column, etc.), and the popularity of the press."(4)

In a society which by tradition was information conscious and oriented toward a pluralistic press, the uniformity and drabness which newspapers displayed during the early years of Communist rule could only lead to a loss of credibility on the part of the press. The journalist, meanwhile, was regarded as an official spokesman of the regime and, as such, tended to be viewed with contempt by the public. It should be recalled that prior to its Bolshevization under Comintern during the late 1920's, and early 1930's, the Communist press in Czechoslovakia took an active interest in national problems, the arts and international affairs. The use of the print media solely as a propaganda tool, therefore, was not even in keeping with the traditions of the KSC press, let alone the high professional standards which the nation's press generally maintained during the interwar and immediate post-World War II years.

The repressive measures adopted by Party leaders in their efforts to mold the press after the Soviet model contributed to their growing isolation and the public's disenchantment with the political order the leaders had created. This was especially the case among the intellectuals. Their disillusionment led to alienation and dissent which first began to surface following Khrushchev's denouncement of the personality cult in 1956. Thus, the raw force employed by the Party hierarchy in an attempt to engineer society and projected through the mass media generated a counterforce that represented the foundation on which the phenomenon of the Prague Spring was later constructed.

De-Stalinization came late to Czechoslovakia, as opposed to most other East European states, but once initiated in 1962 it opened the gates of criticism which could not be easily resealed. Evident shortcomings on practically all levels (especially in the economy), continued attacks against remnants of dogmatism, and new revelations about the illegality of earlier purges all combined to place the Novotny regime on the defensive. The Party leadership was forced to make concessions which led to a more liberal atmosphere. The intellectuals, taking full advantage of the regime's vulnerable position, exerted pressures in the form of demands and, thus, gave expression to the reform movement.

A Czech journalist later described the role played in this endeavor by political publicists who, using Marxist concepts and ideas, conducted a sober but steady campaign against Novotny's deteriorating regime of personal power:

> *Through the veil of censorship these writers kept coming back to the same basic reasons for the petrification of society. The power center tried to organize public argument against this view of things, but found to its dismay that it did not have enough qualified people available to conduct the debate. . . .It was hard for them to put up effective arguments against genuine Marxists with ideas of their own. Nor was it possible to conceal this fiasco from the public.(5)*

Contributing to the overall impetus for change was the creation of friendlier relations with Western states which the regime was induced to pursue largely due to economic pressures but also to be in step with Moscow's foreign policy. With the exception of Radio Free Europe, the jamming of foreign broadcasts ceased during fall 1963 and tourism, especially from the West, was encouraged as a means to secure hard currency. This helped bring new ideas into the country and enabled the broadening of cultural relations.

Due to such exposure, further enhanced by the communications explosion emanating from the West, the mass media in Czechoslovakia could no longer remain stagnant. The necessity to compete effectively with Western transmissions and to raise the media's credibility led to improvements in journalistic standards, reflected in more timely and factual reporting, greater diversity in content and an increase in articles dealing with foreign affairs. Such changes, welcomed and promoted by a new generation of able journalists who were entering the field, aided in reducing the propagandistic role of the press, radio and television, making them more responsive to their respective audiences and enabling them to stimulate public opinion.

The continued activism by writers, journalists and other sectors of the intelligentsia intensified the pressures for change. But due to the regime's unresponsiveness, progressive proposals were more often than not sidetracked through one subterfuge or another. The confrontation between these activists and the proponents of the status quo grew both in sharpness and intensity, reaching its apex during the writers' defiant 1967 Congress. This resulted in the first major break between the Party leadership and an official organization, the SCSS, with the Novotny regime in the end issuing punitive measures against some of the more rebellious writers and their union. These repressive actions failed to intimidate Novotny's opponents, however, or halt the growing demand for reform.

It soon became evident that the frustrations of past years (culminating in such potent grievances as economic stagnation, interference in the creative process, anti-Slovak bias and disregard for basic human rights) had stimulated a popular movement which unleashed itself as a surging force that ultimately found expression at the highest level, the Party Central Committee. It was a nonviolent revolt aimed not against socialism but, as a former editor of the writers' weekly said, "a reaction to those traits of postwar socialist practices that our people were rejecting as deforming and falsifying the first socialist ideals, as something alien to the true programme."(6)

The regeneration of Czechoslovak society undertaken by the new Party leadership has been perhaps best summarized by the liberal writer Milan Kundera who described it as an attempt "to create a socialism without an omnipotent secret police; with freedom of the spoken and written word; with a public opinion of which notice is taken and on which policy is based; with a modern culture, freely developing; and with citizens who have lost their fear."(7) Kundera synthesized, in spirit at least, Czechoslovakia's projected model of 1968, the nation's desired path toward a new socialism with humanism constituting the dominant cohesive agent. It was, as adherents of *Realpolitik* viewed it, a utopian dream projected upon the existing pattern of global power politics. But, then, the Czechs and Slovaks have not been nations of realists, but of poets, philosophers and dreamers.

This fact, perhaps, constitutes the predominant flaw in the fabric of the nation's political culture — an inclination for periods of passivity which has prompted playwright Arthur Miller to refer to the country's inhabitants as a "nowhere-people."(8) Yet from among these 'nowhere-people' have emerged some of the world's leading personalities in fields such as literature, journalism, music and the cinema; individuals who repeatedly have stood for and defended the core ingredient of the creative process — freedom of expression and thought.

No wonder, then, that freedom of expression stood at the very heart of the 1968 revival and that abolition of prior censorship was one of the first major reforms sought following the change in Party leadership. Once censorship was abrogated in early March, it enabled the press to regain its credibility among the population and, thus, to influence public opinion more effectively and, above all, reflect it openly. By so doing, the press, as well as radio and television, became an active participant in the nation's political life, helping to formulate the course of democratization. The critical and pluralistic press which materialized during 1968 was not an unprecedented phenomenon. Freed largely from the confines of Party control, the print media again reflected the traditions and practices developed during their formative years of the last century when national journalism and culture for a time were the only semblance of the existence of the Czech and Slovak nations.

During the short-lived Prague Spring, freedom of expression also served as an impetus for the reorientation of existing, and the formation of new, groups and organizations whose primary goal was to provide their members with an opportunity to fully participate in the decision-making process from which they had been generally excluded under the previous regime. The activism displayed by groups such as these newly founded organizations and the creative unions, including those of the writers and journalists, served to expose the false concept of homogeneity imposed on a society which by tradition was, and again desired to be, pluralistic. Such organizations, in the role of interest groups, exerted influence on the Dubcek administration in the area of policy decisions. Passage of the amendment to the press law is a case in point.

The process that evolved, therefore, was the dismantling of the bureaucratic political structure which, under Novotny, had retained aspects adopted during the Stalinist years, changing it into a more open system of which an independent and uncensored press was very much a part. Once freed, the press accepted its traditional role fully to the point of even criticizing the new Party leadership and expressing views which frequently opposed the basic tenets of Communist ideology. As a close observer of this period so forthrightly said: "Once given freedom, the press demanded license."(9) Thus, the mass media devoted much space and time to exposing and condemning the social and legal deformities which had occurred in the past under Communist rule. This overt criticism of the Party and life under socialism, plus the exchange of widely divergent views in the media, became the main targets of attacks by Soviet leaders against democratization in Czechoslovakia.

It should be noted that, initially, the Soviet leadership was not totally opposed to the Action Program per se. But it soon became evident that it would not accept the manner in which the Program was being interpreted and implemented, especially the concept of the media being allowed to express oppositional views and promote ideas which were heresy to Soviet ideology. This was most evident in discussions and articles concerning the creation of a political opposition and, even, a multi-party system.(10) And although the Dubcek leadership never failed to uphold the principle of the leading role of the Party, the issue was debated in the press. Through appeals by Dubcek and other leaders, attempts were made to pressure the media into controlling themselves and curbing their excessive criticism. But the media continued to fully utilize their freedom until early summer when the Party leadership itself came under attack by the Soviet press.

This appropriately leads to the question of a decontrolled press functioning openly in a one-party dominated political system based on an ideology which rejects the concept of a free and public exchange of opposing ideas. By their actions during the course of the Prague Spring, Czechoslovak journalists who supported democratization expressed the belief that there could be no halfway measures to press freedom. Either a press acts according to its own conscience, its self-perceived social responsibility, and is free, or it serves the dictates of others and becomes a subservient tool. The experiences of the Czechoslovak press after February 1948 could not be erased or easily forgotten.

It is in this vital area where Dubcek made a miscalculated assumption which, according to some observers,(11) proved to be his most basic and fatal mistake. He believed that by freeing the press and promising to end the previous regime's arbitrariness and excesses of power,he had offered sufficient proof of his intentions to gain not only widespread but, more important, unquestioned public support. Then, when this proved not to be the case, as evidenced for instance by the press criticism voiced against the lack of speed with which the Action Program was being implemented, the new Party leader felt he could not issue sanctions against the press, but merely plead for restraint. Freedom of expression, after all, was one of the cornerstones on which Dubcek had based his entire superstructure of democratization. He and his fellow architects failed to anticipate, it seems, that a decontrolled press would give rise in some quarters to an exchange of divergent ideas as to the future political direction of the country — ideas which were generally consistent with the nation's pluralistic past but totally alien to the ideology preached by the Kremlin.

Although the abolition of prior restraint and the actions of a free press were not the sole factors which led to the invasion (there were several other reasons and pretenses — see below), they certainly constituted one of the major and decisive steps which influenced the fateful decision to employ military force. Support for this contention rests in the various documents issued by leaders of the invading countries, especially the Warsaw letter of July 15, 1968, as well as the Soviet response to the Czechoslovak Communist Party Central Committee's answer to that letter.(12) In each case, it should be recalled, one of the first and central points raised was the need for the KSC to regain complete control of the mass media. The same demand was again raised during the tense Cierna nad Tisou meeting at the end of July. During this meeting, the Soviet leadership also demanded that appropriate action be taken to discipline the nation's most critical journalists. Such demands could only be interpreted to mean the reinstitution of the mechanism for pre-publication censorship and, in effect, the silencing of the more outspoken newsmen and broadcasters.

Contributing to the concerns expressed by Soviet and East European Communist leaders was their misunderstanding of the function of the Czechoslovak press during the first eight months of 1968. According to standard Soviet practice, the mass media serve as communication channels in disseminating Party and government pronouncements, generally without comment or opinion. Consequently, views expressed by individual Czechoslovak writers, editors and broadcasters, explicitly representing only their own personal judgments, were frequently misinterpreted in the Soviet Union and elsewhere as reflecting the basic posture adopted by the Dubcek administration. A case in point was the charge that the Soviet secret police had been implicated in Czechoslovakia's political show trials of the early 1950's.

This basic misinterpretation, which prompted repeated criticism of Czechoslovakia's mass media for allegedly expressing and promoting anti-Soviet sentiments, is most clearly evident in the so-called White Book issued by an anonymous group of Soviet journalists shortly after the invasion and widely distributed, in translation, throughout Czechoslovakia. Through the use of excerpts from the Czech, Slovak and Western press, the White Book attempted to justify the invasion by maintaining that under the slogan of 'freedom of expression,' the enemies of socialism were able to wrench the mass media from the control of the KSC and use them as their own obedient organizational implement for the purpose of counterrevolution.(13) During the tense weeks preceding the Warsaw Pact invasion, such misreading of the role of the press in Czechoslovakia only served to further aggravate relations between Soviet and Czechoslovak leaders.

This, then, was the dilemma and irony inherent in Czechoslovakia's experiment in decontrolling the mass media. While the unmuzzled press represented the essential core of democratization, it also served as a primary and decisive cause for the ultimate termination of the process due to the existing political reality that the nation lies within the Soviet sphere of influence.

Without a free press, however, the course adopted by the new leadership could not have been fully realized and the national catharsis — the nonviolent revolution against political and cultural repression which did take place — would not have occurred.

Considerable discussion in the West has focused on the viability of Czechoslovakia's new path toward socialism and the concept of socialism with a human face which was its theoretical base. Was an uncensored press and a more pluralistic system possible without precariously endangering the KSC's leading role in society? Would a decontrolled press in the end have led to the downfall of the Communist Party and the Socialist system as the Soviet leaders claimed in their repeated but fruitless attempts at justifying the intervention? Although answers to these and similar questions must be mostly speculative, certain indicators and trends were evident prior to the abrogation of Czechoslovakia's experiment in freedom which make it possible to at least suggest answers and draw certain conclusions that, hopefully, can serve as possible guidelines for analyzing the future course of states within the Soviet commonwealth.

Perhaps the most convincing indicator that the enacted and proposed reforms, including the abolition of prior restraint, could have been pursued without fatally endangering the Party was the salient fact that never before were the KSC and its top leaders as popular and favorably received by the general public as during 1968. And their popularity stemmed directly from the proposed reform program. This was indicated in opinion surveys conducted by the Czechoslovak Institute of Public Opinion during 1968(14) and, furthermore, by the resurgent interest in Party membership. For the first time since its seizure of power, the KSC and its program were widely and genuinely supported by the people.

Though the press did publish articles by individuals who were critical of the Party and some of its leaders, there was no evident movement to overthrow or depose the existing government. The changes proposed by the critics were to be achieved through legal and peaceful means, not by violence or force, and within a Socialist framework. The press gave voice to a variety of divergent views and was an active participant in the nation's politics, which was in line with the traditions and practices developed during its formative years as a political and pluralistic press. The problem was, however, that the mass media were operating under Western practices in a country situated within the Soviet sphere of influence.

Further support for the contention that Czechoslovakia would have retained its Socialist system and maintained its ties with the USSR was the absence of any significant trend advocating withdrawal from the Warsaw Pact, as had been the case in Hungary in 1956, or a return to the capitalism of the interwar period. Throughout the course of the Prague Spring, Party leaders desired to maintain close and friendly relations with the Soviet Union. What the reformers attempted to create for their country was a new form of socialism — but, indeed, still socialsm. They attempted to formulate a political climate which would be more in tune with the traditions and existing needs of the Czech and Slovak people, including basic civil rights and a freer existence for the individual. In this way, the new program was a departure from the Soviet model of socialism which had been in effect for twenty years in Czechoslovakia but had failed to engender support from among the masses. The main aim, therefore, was to gain public support for the KSC by initiating the basic reforms outlined in the Action Program. But the inherent danger in pursuing this course was that the more the Dubcek administration pleased the people at home, by adopting proposals set forth by the reemerging interest groups, the less it satisfied the demands placed before it by the Soviet leadershp.

Some critics have maintained that the concept of democratization was an idealistic notion. Indeed it was, in the sense that the experiment was an attempt to make one-party rule popular and accepted by the people rather than resented and feared as had been the case under Novotny. But idealism in itself does not necessarily condemn a political program to failure. The same critics have asserted that Dubcek should have limited the press and thus prevented the invasion and assured at least a partial implementation of the Action Program. However, partial reform was not what the new leadership set out to achieve. Although in a different form, perhaps, and with different individuals occupying key positions, such a system would have been merely a continuation of what had existed under Novotny.

Further, it should be remembered that once censorship was restored after the invasion, other reforms initiated during the Dubcek era were expunged. (Even federalization, one of the few, if not the only, remaining reforms of the Dubcek era, has currently deteriorated to the point of little significance. While the institution exists, centralized power has again taken hold.)This contradicts the contention that all the Soviet leaders desired was firm Party control of the press. Although, of course, this was of prime concern, there were other factors which had no less an influence on the Soviet decision to invade. The desire to station troops on Czechoslovak soil, the fear of an emerging formal political opposition inside the country and, above all perhaps, the prospect that the infectious reform movement would spread across Czechoslovakia's borders into the rest of Eastern Europe were all considered.

The independent and critical press of 1968 did contribute to bringing about the invasion, but not because it acted irresponsibly toward the KSC, its leadership or Czechoslovak society. It can be argued convincingly, in fact, that the Party and the nation's press were cooperating in smoothing out the differences which arose following the abolition of prior restraint and which proved to be a constant source of attacks issued against Czechoslovakia's mass media by Soviet leaders and Party dignitaries in other East European states. A prime example of this cooperation was the *aktiv* of Communist journalists which was attached to the Party Central Committee as a consulting body and represented a liaison for solving many of the delicate issues in the relationship between the media and the Dubcek administration. The critical and outspoken yet generally self-disciplined press presented a threat to Soviet leaders because it dared not only to question but also to propose rational suggestions and alternatives to the status quo. For the type of socialism evolving in Czechoslovakia and widely discussed by the mass media threatened the primacy of the Soviet model of socialism within a Communist commonwealth already beset by a myriad of problems.

It is cogent to note here that one of these lingering problems — plaguing Soviet leaders ever since Yugoslavia's expulsion from Cominform in 1948 — was finally acknowledged and dealt with at the congress of European Communist parties held in East Berlin during the summer of 1976. The meeting ended with the signing of a major document recognizing the right of each Communist party to pursue its own path. It was an endorsement in effect of national communism — a milestone in the history of communism — which had been fought for by Yugoslavia's Marshal Josef Tito and vigorously supported by such Euro-Communists as Italy's Enrico Berlinguer, Spain's Santiago Carrillo and France's Georges Marchais. But there is no doubt that major events occurring during the past years vis-a-vis Yugoslavia, Poland, Hungary, the People's Republic of China, Albania, Rumania and Czechoslovakia all had an impact on the formation of the new policy concerning the Soviet

Union's changing role in the international Communist movement. Those who initially stand to gain the most from the agreement are Yugoslavia and the larger Communist parties of Western Europe. But the future potential for the East European states cannot and should not be discounted. For, while the USSR continues to maintain a strong hold over these countries, through economic, military and political ties, the door has been unlocked, thus providing the East European parties with the possibility for a freer hand in their own affairs. Whether future generations of idealists and dreamers will attempt to open the door toward a freer existence only time will tell. But the potential exists. This was not the case when the Dubcek leadership attempted to nudge the door open nearly a decade ago.

As noted earlier, the Czechoslovak experiment was still in a formative stage when it was aborted. It was as yet imperfect and faced many trials. But the fact that it was forcibly arrested in its development seems to strongly indicate that democratization was succeeding. The popular and voluntary support which the Czechoslovak public displayed and the manner in which the nation's mass media united behind the country's leadership when it was subjected to external threats are positive indicators that the new course and the ideals which its formulators espoused were in line with the people's basic needs and desires as well as their cherished national traditions.

In essence it was the potential success of the Prague Spring which most concerned the Soviet and other Warsaw Pact leaders. They feared that the nucleus of a new ideology was germinating in Czechoslovakia — a combination of Marxist socialism and Masarykian democracy — which would constitute yet another alternative to the Soviet model. Such an alternative, if proved successful, could appeal to those subjected peoples whose historical development and traditions were closely tied to the West, the Poles and Hungarians for instance, or else inspire separatist movements in such areas as the Ukraine and the former Baltic states. A means had to be found to arrest the growth of this new ideological alternative before it could seed in other fertile soils. Hence, the military intervention.

Altogether, the above suggests that socialism and a free press are not necessarily opposing concepts or incompatible, and that socialism with a human face, including a decontrolled press with legal safeguards against arbitrary government encroachment, could indeed have been viable in Czechoslovakia. For, socialism as a political, economic and social system was an established fact. The reformers strove to eradicate only the negative aspects of political censorship, arbitrary political power and public fear, not the system itself. The reformers tended to believe that the people did not have to be coerced into accepting Communist rule but would voluntarily support such a government if it were responsive to the public's needs and desires. (It is germane to point out that during what is generally referred to as the last free national election in Czechoslovakia, the Communist Party won some thirty-eight percent of the total vote. Agreed, this election was held at a different time and under rather different circumstances. Nevertheless, the KSC's plurality in the May 1946 election was decisive, especially when considering that President Eduard Benes' National Socialist Party placed second with less than nineteen percent of the vote.)

Since Czechoslovakia was not without powerful external influences, however, it was politically naive on the part of the liberals to think that they could maintain their desired high level of self-determination in internal affairs and implement such extensive reforms, especially a decontrolled press, unimpeded. A controlled and obedient press, after all, is central to the modus operandi of the Soviet system and can function only within limits prescribed by that system. As long as Soviet influence predominates in Eastern Europe, then, the implementation of such democratic concepts as freedom of expression as envisioned by Czechoslovakia's reformers and expressed in the amended press law of 1968 is not feasible, for it undercuts the very essence of one of the basic tenets of a closed society — the suppression of oppositional views.

Yet it should be kept in mind that even if not readily possible under the prevailing global pattern of political influence and control, press freedom is inherently a *potential* phenomenon in those East European states with Western traditions and ties. Thus, Czechoslovakia's experience in decontrolling its mass media can serve as a potent reminder and significant precedent for new generations of reformers in the continuing struggle against absolutism and oppression.

EPILOGUE: THE CONSEQUENCES

The Kremlin's proclaimed justification for the August 1968 Warsaw Pact invasion was to suppress what the Soviet leaders called a "counterrevolution" in Czechoslovakia.(1) This was supposed to have enabled Communists loyal to the USSR and the cause of Socialist solidarity to take over leadership of the KSC and form a new government. But after the Soviet tanks had been deployed throughout Prague and troops had occupied key buildings and facilities, including the Party headquarters, radio stations, newspaper offices(2) and television studios, not only were there no counterrevolutionaries to be found, but no 'loyal' Communist was willing to step forward and head a puppet government.

Instead, the invading armies of five Warsaw Pact states (Soviet Union, Bulgaria, Hungary, East Germany and Poland) were faced with a stubborn nonviolent resistance directed for the most part through the alleged instruments of counterrevolution — the mass media — which were supposed to have been silenced. Ultimately, however, the free press was again regimented and the causes it had espoused and defended were suppressed, but not before a final defiant stand against the occupation.

The Invasion

The crusading spirit and political activism displayed by the communication media during Czechoslovakia's euphoric spring and early summer were accentuated by the media's performance during the week of invasion, August 21-27. While the country's top leaders were being forcibly detained in Moscow, the press, radio and television constituted what can justifiably be termed a surrogate government. As such, they kept the public appraised of the day-to-day situation and, at the same time, helped to maintain order and to responsibly guide the nonviolent resistance movement which had materialized throughout the country.

Later, Zdenek Hejzlar, appointed director of Czechoslovak Radio just a month prior to the invasion, assessed the then existing climate: " 'The journalists saved the situation in August and, in a real sense, saved the nation.' " And although individuals who helped publish and disseminate newspapers and produce television programs (often under the very noses of the occupying forces) displayed sustaining courage, it was the radio which played the vital role because of its ability, more than any other medium, to quickly reach a maximum number of people in virtually every corner of the nation. " 'In those August days,' " Hejzlar added, " ' everyone in Czechoslovakia carried a transistor, and our people, many of them at great personal risk, worked hard to keep them informed.' "(3)

Thus, clandestine radio stations transmitted news and instructions to the citizenry, television crews staged spontaneous programs and interviews in makeshift studios, and newspaper extras, as well as numerous fliers, carried declarations supporting the Dubcek administration and denouncing the occupation. In short, the public was not a headless mob acting blindly and irrationally, as so often happens in similar crises, but was generally well organized and kept abreast of major events. In this way, the stand taken by the Party Central Committee and the Dubcek government against the invasion became known throughout the world, as did the decisions made at the Extraordinary Fourteenth Party Congress held in an industrial suburb of Prague during the invasion week.

Despite adverse conditions, virtually all Prague dailies continued publication, carrying proclamations and statements from leading Party and government bodies, as well as from other organizations and the respective editorial offices. The editorial staff of *Mlada fronta,* for instance, said in part:

> *We stand firmly behind the only representative government of our republic: President Ludvik Svoboda, Presidium of the Central Committee of the KSC headed by Alexander Dubcek, (and the) Presidium of the National Assembly. At this hour, we stand behind everything progressive which has been created in this country since January. We stand behind our homeland's sovereignty which has been infringed upon. We reject anyone who would proclaim himself to be the nation's spokesman.*
>
> *We promise that should this issue of Mlada fronta be the last in which we had a part, so be it. We cannot change our views because we are socialists and because socialism without a human face is not socialism. No one can count on our support for anything else.*

> *Should a different Mlada fronta appear in the near future, even if set in the same type, it won't be ours. We want you to know that.(4)*

The editorial collective of *Rude pravo,* meanwhile, also declared its full support for the Dubcek leadership, then added: "In this grave moment of our history, nothing is so essential as that we all maintain a dignified calm and deliberation. It's the only possible path toward creating conditions to speedily resolve the emergent situation. Let us demonstrate," the editorial continued, "that the Czechoslovak people are capable of resolving their own serious problems in life independently, with dignity and boldness, as they once already have demonstrated in their history."(5) The reference to "once already," no doubt, was a comparison to the Nazi occupation.

Zemedelske noviny, besides publishing the official Party and government proclamations denouncing the invasion, also carried a statement by the Union of the Czech Journalists. Firmly supporting Dubcek and the national government, the Union declared: "We do not want and will not serve anyone else. We appeal to all journalists to conduct themselves in the spirit of the progressive and democratic traditions of our people, and to do nothing of which they later may be ashamed."(6) Under the headline "Truth Will Prevail," President Masaryk's famous motto, the editorial staff of the Socialist Party's daily, *Svobodne Slovo* (Free Word), urged the population to remain calm and to preserve the democratic ideals upon which the Republic was founded and with which the nation had lived since January. "That's the only path, the only possibility. Inner strength, with whose help we lasted through the years of occupation, the past twenty years, will (help us to) survive the years to come. With firm hope. With firm faith. With unbroken determination."(7)

Such forceful statements, published and broadcast throughout the week of invasion, helped to fortify the public will to resist. Due largely to such efforts by the media, the population did not panic and bloodshed was kept to a minimum (in contrast to the Hungarian intervention some twelve years earlier), greatly undercutting the Kremlin's claim that a counterrevolutionary force was preparing to seize power in Czechoslovakia.

The mass media were well prepared for the task — they had fought the excesses of the Novotny regime and, during the course of the first eight months of 1968, had matured into an effective communication system. In addition, technical facilities were not lacking. Emergency broadcasting equipment issued by the Warsaw Pact to be used in rallying the population in the event of an attack from the West was used effectively by radio personnel, many of whom were trained army reservists in signal units,(8) to unite and rally the population against the attack from the East. The spirit of national unity resulting from the journalists' work, moreover, created a certain psychological climate in which it was virtually impossible for an individual — even if willing — to openly collaborate with the Soviets. And while there were those who did the occupiers' bidding under the cover of anonymity, the prevailing spirit of resistance forced Soviet leaders to alter their plans. Thus, it took several months of continual pressure, rather than the few days anticipated, to finally install a pro-Soviet regime willing to unquestioningly accept the conditions of occupation.

In retrospect, one can see the ironic situation in terms of the mass media that prevailed during the critical period immediately following the invasion when the truly legal media had to work as clandestine operations and were regarded as such by the occupation troops while the illegal newspaper *Zpravy* (Reports), published under the auspices of the Warsaw Pact command, was distributed rather freely. The paper was aided in its propagandistic task by the radio station *Vltava* (Moldau) which began transmitting in Czech and Slovak out of Dresden, East Germany, on the morning of August 21. Numerous anonymous fliers, most with an unusually strong conservative and anti-Semitic tone, also appeared in the capital soon after the invasion.

The effectiveness of the two main Warsaw Pact outlets, however, was practically nil. This was due primarily to the absurd statements broadcast and printed which, for the most part, were readily and rationally countered by the Czech media. What is more, the heavily accented speech of the *Vltava* announcers was a source of ridicule among the public, helping to alleviate some of the existing tension. The credibility of the two operations was further reduced when the Prague media identified collaborators who were working on the respective staffs.(9) It is cogent to note that the change in propaganda approach taken by *Zpravy* and *Vltava* supports the above-mentioned alteration in strategy pursued by the Soviets. At the outset, the output of both tended to be friendly and almost conciliatory in tone; however, their articles and broadcasts turned into vicious attacks against institutions and individuals as soon as it became evident that a puppet government could not be quickly established. Frequent targets of these attacks were the mass media and key individuals involved who condemned the invasion and continued to oppose the occupation.

A certain degree of normality was restored when the Czechoslovak delegation headed by President Svoboda and including the detained leaders Dubcek, Smrkovsky and Oldrich Cernik returned to Prague on August 27 after signing the Moscow Protocol the previous day. Among the main provisions in this document were the control of the mass media by the KSC and the reimposition of censorship.(10) The Protocol also called for the banning of all 'illegal' groups (such as K-231 and KAN) which had been organized outside the National Front.

What followed during the ensuing months was an attempt to salvage at least some provisions of the post-January program. But despite efforts of the press toward this end, as well as actions taken by pressure groups such as the journalists' and writers' Unions, the freedoms gained and savored during the Prague Spring were progressively curtailed under the shadow of military power. Czechoslovakia's experiment in humanizing socialism was thus forcibly halted.

Final Resistance

In protest of the signing of the Moscow Protocol, which it compared to the Munich Agreement of 1938, the staff of the weekly *Student* voted to "no longer publish the magazine (sic), not even if the current conditions permitted it."(11) The outspoken publication thus became the first victim of post-invasion efforts to normalize the situation, that is, to return to conditions prescribed by the Soviet leadership. In a similar vein, the editorial department of *Literarni listy* decided to stop publication until such time " 'when we can work in accordance with our convictions and conscience. Never again will we consent to 'realistic' politics of filtered truths.' "(12) Despite such opposition, reinforced by widespread public sentiment against the document, the Protocol was accepted by both the Party Central Committee and the Dubcek government. Then, on September 13, 1968, the National Assembly passed a law reinstituting censorship.(13) It was not a severe law, though, because instead of establishing a censorship agency, the law provided that the chief editors were to serve as their own censors. Pursuits in the sciences and arts were not affected by the statute.

Meanwhile, an early September issue of *Kulturny zivot* was censored by the new Slovak Party leadership formed during the KSS Congress held at the onset of the month and headed by Husak as Party First Secretary in Slovakia. Due to this censorship, but also because of a conflict among the staff concerning post-invasion policies, the Slovak writers' weekly was also discontinued. The following spring, an attempt was made to revive the paper under the title *Literarny zivot* (Literary Life), but the effort failed.

Under Husak's leadership, the Party in Slovakia was initially more effective in suppressing resistance against occupation policies, including censorship, than was the case in the Czech lands. This was attested to by letters from Slovak readers published in various issues of *Reporter.* A letter printed in the journalists' weekly on February 13, 1969, for example, stated that the magazine's first issue for 1969 was not distributed in Slovakia because of "certain things" it contained. The Bratislava letter writer succinctly described existing conditions when he quoted a Postal Newspaper Service official's response to a query about the situation: "It's not as it used to be." *Reporter* also disclosed that only 4,141 issues of Czech-language dailies were distributed throughout Slovakia, including 1,698 in the Slovak capital. (14)

The discontinuation of *Student* and the writers' weeklies, however, did not mean that the liberals simply gave up hope and capitulated. Despite growing pressure (*Reporter,* for instance, which had been criticized in the White Book for publishing political articles "permeated with an anti-Soviet spirit," (15) was frequently attacked in the press of the invading Warsaw Pact countries), those remaining in operative editorial offices attempted to sustain the effort to safeguard what was left of the Action Program. This was especially the case with the political-cultural weekly press that emerged in Prague.

During fall 1968, new weekly publications, along with the still existing *Reporter,* continued to support the liberal view and criticize the occupation. Among them were *Zitrek* (Tomorrow) and *Obroda* (Rebirth), published by the Socialist and Populist Parties, respectively. Also, *Politika* (Politics) replaced *Kulturni tvorba* as an organ of the Party Central Committee. It appeared as early as the week of the invasion in a special edition, although its regular publication was delayed for several weeks. The new magazine's political outlook was evident from the start because, instead of the usual "Workers of the World Unite" slogan, its staff chose the motto "Truth Is Revolutionary," a phrase associated with Antonio

Gramsci, the Italian Communist leader of the 1920's and 1930's.

In November these publications were joined by *Listy* (Pages), a new weekly started by the Czech writers. As explained in the first issue, the writers involved felt that they could not remain silent while their nation and fellow countrymen were being slandered by foreign propaganda.(16) This referred to the continued criticism of the media and Party leadership, as well as attacks against prominent reformers, voiced by the media of the invading countries, especially through radio station *Vltava* and the occupation paper *Zpravy.*

An example of the latter's content was an article charging that seven journalists and publicists regularly had contacted a certain British press attache and provided him with military secrets.(17) Letters protesting the allegation, written by several of those named in the *Zpravy* article, were published in the February 23, 1969, issue of *Reporter* under the headline "Liars and Slanderers." As the heading exemplifies, the struggle between the Warsaw Pact propaganda outlets and Czech publications — particularly the weeklies — resulted in bitter exchanges which intensified, especially on the part of *Zpravy* and *Vltava,* as both external and internal pressures on the nation's mass media increased in frequency and force.

The principal targets of the political-cultural weeklies were the military occupation and the gradual strangulation of freedoms and liberal policies initiated during the first half of 1968. The press also continued to deny the charges of counterrevolution and anti-Soviet activism being leveled by Soviet publications against the media and individual reformers. In addition, the nation's print media demanded that the distribution of *Zpravy* be halted, contending that it was an illegal publication because it was not licensed in Czechoslovakia as required by law. Toward the end of the year, the media were joined in this demand by the National Assembly and some Party organizations.(18)

Protest against the occupation, curtailment of freedoms, and accusations by Soviet and Warsaw Pact media was tragically emphasized with the death by self-immolation of Jan Palach on January 16, 1969. In a letter which was signed Torch No. 1, the twenty-one-year-old student warned that other torches would burn if certain demands were not met and the nation did not adequately support these demands by a general strike. The conditions listed were: 1) immediate abolition of censorship and 2) prohibition of the distribution of *Zpravy.*(19) Palach's death prompted student demonstrations throughout the country, declarations for the right of individual and national self-determination by the writers' Union, and other similar manifestations of protest.

The tragic act of desperation by Palach and the vocal dissent that followed, however, had little effect on the dismal atmosphere, aside from pointing up the hopelessness of the situation. Although radio station *Vltava* stopped transmitting during February 1969, censorship was maintained and *Zpravy* continued to be distributed, primarily through indirect methods, until May 1969 by which time the necessary changes had been initiated to assure that normalization, according to Kremlin specifications, would be achieved.

Steps Toward Normalization

Coinciding with the mass media's resistance to the policies of occupation was the introduction of changes within both Party organizations and the communication field. Individuals who proved to be most offensive to the Soviet leadership were relieved of their posts. Such was the case with the directors of Czechoslovak radio and television. In some instances, potentially threatened liberal journalists managed to be transferred to posts abroad while others chose exile in the West. The vacated posts, meanwhile, were filled either by journalists who had served under Novotny or others who were willing to back the policy of occupation and comply with Soviet demands.

Such staff changes became more frequent during 1969 as, under Soviet pressure, liberal officials were replaced within the Party hierarchy and state administration. The replacement of certain Party officials and the disciplining of media personnel, it should be remembered, were among the demands presented by the Soviet representatives at the Cierna talks held less than a month prior to the military intervention. Thus, the Soviets were finally having it their way. The gradual change in the liberal press was also a reflection of increased media harassment.

As early as November 1968, for example, *Reporter* and *Politika* (after only eleven issues had been published) were suspended for periods of one and three months, respectively. The journalists' Union protested the suspension of its magazine with a threat of court action and, as a result, the ban on *Reporter* was lifted. The suspensions, however, served as a clear indication that measures would be taken by the government against publications which proved to be too critical and bothersome.

Later that month (November 14-17), a sharp debate concerning the communication media developed at the plenum of the Party Central Committee. Dubcek devoted a considerable portion of his opening speech to the issue, criticizing the media for "political irresponsibility" and for departing in their polemics from political reality. He stressed that if inadequacies in the media were to be overcome, it was necessary to "unconditionally strengthen the leading task of the Party in the area of radio, press and television and their control by the state."(20) The debate which followed revealed a division within the Committee as to those willing to continue defending the reform program and those supporting the policy of occupation.

The final resolution adopted by the Party body, however, indicated that the prevailing trend would be one of compliance with Soviet directives. The main thrust of the resolution was contained in the following sentence: "The press, radio and television are, above all, the instruments which carry into life the politics of the Party and state."(21) Despite such warnings, the press continued its criticism of the occupation and the restrictive policies being implemented. It was assisted in this effort by the journalists' organization.

A day following the Party plenum, the Prague Branch of the SCSN met to voice its views on the existing political atmosphere and issued a resolution, addressed to the Party leadership and government bodies, to this effect. The journalists present expressed grave concern over the suspension of *Reporter* and *Politika,* prohibition of political commentaries on radio and television, and staff changes being initiated in editorial offices, all of which, they said, "alarms us and compels us toward a decisive protest." The resolution also warned that the liquidation of freedom of expression could have a crippling effect on the unity between the people and their leading representatives. "It is not only a question of attacks against the press, radio and television. It is, above all, a question of this socialist country's population being able to responsibly express itself about the fate of its own future."(22) The document further noted that efforts were being made to push journalism back not only to the pre-January 1968 period but all the way to the 1950's. The warning proved all too prophetic.

As noted earlier, resistance to the occupation was accentuated by Palach's death at the onset of 1969. But the full force of the nation's frustrations was released through the major demonstrations which followed the March 21 and 28 victories of the Czechoslovak ice hockey team over the Soviets. Describing the demonstrations as renewed anti-Soviet activism, the Kremlin leadership intensified its pressures on the Dubcek leadership. This eventually led to Dubcek's resignation as Party First Secretary, which was approved during the April 14-15 session of the Party Presidium. Ironically, Husak, the same man who but a year earlier had so compellingly supported the democratization process initiated under Dubcek, became the new Party chief.

At the beginning of April, meanwhile, prior censorship was reinstituted under the pretense that the press had aided in establishing the anti-Soviet mood of the March riots. The decision met with forceful, if unavailing, protests. On April 3, for instance, the Union of Czech Journalists declared that the reimposition of pre-censorship would seriously endanger the mass media's ability to continue in their dialogue with the citizenry, a media function which represented "an expression of mutual trust between the people and their government."(23) The carefully worded protest was one of the last the Union, as it then existed, was to issue. Further resistance by the press was made even more difficult when, during the next few weeks, the most outspoken weeklies and cultural journals were either permanently suspended or voluntarily ceased publication, including *Reporter, Listy, Politika* and *Zitrek.* Purging of the press continued into 1970. The willingness of the remaining journalists to comply with the realities of occupation soon became apparent.

In mid-May, several dozen journalists and publicists signed a proclamation, published in *Rude pravo* under the title "A Word To Our Own Ranks," which in essence condemned the liberal journalists who opposed the occupation and gave support to the Husak leadership and its policy of normalization.(24) This was followed two months later by a meeting of some 500 journalists called by the Party Presidium. The conference was addressed by Husak and other members of the new leadership whose pronouncements constituted the directives to be followed by the mass media. These included "paralyzing" the so-called rightists who remained active in the press, strengthening ties with the Soviet Union and other Warsaw Pact countries, and carrying out the policies of the new regime.(25)

Due to the suspension of the liberal papers and dismissal of their staff members, which also meant their expulsion from professional organizations, the journalists' Union was greatly weakened. The existing leadership was forced to resign in September 1969 and was replaced by a thirty-member commission as the leading body. The active Prague Branch was disbanded and a process of cleansing the Union of "counterrevolutionary elements" was begun. The procedure employed was reminiscent of the purges undertaken following the end of World War II and the Communist takeover in 1948. Anyone recognized as an active supporter of democratization failed to retain Union membership and, thus, was deprived of work in the journalistic field. This was subsequently followed by arrests and trials of journalists.(26) As a result, both the SCSN and SSN were once again molded into willing servants of the Party leadership.

A similar fate occurred with the writers' Union which, in June 1969, had been federalized into two autonomous sections under a combined leadership. The Slovak group was soon forged into a compliant body, but the Union of Czech Writers (SCS) resisted. Although a new leadership was elected, the Czechs refused to expel reformists and swear allegiance to the Husak regime. Due to its defiance, the SCS was ordered disbanded in October 1970 and all its assets were confiscated by the state. The Czech section was not officially reactivated until May 1972, and the new SCS publication, *Literarni mesicnik* (Literary Monthly), was virtually devoid of any meaningful political writing. Thus, with the purging of the journalists' and writers' organizations, the political force which they had represented ceased to be. The organizations again became primarily transmission belts for the heralding of official Party policy.

Winter Once Again

Nearly a decade has elapsed since Czechoslovakia's political experiment was negated by the Soviet-led Warsaw Pact intervention. Since then the country has again become an obedient member of the Soviet commonwealth, and the nation's press no longer criticizes the Soviet Union or seriously ponders such "subversive" ideas as Czechoslovakia's own path toward socialism. This submissiveness, however, was reinstituted only with the use of military force and only after a lengthy process during which the press, radio and television were purged of the critical spirit and individualism which they had displayed during 1968.

Thus, the mass media again have been forcibly transformed from distinct information channels which served as a critical and independent political force into a controlled instrument of propaganda. This was made evident in the January 1973 address of Svestka, former chief editor of *Rude pravo* and a Party Central Committee secretary, to a combined meeting of the leaderships of the journalists' organizations. Referring to the tasks given the mass media by Husak during the Party Congress held May 25-29, 1971, Svestka said:

> *The primary missions of the mass media in a socialist state are to be an active organizer and propagator of the politics of the Communist Party, to unceasingly develop socialist consciousness among the broad segments of the population and to purposefully, and in the spirit of socialist thought, formulate public opinion and gain the workers' active support for the Party's politics, for participation and commitment and for work and civic initiative. (It is also their task) to fight against enemy propaganda, against the influence of bourgeois ideology, against petit bourgeois remnants in thought and practice. (27)*

In these primary tasks, there is no mention of the function of informing the public. As it stands, the statement of purpose does credit to the type of material which frequently was included in the gray press of the late 1950's.

Various statements of protest have appeared in the West since the early 1970's, a time which witnessed severe repressive actions against individuals who refused to recant convictions expressed during 1968-69 and saw the new regime consolidate power with the posts of President and Secretary General of the Party again resting in the hands of a single individual. Prime examples of these protestations are Dubcek's defense of his program in a lengthy letter to the Federal Assembly, several interviews granted by Vaculik as well as his plea to United Nations Secretary General Kurt Waldheim, a public letter from Havel to Husak, numerous communiques by Czech dissidents sent to colleagues in the West and the Charter 77 declaration attempting to hold the Czechoslovak government accountable for adherence to the human rights provisions of the Helsinki Agreement. Such documents provide at least a glimpse at the depressing Kafkaesque situation that now exists inside the country where general apathy, resignation and cultural stagnation prevail amidst a projected image of consolidation and well being.

As Havel so aptly stated in his 1975 letter to Husak:

> *Your aim of winning the support of the people and of consolidating the situation in the country seems to have been achieved. People go to work, procreate, buy cars, flats and houses; the living*

> *standard is rising. Moreover, they publicly endorse whatever your Government asks them to endorse; there are no overt signs of dissent against any government decisions.*
>
> *Yet this public image of total consolidation . . . is being daily undermined by an ever deepening inner crisis in our society.*
>
> *The idyllic image is artificial. It is not based on any real belief in the regime's goals, any trust in your Government nor even on any vague agreement with your overall policies, but on fear, corruption and apathy. The much advertised consolidation is phoney, the crisis is real.*

Then, turning to the cultural scene, the playwright pointed to the absence of once available specialized literary, artistic and scientific journals and the dearth of any new poetry and fiction, with the exception of a few scattered manuscripts which circulated by means of *samizdat.* "Who can fathom the irreparable damage done to all the fields of man's cultural endeavors?" he asked. "It is not only our cultural activity which has been paralyzed; the very history of our nation has been suspended. In fact, it (has) ceased to exist."(28)

In an attempt to reverse this trend of unconcealed apathy and covert disagreement, the Husak regime extended an open invitation to the nation's inactive intelligentsia to once again join the mainstream of creative pursuits — as sorrowful as it is — by renouncing their political views and accepting the status quo. A few individuals have bent to such pressures, but countless others continue to persist in their ways and, consequently, continue to be exposed to the regime's harassment and deprivations. It should be said, however, that the repressive atmosphere accompanying the normalization process during 1971-72 has eased somewhat. Relations with Western states, particularly West Germany, are on the upswing, and a few concessions have been made on the domestic front.

The mass media, nevertheless, continue obediently to function as a transmission belt for Party dictates and government pronouncements. Following the signing of the Helsinki Agreement, for instance, the Party press cautioned that provisions of the document "must be interpreted and applied to conform to the Marxist-Leninist world outlook and the requirements of the anti-imperialist class struggle."(29) Despite their compliance, however, media personnel are still subjected to repeated exhortations by the Party due, apparently, to the low level of achievement by the journalistic field since the cleansing of its top echelon. The strata hit hardest during this purging process was the thirty to forty-year-old age group, which was true of other professions as well.

In May 1972 this age group comprised only 19 percent of the Union of Journalists' membership, or 714 of a 3,759 total, and by October 1974 the figure had slipped to 18.6 percent, or 890 members out of a total of 4,790. The article citing these statistics, published in the Union's quarterly journal *Sesity Novinare* (Newsman's Notebooks), criticized various structural aspects of the organization as well as the nation's journalism in general, the low educational level of the Union membership and the lack of sufficient Socialist consciousness among journalists. The author, Union Chairman Zdenek Horeni, stated that less than 42 percent of the nation's journalists held higher education diplomas and 10 percent had not progressed beyond a basic education. Horeni compared this to the situation in Poland where, he asserted, journalism had developed along similar lines during the past thirty years, yet 61 percent of Polish journalists held university degrees. Moreover, of the 901 Czechoslovak journalists assigned to primary and secondary publications, Horeni maintained that 502 had no higher education and 489 (including 17 chief editors, 22 deputy chief editors and 54 department heads) did not possess the required and correct political preparation.(30)

This reference to and concern with political preparation reflects a Party Presidium decree that every journalist, whether a Communist or not and regardless of Party affiliation, must successfully complete an evening course sequence in Marxism-Leninism unless he or she already possesses an equivalent level of political preparedness. Such measures are intended to assure the Socialist purity of the nation's mass media and to guarantee that all journalists become politically aware and thus part of a unified political *aktiv* of the Communist Party and the National Front.

It is evident, from Horeni's articles and others,(31) that a new approach has been adopted in journalism education so as to fulfill the mission set forth during the Fourteenth Congress of the KSC. As stated in the Congress documents, the mass media are " ' *significant and powerful ideological instruments of the communist party and socialist state for the formation of a socialist person's character.*' " Their basic task is to " '*raise and expand socialist consciousness among broad strata of the inhabitants* (and) *purposefully, in the spirit of socialist ideals, to form public opinion.*' "(32) Again, there is no mention of the media's informational function. The mass media are viewed instead as propaganda channels for the regime. Sadly enough, this is a familiar role for the Czechoslovak press.

Thus, a cycle in the nation's history and that of its press under Communist rule was terminated by the Soviet-led military intervention. A new evolutionary cycle is already underway. Only time will tell if the spark of freedom, self-determination and humanism, rekindled and reaffirmed during 1968, will survive the current winter freeze and be set aflame again in another spring by some future generation of journalists and writers with the same convictions, hopes and dreams. The precedent has been set.

NOTES

INTRODUCTION

For background on the history of modern Czech and Slovak journalism and the beginnings of a Communist press in Czechoslovakia, see my "The Czech and Slovak Press: The First 100 Years." Journalism Monographs, No. 47 (January, 1977).

1. During this century, the Czechs and Slovaks have experienced three forms of totalitarian rule, each accompanied by varying degrees of oppression. Until its independence, present-day Czechoslovakia was part of the Austro-Hungarian Empire. During World War II, Bohemia-Moravia was a protectorate of the Third Reich, while Slovakia was a separate state under a puppet government. Following the February 1948 Communist coup d'etat, the nation became a people's democratic republic, part of the Soviet commonwealth.

2. By the end of 1967, the Union of Czechoslovak Journalists included a total of 4,332 members. See *Novinar,* XIX, No. 12 (1967), p. 421. In April 1972, it was announced that 368 individuals had lost membership standing in the Union's Slovak section and 1,212 persons in the Czech section. See *Novinar,* XIV, No. 5 (1972) Supplement, pp. 5, 16.

3. This refers to the steps taken by the Gustav Husak regime to stabilize the situation inside the country by regaining control of the levers of power in directing society. In brief, it was a return to conditions which complied with Soviet demands.

4. Although de-Stalinization will be discussed at greater length later, here it need be said that whereas the USSR, Hungary and Poland, for instance, began to de-Stalinize during 1956, Czechoslovakia's leadership did not commence the process in the true meaning of the term until the Twelfth Congress of the KSC in December 1962. Also, liberalization and democratization have generally been used interchangeably. However, it is more accurate to consider liberalization as an outgrowth of de-Stalinization, a phase lasting until Antomin Novotny's dismissal as Party First Secretary in January 1968. Democratization, then, was the process which followed until the military intervention.

5. Milovan Djilas, "The Unquenchable Fires of Czechoslovakia," translated by Michael M. Milenkovitch, *The Central European Federalist,* XVI (December, 1968), p. 9.

6. Hugh Seton-Watson, *Eastern Europe Between the Wars 1918-1941,* Harper Torchbooks (3rd. ed., revised; New York: Harper & Row, 1967), p. 140.

7. Herbert Passin, "Writer and Journalist in the Traditional Society," in *Communications and Political Development,* ed. by Lucian W. Pye, Studies in Political Development, No. 1 (Princeton, N.J.: Princeton University Press, 1963), pp. 82-123.

8. *Prirucni slovnik naucny.* (Encyclopedia of the Czechoslovak Academy of Sciences"), III (Prague: Academia, 1966), p. 773.

9. "Cim ziju umelecke svazy?" ("What Do Creative Unions Live By?") *Nova mysl,* XX, No. 9 (1966), p. 17. For a more comprehensive account of the activist writer, see my "The Writer as Political Actor in Czechoslovak Society: A Historical Perspecpive," *East European Quarterly,* VII (September, 1973), pp. 199-220.

10. Milovan Djilas, *The Unperfect Society: Beyond the New Class,* translated by Dorian Cooke (New York: Harcourt, Brace & World, 1969), p. 50.

11. See the contributions in Frederic J. Fleron, Jr., ed., *Communist Studies and the Social Sciences: Essays on Methodology and Empirical Theory* (Chicago: Rand McNally, 1969).

12. While Andrew Janos does not altogether reject the application of the pluralistic model in explaining Communist politics, he nevertheless does express certain reservations about its use. See his chapter "Group Politics in Communist Society: A Second Look at the Pluralistic Model," in *Authoritarian Politics in Modern Society: The Dynamics of Established One-Party Systems,* ed. by Samuel P. Huntington and Clement H. Moore (New York: Basic Books, 1970), pp. 437-50.

13. Michal Lakatos, "K niektorym problemom struktury nasej politickej sustavy" ("Toward Some Problems of the Structure of Our Political System") *Pravny obzor,* XLVIII, No. 1 (1965), p. 31.

14. Michal Lakatos, "Dvatsad rokov budovania socialistickej demokracie" ("Twenty Years of Building Socialist Democracy") *Pravny obzor,* XLVIII, No. 5 (1965), pp. 273-74. The two articles by Lakatos and other of his writings on the role of interest groups in Socialist society are discussed in Morton Schwartz, "Czechoslovakia: Toward One-Party Pluralism?" *Problems of Communism,* XVI (January-February, 1967), pp. 21-27; H. Gordon Skilling, "Interest Groups and Communist Politics: An Introduction," in *Interest Groups and Soviet Politics,* ed. by Skilling and Franklyn Griffiths (Princeton, N.J.: Princeton University Press, 1971), pp. 3-18; and Galia Golan, "The Short-lived Liberal Experiment in Czechoslovak Socialism," *Orbis,* XIII (Winter, 1970), p. 1096-1116.

15. The approach was employed in studies contained in Skilling and Griffiths, eds., *Interest Groups and Soviet Politics.* Aside from Skilling's contributions, another chapter of interest is Ernest J. Simmons, "The Writers," pp. 253-89. Also see George Mond and R. Richter, "Writers and Journalists: A Pressure Group in East European Politics," *Journalism Quarterly,* XLIII (Spring, 1966), pp. 95-106.

16. *Zitrek,* November 13, 1968, p. 2.

17. Djilas, "The Unquenchable Fires of Czechoslovakia," p. 9.

18. Mond and Richter, "Writers and Jurnalists," p. 106.

19. Ghita Ionescu, *The Politics of European Communist States* (New York: Frederick A. Praeger, 1967), p. 209.

20. Mond and Richter, "Writers and Journalists," p. 106.

21. Dan N. Jacobs, "Area Studies and Communist Systems," in *Communist Studies and the Social Sciences,* ed. by Fleron, p. 204.

CHAPTER I

1. Jiri Hajek, *Mytus a realita ledna 1968* ("Myth and Reality of January 1968") (Prague: Svoboda, 1970), pp. 13-14.
2. *Literarni noviny,* April 25, 1956, p. 13.
3. *Literarni noviny,* May 26, 1956, p. 7.
4. *Vladislav Jisl, "Lina kuze nebo ostry mec?" ("Lazy Hide or a Sharp Sword?") Ceskoslovensky novinar,* VIII (January, 1956), p. 5.
5. Karel Storkan, "Promeny publicistiky" ("Transformations in Journalism") *Sesity novinare,* II, No. 4 (1968), p. 44.
6 Karel Jezdinsky, "Impact of Mass Communications Media on the Czechoslovak Reform Movement of 1968" (paper presented at the proceedings of a seminar held at the University of Reading (England), July 12-17, 1971), p. 19.
7. Vojtech Dolejsi, "Patnact let novinarske organizace" ("Fifteen Years of the Journalists' Organization") *Novinarsky sbornik,* V, No. 3 (1960), p. 364. Also see Jan Korecky, "Novinarska organizacia na Slovensku v rokoch 1945-1950" (sic) ("The Journalist Organization in Slovakia During 1945-1950" (1960) *Novinarsky sbornik,* VII, No. 1 (1962), p. 75.
8. *Novinarsky sbornik,* II, No. 3 (1957), p. 301, cited in Jaroslav Vesely, "Vyvoj ceskoslovenskeho tisku, jeho struktura a perspektiva" ("Development of the Czechoslovak Press, Its Structure and Perspective") *Novinarsky sbornik,* VI, No. 2 (1961), p. 132.
9. *Ibid.,* p. 129. In May 1948, the number of periodic publication licenses amounted to only one-third of the number of papers and periodicals published in 1929 and one-half of those published in 1940 under the Protectorate administration in the Czech lands. See Jan E. Sedlacek, "Tisk — jako nastroj ekonomicke propagandy" ("The Press — As an Instrument of Economic Propaganda") *Novinarsky sbornik,* X, No. 4 (1965) p. 848.
10. *Svobodne slovo,* May 6, 1953, cited in Vratislav Busek and Nicolas Spulber, eds., *Czechoslovakia* (New York: Frederick A. Praeger for the Mid-European Studies Center of the Free European Committee, 1957), p. 118.
11. *Sbirka zakonu a narizeni republiky Ceskoslovenske* ("Collection of Laws and Statutes of the Czechoslovak Republic"), No. 184/1950, p. 716. Besides the KSC, other parties included in the political union of the National Front were the Populist (Catholic) and Socialist Parties of Czechoslovakia and the Freedom and Revival Parties of Slovakia. Following the Communist takeover, the National Socialist and Democratic Parties were abolished while the Czechoslovak Social Democratic Party merged with the KSC.
12. *Ibid.,* p. 717.
13. *Ibid.,* No. 68/1951, p. 215.
14. Cited in Dolejsi, "Patnact let novinarske organizace," p. 365.
15. *Ibid.,* p. 366.
16. Vojtech Dolejsi, "Zmeny ve strukture nasich redakci" ("Structural Changes in Our Editorial Offices") *Novinarsky sbornik,* III, No. 4 (1958), p. 420.
17. A. Strakova and Vit. Janacek, "Nekolik poznamek k zahranicnimu zpravodajstvi CTK" ("Some Comments About Foreign Reporting of CTK")

Ceskoslovensky novinar, VIII (March, 1956), p. 75.

18. *Ibid.,* p. 76.

19. *Dolejsi,* "Zmeny ve strukture nasich radakci," p. 424.

20. *Ibid.,* p. 421.

21. Dusan Havlicek, "Czechoslovak Mass Media in 1968" (paper presented at the proceedings of a seminar held at the University of Reading (England), July 12-17, 1971), p. 4.

22. *Ibid.,* p. 5.

23. For a revealing examination of this situation, see Jiri Ruml , "Mych dvacet let" ("My Twenty Years") *Reporter,* February 28 — March 6, 1968, p. 5.

24. *Reporter,* March 20-27, 1968 (special section), p. II.

25. Ladislav Mnacko, *The Seventh Night,* translated from Slovak (London: J.M. Dent & Sons, 1969), p. 70.

26. Vladimir Till, "O kvalifikaci, postaveni a moznostech ceskoslovenskeho novinare" ("Concerning Qualifications, Standing and Opportunities of Czechoslovak Journalists") *Ceskoslovensky novinar,* VIII (May, 1956), p. 144.

27. Josef Stanek, "Dokud nebude pozde" ("As Long as It Won't Be too Late") *Ceskoslovensky novinar,* VIII (June, 1956), p. 183. Also see Dolejsi, "Patnact let novinarske organizace," p. 372. Actually, as of May 1957, the SCSN had a total of 3,344 members and candidate members. Dolejsi noted, however, that between 200 and 300 of these had left the journalistic profession for various reasons.

28. Ruml, "Mych dvacet let," p.5.

29. Storkan, "Promeny publicistiky," p. 44.

30. The cause of the riots, little publicized in the West at the time, was a major change in the nation's monetary system which resulted in the devaluation of workers' savings. The unrest lasted for two days before being suppressed by police and armed militia units.

31. "Government Affairs," *News from behind the Iron Curtain, II* (September, 1953), p. 12.

32. Interview with Karel Jezdinsky, former staff member of Czechoslovak Radio, Munich, West Germany, June 29, 1972.

33. Dana A. Schmidt, *Anatomy of a Satellite,* Atlantic Monthly Press Book (Boston: Little, Brown and Company, 1952), p. 46. The circumstances surrounding Oatis' arrest and trial are fully described in Chapter IV.

34. *Kvety,* No. 42 (November 20, 1955), p. 13. Additional information was gained during several interviews with Alexej Kusak in Bad Aibling and Munich, West Germany, in winter 1971-72.

35. *Kvety,* No. 38 (September 22, 1955), p. 2.

36. Dolejsi, "Patnact let novinarske organizace," p. 371.

37. *Literarni noviny,* April 21, 1956, p. 2.

38. *The New York Times,* May 28, 1956, p. 2. During the mid-1950's Sydney Gruson maintained *The Times* bureau in Prague before relocating it to Poland.

39. *The New York Times,* June 5, 1956, p. 18.

40. A. Pospisilova, "Jak ostrime sve zbrane" ("How We Sharpen Our Weapons") *Ceskoslovensky novinar,* VIII (June, 1956), p. 184.

41. Quoted in *The Times* (London), June 13, 1956, p. 10.
42. Dolejsi, "Patnact let novinarske organizace," p. 371.
43. UV SCSN, "Usneseni o odlozeni II. sjezdu" ("Resolution on the Postponement of the Second Congress") *Ceskoslovensky novinar,* VIII (August, 1956), p. 241.

CHAPTER II

1. Victor A. Velen, "Czech Stalinists Die Hard," *Foreign Affairs,* XLII (January, 1964), p. 322.
2. *Svoboda,* December 23, 1961, p. 1.
3. For literature pertaining to the economic and political situation during this period, see for instance Galia Golan, *The Czechoslovak Reform Movement: Communism in Crisis 1962-1968* (Cambridge: Cambridge University Press, 1971), especially Introduction and Chapters III and V; Velen, "Czech Stalinists Die Hard;" A.H. Brown, "Pluralistic Trends in Czechoslovakia," *Soviet Studies,* XVII (April, 1966), pp. 453-72; Harry G. Shaffer, "Out of Stalinism," *Problems of Communism,* XIV (September-October, 1965), pp. 31-40; and Ota Sik, "The Economic Impact of Stalinism," *Problems of Communism,* XX (May-June, 1971), pp. 1-10.
4. *Host do domu,* IX, No. 2 (1962), p. 85. Also see Richard Blech in *Smena,* April 4, 1962; A. Suchy in *Film a doba,* VI, No. 3 (1962); and V. Kaucky in *Literarni noviny,* February 17, 1962.
5. *Nova mysl,* XVI, No. 6 (1962), p. 656. The article stated that 41,776 letters had been dealt with the previous year by the Office of the President alone, while 4,249 workers had made their appeals personally.
6. H. Gordon Skilling, *Communism National and International: Eastern Europe after Stalin* (Toronto: University of Toronto Press, 1964), p. 129.
7. *Nova mysl,* XVI, No. 12 (1962), pp. 1431-38; *Nova mysl,* XVII, No. 3 (1963), pp. 296-304.
8. Hans Bjorkegren, *Aleksandr Solzhenitsyn: A Biography,* translated by Kaarina Eneberg (New York: The Third Press, Joseph Okpaku Publishing Co.,1972), p. 11.
9. Ladislav Mnacko, *The Seventh Night,* translated from Slovak (London: J.M. Dent & Sons, 1969), pp. 151-52.
10. *Kulturny zivot,* May 4, 1963, p. 1.
11. For a discussion of the DAV rehabilitation issue see Golan, *The Czechoslovak Reform Movement,* p. 35.
12. *Rude pravo,* June 13, 1963, p. 4. The entire issue was not resolved until December and not made public until January 1964.
13. *Kulturny zivot,* May 4, 1963, p. 3.
14. *Kulturny zivot,* January 4, 1963, p. 2.
15. *Kulturny zivot,* May 4, 1963, p. 6.
16. *Plamen,* IV, No. 12 (1962), p. 131.
17. *Literarni noviny,* January 5, 1963, p. 12.
18. *Literarni noviny,* February 16, 1963, pp. 4-5. A slightly revised version of the article was reprinted in Eduard Goldstucker, *Na tema Franz Kafka; clanky a studie* ("On the Theme of Franz Kafka: Articles and Studies")

(Prague: Ceskoslovensky spisovatel, 1964), pp. 23-27. Goldstucker's original article preceded the now famous Kafka Conference, held in Liblice during May 1963, which gave rise to an extensive debate extending beyond the topic of literature and the borders of Czechoslovakia. The discussion also encompassed the problem of alienation in Socialist society, thus providing the impetus for the later discourse on the need of the public's participation in politics via interest groups. It is pertinent to note that *Neues Deutschland* later (September 10, 1968) referred to the Kafka Conference as "an important milestone in increasing the influence of revisionist and bourgeois ideology," adding that it was during this meeting when, for the first time, "revisionism in the CSSR emerged collectively and openly." Quoted in *Politika* (Prague), September 26, 1968, p. 38.

19. *Rude pravo,* March 24, 1963, p. 4.

20. *Rude pravo,* February 26, 1963, p. 3.

21. During the 1950's Kriz, as secretary of the writers' Union Brno branch, was considered a stalwart follower of the Party line. In 1960, however, he published *The Great Solitude,* describing the terror imposed by the Party in its establishment of collective farms. Ptacnik, author of *Frontier Town* (1958), had been criticized for his work's negative aspects in depicting life after the war in areas bordering Germany. Besides, he also defended Josef Skvorecky's *The Cowards,* published the same year and also focusing on the negative, when it was unpopular and even risky to do so. See Jaroslav Dresler, "Writers in Czechoslovakia," *Survey* (London), No. 49 (October, 1963), pp. 149-53.

22. *Nova mysl,* XVII, No. 7 (1963), pp. 868-69.

23. *Ibid,* p. 872.

24. *Literarni noviny,* June 1, 1963, p. 1.

25. During the Third Congress of Czechoslovak Writers, Jesenska explicitly linked the name of Premier Siroky to trials of the bourgeois nationalists but did not elaborate. See *Literarni noviny,* June 8, 1963, p. 8.

26. *Pravda,* June 3, 1963, pp. 2-3. A brief report of his speech also was published in *Praca,* May 28, 1963, p. 3.

27. *Kulturny zivot,* June 1, 1963, p. 1.

28. *Rude pravo,* April 23, 1963, pp. 1-2.

29. *Kulturny zivot,* June 1, 1963, pp. 1, 9.

30. *Pravda,* June 12, 1963, p. 2.

31. Besides the demotion of Bacilek and a few other top Party stalwarts (e.g., Bruno Kohler), Novotny was also forced to replace Siroky with the more popular Jozef Lenart as Premier.

32. *Rude pravo,* April 6, 1963, p. 2.

33. *Nova mysl,* XVIII, No. 4 (1964), p. 386. The document also appeared in *Pravda* and *Rude pravo,* April 3, 1964. Although the weeklies' total circulation for January was given as 278,500 in the *Nova mysl* text, the true total when adding the individual figures provided — *Kulturni tvorba* 118,500, *Literarni noviny* 133,000, *Kulturny zivot* 33,000 — amounts to 6,000 issues more.

34. *Nova mysl,* XVIII, No. 4 (1964), p. 392.

35. *Ibid.,* p. 403.

36. *Ibid.,* p. 404.

37. *Rude pravo,* April 6, 1964, p. 2.
38. *Literarni noviny,* April 11, 1964, p. 2.
39. *Kulturny zivot* May 1, 1964, p. 3.
40. Antonin J. Liehm, *The Politics of Culture,* translated by Peter Kussi (New York: Grove Press, 1972), p. 42.
41. Kamil Winter, "Introduction," in Radoslav Selucky, *Czechoslovakia: The Plan that failed,* translated by Derek Viney (London: Thomas Nelson and Sons, 1970), p. x.

CHAPTER III

1. Interview with Emil Stefan, former director of Bratislava Television, Munich, West Germany, July 1971.
2. A prime example was the coverage of President Kennedy's June 10, 1963, speech announcing the Moscow talks on the cessation of nuclear testing. With the exception of *Rude pravo,* the press summed up the speech in three or four lines, even though it had been reprinted in full in the Soviet press. Recalling the journalists' Congress, held less than two months earlier, during which inadequacies in foreign reporting were criticized, Liehm wrote: "At a time of the existence of television and radio, this type of reporting is not even journalistic, wise or, in the end, really worth anything." See *Literarni noviny,* June 15, 1963, p. 2, also Antony Buzek, *How the Communist Press Works,* Praeger Publications in Russian History and World Communism, No. 147 (New York: Frederick A. Praeger, 1964), p. 183.
3. Dusan Havlicek, "Czechoslovak Mass Media in 1968" (paper presented at the proceedings of a seminar held at the University of Reading (England), July 12-17, 1971), p. 12. Also see Tad Szulc, *Czechoslovakia Since World War II* (New York: Viking Press, 1971), p. 194.
4. *Nova mysl,* XIX, No. 10 (1965), p. 1191.
5. *Nova mysl,* XVIII, No. 6 (1964), pp. 649-51.
6. *Ibid.,* p. 657.
7. *Zivot strany,* XIV, No. 18 (1964), p. 1096.
8. *Kulturni tvorba,* September 29, 1966, p. 6.
9. *Zivot strany,* XV, No. 5 (1965), p. 283.
10. Karel Tejkal, *Rozhlasove zpravodajstvi: K nekterym problemum rozhlasove specificnosti* ("Broadcast Reporting: Toward Some Problems of Broadcasting Specification") (Prague: Statni pedagogicke nakladatelstvi, 1967), p. 3.
11. *Zivot strany,* X, No. 12 (1960) p. 743. Included among the criticism issued against broadcasting was its lack of a "national character," meaning that stations transmitting in Czech did not have a proportionate amount of Slovak language programs. As a result, the 1960 Party directive projected that by 1965 between 30 and 35 percent of all statewide programing would be conducted in Slovak.
12. *Kulturni tvorba,* September 29, 1966, p. 6.
13. *MY 65,* II (November, 1965), p. 64.
14. International Press Institute, *"Svoboda" The Press in Czechoslovakia 1968* (Zurich: International Press Institute, 1969. p. 42.

15. *Zivot strany,* X, No. 12 (1960), p. 736.
16. IPI, *"Svoboda,"* p. 43.
17. *Zivot strany,* XV, No. 5 (1965), p. 288.
18. IPI, *"Svoboda,"* p. 42.
19. *Vecerni Praha,* March 12, 1965, as cited in "Television in Eastern Europe," *East Europe,* XV (April, 1966), p. 14.
20. "Television in Eastern Europe," p. 13. An indication of the wide appeal of Western and domestically produced films was contained in a report published in *Osvetova prace* (Work of Enlightenment), No. 24 (1965), which said that of the 182 Soviet and Socialist bloc films shown in Czechoslovakia during 1964 and the first half of 1965, a total of 58 or 31.8 percent attracted less than 100,000 viewers, or less than 1 percent of all moviegoers — the established mark of failure or success. This included 18 of 32 (59.4 %) Soviet films and 26 of 52 (50.0 %) Socialist bloc films. In comparison, only 6 of 42 (14.3 %) domestically produced movies failed to meet the established standard as did 8 of 51 (15.3 %) Western films screened during the same period. See *East Euorpe,* XV (March, 1966), p. 46.
21. Quoted in "Television in Eastern Europe," p. 13-14.
22. *Zivot strany,* XV, No. 5 (1965), p. 289.
23. *Ibid.,* p. 285.
24. *Zivot strany,* XVI, No. 22 (1966), p. 46.
25. *Zivot strany,* XVI, No. 1 (1966), pp. 12-17.
26. *Literarni listy,* March 14, 1968, p. 8.
27. *Literarni noviny,* January 1, 1966, p. 2.
28. *Zivot strany,* XVI, No. 8 (1966), p. 17.
29. *Orientace,* I, No. 1 (1966), p. 1.
30. *Literarni noviny,* October 8, 1966, p. 2. The term dates back to the press law of 1862 which stipulated that the 'responsible editor,' not necessarily the true editor-in-chief, of a given publication was the individual responsible for its content. Thus, if an article constituted a breach of law, it was the responsible editor who was held to answer in court unless he revealed the author's name.
31. Buzek, *How the Communist Press Works,* p. 200.
32. Jiri Goldschmidt, "Skola pro Africke novinare" ("School for African Journalists") *Svet v obrazech,* XXI, No. 43 (1965), p. 19.
33. Buzek, *How the Communist Press Works,* p. 205.
34. Havlicek, "Czechoslovak Mass Media in 1968," p. 11.
35. *Pravda,* September 28, 1966, p. 3. (This was the last article in a two-part series.)
36. *Pravda,* October 19, 1966, p. 3.
37. A phrase used by Zdenek Hejzlar, appointed director of Czechoslovak Radio shortly before the invasion, to describe the liberalization period in Czechoslovakia under Novotny. See Donald R. Shanor, *Soviet Europe* (New York: Harper & Row, 1975), p. 85.

CHAPTER IV

The latter portion of this chapter served as the basis for my "Czechoslovakia's Press Law, 1967-68: Decontrolling the Mass Media." Journalism Quarterly, LII (Autumn, 1975), pp. 450-57.

1. Galia Golan, *The Czechoslovak Reform Movement: Communism in Crisis 1962-1968* (Cambridge: Cambridge University Press, 1971), pp. 146-47.
2. UV SCSN, "Stanovisko UV Svazu Cs. Novinaru k tezim pro pripravu XIII. Sjezdu KSC" ("Position of the Central Committee of the Union of Czechoslovak Journalists Toward the Theses in Preparation for the XIII Congress of the KSC") *Novinar,* XVIII (February, 1966), pp. 33-34.
3. UV KSC, "O stranickem vedeni tisku, rozhlasu a televize" ("Concerning the Party's Direction of the Press, Broadcasting and Television") *Zivot strany,* XVI, No. 18 (1966), pp. 1-4.
4. UV SCSN, "Stanovisko UV Svazu cs. novinaru k praci tisku, rozhlasu a televize od XII. sjezdu KSC" ("Position of the Central Committee of the Union of Czechoslovak Journalists Toward the Work of the Press, Radio and Television Since the XII Congress of the KSC") *Novinar,* XVIII (June, 1966), p. 4.
5. Interview with Karel Jezdinsky, former staff member of Czechoslovak Radio, Munich, West Germany, June 29, 1972.
6. "Znepokojujici tendence" ("Disquieting Tendencies") *Zivot strany,* XVI, No. 1 (1966), p. 16.
7. Vladislav Jisl, "Sedma velmoc . . . a verejne mineni" ("The Seventh Power . . . and Public Opinion") *Novinar,* XVIII (April, 1966), p. 107.
8. *Kultura,* I, No. 2 (1958), p. 1.
9. Marie Simakova, "Noviny a interview" ("Newspapers and the Interview") *Novinarsky sbornik,* X, No. 4 (1965), p. 444.
10. *Ibid.,* p. 446.
11. *Kulturny zivot,* April 22, 1966, p. 6; *Literarni noviny,* April 23, 1966, pp. 1, 3.
12. *Kultura,* I, No. 32 (1958), p. 2.
13. Karel Storkan, "Promeny publicistiky" ("Transformations in Journalism") *Sesity novinare,* II, N. 4 (1968), p. 47.
14. *Novinarsky sbornik,* X, No. 3 (1965), p. 234 as cited in Storkan, "Promeny publicistiky," p. 35.
15. *Ibid.,* p. 48.
16. Interview with Alexej Kusak, former editor of *Student,* Bad Aibling, West Germany, November 15, 1971.
17. Jean-Paul Sartre, "Introduction: The Socialism that Came in from the Cold" in Antonin J. Liehm, *The Politics of Culture,* translated by Peter Kussi (New York: Grove Press, 1972), p. 31.
18. Jan Hrabanek, "Press and Editorial Rights in Czechoslovakia," *Democratic Journalist,* XV (July-August, 1967), p. 88.
19. *Sbirka zakonu Ceskoslovenske socialisticke republiky* ("Collection of Laws of the Czechoslovak Socialist Republic"), No. 81/1966, p. 436. (Key sections of the law were published in *The Soviet Press,* VI, (Fall, 1967), pp. 31-37).

20. *Sbirka zakonu,* p. 433.
21. *Ibid.*
22. *Ibid.,* p. 435.
23. *Ibid.,* pp. 436-37.
24. *Mlada fronta,* March 6, 1968, p. 2. Also see Dusan Havlicek, "Czechoslovak Mass Media in 1968" (paper presented at the proceedings of a seminar held at the University of Reading (England), July 12-17, 1971), p. 7.
25. Lubos Sefcak, "Svoboda tlace, zakon a cenzura" ("Press Freedom, the Law and Censorship") *Novinar,* XX (June, 1968), p. 158.
26. "Takove to bylo" ("That's How It Was") *Reporter,* March 27-April 3, 1968, p. 5.
27. Dusan Hamsik, *Spisovatele a moc* ("Writers and Power") (Prague: Ceskoslovensky spisovatel, 1969), p. 172.
28. UV KSC, "O stranickem vedeni tisku," p. 2.
29. *Rude pravo,* December 21, 1966, p. 3.
30. Pavel Kohout, *From the Diary of a Counterrevolutionary,* translated by George Theiner (New York: McGraw-Hill, 1972), p. 219. Also see Kohout's speech to the 1967 writers' Congress in Svaz Ceskoslovenskych spisovatelu, *IV. Sjezd Svazu ceskoslovenskych spisovatelu/Protokol/Praha 27-29. cervna 1967* ("Fourth Congress of the Union of Czechoslovak Writers/Minutes Prague 27-29 June 1967") (Prague: Ceskoslovensky spisovatel, 1968), pp. 39-44.
31. Sefcak, "Svoboda tlace, zakon a cenzura," p. 158.
32. A good example was an article describing how members of the People's Militia, in not too respectful a manner, prevented newsmen and television cameramen from entering the grounds of a large clothing factory damaged by a major fire, the worst such disaster in the area in twenty years. The author, a reporter for the daily *Rovnost* (Equality), managed to cover the story *only* because he was personally acquainted with the factory director and several of the militiamen. He concluded the account by asking: "Where is the new press law which clearly states the duty of economic conerns and all responsible functionaries is to inform the mass information media, that is the press, radio and TV and their personnel?" *Reporter,* April 24-May, 5, 1967, p. 13.
33. Sefcak, "Svoboda tlace, zakon a cenzura," p. 157.
34. Hamsik, *Spisovatele a moc,* p. 8.

CHAPTER V

1. *Literarni noviny,* March 26, 1966, p. 2; *Literarni noviny,* June 25, 1966, p. 2; *Literarni noviny,* October 8, 1966, p. 2.
2. *Zivot strany,* XVI, No. 18 (1966), pp. 1-4; *Zivot strany,* XVI, No. 21 (1966), pp. 1-5. An additional indicator was the arrest during August 1966 of young liberal writer Jan Benes and cinema student Karel Zamecnik for allegedly being in contact with a Paris-based Czech emigre publication. The following July, Benes was sentenced to five years in prison while Zamecnik was acquitted.

3. "The old gray press isn't any longer," *Economist*, February 25, 1967, p. 723.
4. Boleslav Rohac and Rudolf Vlcek, "Vysledky registrace periodickeho tisku podle noveho tiskoveho zakona" ("The Results of Press Registration According to the New Press Law") *Novinar*, XX, No. 3 (1968), p. 79.
5. Radio Bratislava, December 29, 1966.
6. CTK, December 22, 1966.
7. Rohac and Vlcek, "Vysledky registrace periodickeho tisku," p. 78.
8. *Sbirka zakonu Ceskoslovenske socialisticke republiky* ("Collection of Laws of the Czechoslovak Socialist Republic"), No. 81/1966, p. 434.
9. Rohac and Vlcek, "Vysledky registrace periodickeho tisku," p. 79.
10. *Pravda*, December 29, 1966, p. 2.
11. *Svobodne slovo*, April 23, 1967, p. 1.
12. *Literarni noviny*, June 24, 1967, p. 2.
13. *Kulturni tvorba*, December 1, 1966, p. 3.
14. See *Pravda*, July 4, 1967, p. 3. A reporter described the bureaucarcy and frustrations he encountered while attempting to obtain information about a railway accident in Slovakia.
15. "Cim ziju umelecke svazy?" ("What Do Creative Unions Live By?") *Nova mysl*, XX, No. 9 (1966), pp. 16-17.
16. Vladimir V. Kusin, *Political Grouping in the Czechoslovak Reform Movement* (London: Macmillan, 1972), p. 70.
17. Interview with Karel Jezdinsky, former staff member of Czechoslovak Radio, Munich, West Germany, June 29, 1972.
18. *Rude pravo*, March 13, 1967, p. 2.
19. Dusan Hamsik, *Spisovatele a moc* ("Writers and Power") (Prague: Ceskoslovensky spisovatel, 1969), p. 137.
20. *Ibid.*, p. 172. The total number of interventions listed actually amounts to 432, the difference being the number of interventions made between the June Congress and the weekly's removal from the SCSS's control in late September.
21. *Kulturny zivot*, May 19, 1967, p. 3.
22. *Kulturny zivot*, May 12, 1967, p. 8.
23. Galia Golan, *The Czechoslovak Reform Movement: Communism in Crisis 1962-1968* (Cambridge: Cambridge University Press, 1971), p. 130.
24. Svaz Ceskoslovenskych spisovatelu, *IV. Sjezd Svazu ceskoslovenskych spisovatelu/Protokol/Praha 27.-29.cervna 1967* ("Fourth Congress of the Union of Czechoslovak Writers/Minutes Prague 27-29 June 1967") (Prague: Ceskoslovensky spisovatel, 1968), p. 40.
25. For example, see *Ibid.*; Hamsik, *Spisovatele a moc;* Dusan Hamsik, *Writers and Rulers*, translated by D. Orpington (New York: Vintage Books, 1971); Pavel Kohout, *From the Diary of a Counterrevolutionary*, translated by George Theiner (New York: McGraw-Hill, 1972); Harry Schwartz, *Prague's 200 Days: The Struggle for Democracy in Czechoslovakia* (London: Pall Mall Press, 1969), Chapter 2; and Tad Szulc, *Czechoslovakia Since World War II* (New York: Viking Press, 1971), Chapter XIII.
26. "Literatura po sjezdu" ("Literature After the Congress") *Nova mysl*, XXI, No. 15 (1967), pp. 6-7. Also see *Kulturny zivot*, March 28, 1968, pp. 3, 8.
27. "Dopis delegatu V. sjezdu SCSN ustrednimu vyboru KSC" ("Letter of

the Delegates of the Fifth Congress of the SCSN to the Central Committee of the KSC") *Novinar,* XIX, No. 11 (1967), p. 343.

28. In a sociological survey on job status and prestige conducted prior to 1968, the position of journalist was included among a list of 30 occupations. The public sample rated journalists as 19th in social utility and usefulness, 25th in salary and 26th in terms of occupational importance. See Vladimir Brenner and Milan Hrouda, "Veda a vysokoskolske vzdelani v prestizi povolani" ("Scholarship and Higher Education in the Prestige of Occupations") *Sociologicky casopis,* IV, No. 1 (1968), p. 51.

29. "The old gray press isn't any longer," p. 723. Interview with Antony Buzek, former CTK correspondent, London, England, September 19, 1972.

30. *Novinar,* XIX, No. 12 (1967), p. 421.

31. Karel Jezdinsky, "Impact of Mass Communications Media on the Czechoslovak Reform Movement of 1968" (paper presented at the proceedings of a seminar held at the University of Reading (England), July 12-17, 1971), p. 26.

32. *Ibid.*

33. Jaroslav Diblik, "Svaz a nase profesionalni zajmy" ("The Union and Our Professional Interests") *Novinar,* XIX, No. 9 (1967), p. 263.

34. For an account of actions taken against the writers by the regime, see Hamsik, *Spisovatele a moc,* Chapter 3, especially pp. 90-91. Also see Szulc, *Czechoslovakia Since World War II,* pp. 234-35.

35. *Literarni listy,* April 18, 1968, p. 6.

36. Jan Skacel, "Mala recenze na Literarni noviny" ("A Little Review of 'Literarni noviny' ") *Host do domu,* XIV, No. 11 (1967), p. 80.

37. *Rude pravo,* September 21, 1967, p. 1.

38. *Pravda,* September 16, 1967, p. 1.

39. *Praca,* September 21, 1967, p. 3.

40. Both *Mlada fronta* and the Slovak daily *Praca* carried brief reports of the incident on November 2, 1967, while *Rude pravo* and the Prague daily *Prace* reprinted the brief CTK report (dated November 2) in their November 3, 1967, issues.

41. *Reporter,* December 16, 1967, pp. 4-7.

42. *Kulturni tvorba,* November 16, 1967, p. 1.

43. Michel Salomon, *Prague Notebook: The Strangled Revolution,* translated by Helen Eustis (Boston: Little, Brown and Co., 1971), p. 20.

44. Radoslav Selucky, *Czechoslovakia: The Plan that failed,* translated by Derek Viney (London: Thomas Nelson and Sons, 1970), p. 96.

45. *Christian Science Monitor,* December 23, 1967, p. 2.

46. *The New York Times,* December 26, 1967, p. 32.

47. Salomon, *Prague Notebook,* pp. 62-63. Also see *The New York Times,* December 20, 1967, p. 3.

48. CTK, January 18, 1968.

49. *Kulturny zivot,* January 12, 1968, pp. 1, 8.

50. *Ibid.,* p. 8.

51. *Rude pravo,* January 14, 1968, p. 4.

52. *Prace,* February 1, 1968, p. 5.

53. TAJUNG, February 15, 1968.

54. Radio Prague, February 23, 1968.

55. *Zemedelske noviny,* February 27, 1968, p. 1.

56. Ustredni vybor Svazu cs. novinaru, "Dopis prvnimu tajemniku UV KSC A. Dubcekovi" ("Letter to the First Secretary of the Central Committee of the KSC A. Dubcek") *Novinar,* XX, No. 2 (1968), p. 34.

57. *Reporter,* February 14, 1968, p. 3.

58. Salomon, *Prague Notebook,* p. 65.

59. *The Times* (London) March 1, 1968, p. 7. Although circulated on February 29, 1968, the first issue of the new writers' weekly was actually dated March 1.

60. *Literarni listy,* March 1, 1968, p. 1.

CHAPTER VI

1. For example, see *Reporter,* February 7, 1968, p. 9.

2. International Press Institute, *"Svoboda" The Press in Czechoslovakia 1968* (Zurich: International Press Institute, 1969), p. 25. Also see Jaroslaw Piekalkiewicz, "Public Political Opinion in Czechoslovakia During the Dubcek Era," in his and E.J. Czerwinski, eds., *The Soviet Invasion of Czechoslovakia: Its Effects on Eastern Europe,* Praeger Special Studies in International Politics and Public Affairs (New York: Praeger Publishers, 1972), p. 17.

3. Dusan Havlicek, "Czechoslovak Mass Media in 1968" (paper presented at the proceedings of a seminar held at the University of Reading (England), July 12-17, 1971), p. 21.

4. *Literarni listy,* April 4, 1968, p. 4.

5. V.V. Kusin, ed., *The Czechoslovak Reform Movement, 1968,* Proceedings of the Seminar held at the University of Reading on 12-17 July, 1971 (Santa Barbara, Calif., : ABC-Clio Press, 1973), p. 283.

6. *Rude pravo,* February 10, 1968, p. 3.

7. *Literarni listy,* March 1, 1968, pp. 4, 12.

8. *Mlada fronta,* March 5, 1968, p. 2.

9. *Zemedelske noviny,* March 16, p. 6.

10. *Ibid.*

11. *Reporter,* May 1, 1968, p. 5.

12. *Rude pravo,* June 27, 1968, p. 1.

13. *Sbirka zakonu Ceskoslovenske socialisticke republiky* ("Collection of Laws of the Czechoslovak Socialist Republic"), No. 84/1968, p. 238.

14. Ithiel de Sola Pool, "Public Opinion in Czechoslovakia," *Public Opinion Quarterly,* XXXIV (Spring, 1970), p. 10.

15. The Action Program of the Communist Party of Czechoslovakia has been published in translation in Paul Ello, ed., *Dubcek's Blueprint for Freedom* (London: William Kimber, 1969), pp. 123-212.

16. *Lidova demokracie,* June 23, 1968, p. 1.

17. Dusan Hamsik, *Writers Against Rulers,* translated by D. Orpington (New York: Vintage Books, 1971), p. 162.

18. *Reporter,* April 3, 1968, p. 2.

19. *Prace,* March 20, 1968, p. 4.

20. *Student,* March 6, 1968, pp. 1, 5.

21. *The Guardian* (London), March 19, 1968, p. 9.

22. *Rude pravo,* March 20, 1968, pp. 1-2.

23. *Novinar,* XX, No. 5 (1968), p. 160. Also see Emil Sip, "How the press won its freedom," *IPI Report,* XVI (April, 1968), p. 5.

24. *Ibid.* (Box insert)

25. Karel Jezdinsky, "Impact of Mass Communications Media on the Czechoslovak Reform Movement of 1968" (paper presented at the proceedings of a seminar held at the University of Reading (England), July 12-17, 1971), p. 19.

26. "Ruch v novinarske organizaci" ("Activity Within the Journalists' Organization") *Novinar,* XX, No. 3 (1968), p. 72.

27. Ustredny Vybor SSN, "Uznesenie UV SSN" ("Resolution of the Central Committee of the Union of Slovak Journalists") *Novinar,* XX, No. 4 (1968), p. 110; "Rezoluce Klubu nezavislych novinaru" ("Resolution of the Club of Independent Journalists") *Novinar,* XX, No. 5 (1968), p. 183.

28. "Pred svolanim mimoradneho sjezdu svazu cs. novinaru" ("Prior to the Convocation of the Irregular Congress of the Union of Czechoslovak Journalists") *Novinar,* XX, No. 4 (1968), p. 111.

29. *Reporter,* April, 3, 1968, p. 2.

30. "Aktiv Prazskych novinaru" ("Meeting of Prague Journalists") *Novinar,* XX, No. 4 (1968), p. 112.

31. *Ibid.*

32. "Politicka rezoluce mimoradneho sjezdu SCSN" ("Political Resolution of the Irregular Congress of the SCSN") *Novinar,* XX, Nos. 7-8 (1968), p. 259.

33. "Projev Alexandra Dubcka, prveho tajomnika UV KSC" ("The Address of Alexander Dubcek, First Secretary of the Central Committee of the KSC") *Novinar,* XX, Nos. 7-8 (1968), p. 249.

34. "Rezoluce mimoradneho sjezdu cs. novinaru k tiskovemu zakonodarstvi" ("Resolution of the Irregular Congress of the Union of Czechoslovak Journalists on Press Legislation") *Novinar,* XX, Nos. 7-8 (1968), p. 261.

35. "Politicka rezoluce mimoradneho sjezdu," p. 261.

36. Vlado Kaspar, "Nekolik slov k mimoradnemu sjezdu" ("A Few Words Concerning the Irregular Congress") *Novinar,* XX, No. 6 (1968), p. 197.

37. IPI, *"Svoboda,"* p. 92.

38. *Current Digest of the Soviet Press,* XX (May, 1968), pp. 8-10.

39. *Zemedelske noviny,* May 16, 1968, p. 1.

40. *Literarni listy,* May 23, 1968, p. 2.

41. Radio Prague, May 23, 1968.

42. *Literarni listy,* April 4, 1968, p. 4.

43. *Current Digest of the Soviet Press,* XX (June, 1968), p. 10.

44. Ello, ed., *Dubcek's Blueprint for Freedom,* p. 252.

45. *Reporter,* May 8, 1968, p. 3.

46. Jezdinsky, "Impact of Mass Communications Media," p. 17.

47. Interview with Karel Jezdinsky, former staff member of Czechoslovak Radio, Munich, West Germany, June 29, 1972. Jezdinsky explained that once censorship had been abolished, the main fear among reformist journalists

was that it would be reinstated after the Dubcek leadership had secured its power. They based their suspicions on the experience of the Polish press after 1956. To gain public support, Gomulka had allowed a certain degree of freedom to prevail in his country, including less restrictive censorship. But once having secured his political position, he gradually rescinded these freedoms and imposed strict restrictions on the press.

48. *Literarni listy,* June 27, 1968, p. 3. The manifesto also appeared in *Mlada front, Prace* and *Zemedelske noviny.*

49. *Literarni listy,* June 27, 1968, p. 3.

50. Harry Schwartz, *Prague's 200 Days: The Struggle for Democracy in Czechoslovakia* (London: Pall Mall Press, 1969), p. 159.

51. *Current Digest of the Soviet Press,* XX (July, 1968), p. 4.

52. *Ibid.*

53. *Rude pravo,* July 19, 1968, p. 2.

54. *Ibid.*

55. *Student,* July 24, 1968, p. 1.

56. Havlicek, "Czechoslovak Mass Media in 1968," p. 31.

57. IPI, *"Svoboda,"* p. 70. For reactions to the *Student* article, see *Rude pravo,* July 24, 1968, p. 2; *Vecerni Praha,* July 24, 1968, p. 3; and *Literarni listy,* July 25, 1968, p. 2.

58. *Mlada fronta,* August 4, 1968, p. 3.

59. Josef Smrkovsky, *Nedokoncene Vzpominky* ("Unfinished Recollections") (Typewritten manuscript translated from the Italian, 1975). Smrkovsky's memoirs were made public by Davido Lajola, editor of *Giorni-Vie Nuove* and former member of the Central Committee of the Italian Communist Party. The first part of the memoirs was made public in pamphlet form on February 20, 1975.

60. *Current Digest of the Soviet Press,* XX (August, 1968), pp. 10-11.

CHAPTER VII

1. Vladimir V. Kusin, *The Intellectual Origins of the Prague Spring: The Development of Reformist Ideas in Czechoslovakia 1956-1967* (Cambridge: Cambridge University Press, 1971), p. 142.

2. Radoslav Selucky, *Czechoslovakia: The Plan that failed,* translated by Derek Viney (London: Thomas Nelson and Sons, 1970), p. 135.

3. *Literarni listy,* April 11, 1968, p. 2.

4. *Novinarsky sbornik,* II, No. 4 (1957), pp. 446-47, quoted in Antony Buzek, *How the Communist Press Works,* Praeger Publications in Russian History and World Communism, No. 147 (New York: Frederick A. Praeger, 1964), p. 82.

5. Selucky, *Czechoslovakia,* p. 78.

6. Dusan Hamsik, *Writers and Rulers,* translated by D. Orpington (New York: Vintage Books, 1971), p. 161.

7. Quoted in *Ibid.,* pp. 161-62.

8. *The New York Times,* July 16, 1975, p. 37.

9. V.V. Kusin, ed., *The Czechoslovak Reform Movement 1968,* Proceedings

of the Seminar held at the University of Reading on 12-17 July, 1971 (Santa Barbara, Calif.: ABC-Clio Press, 1973), p. 283.

10. For instance, see the articles translated in "On the Theme of Opposition" in Andrew Oxley, Alex Pravda and Andrew Ritchie, eds., *Czechoslovakia: The Party and the People* (London: Allen Lane, 1973), pp. 101-148.

11. V.V. Kusin, ed., *The Czechoslovak Reform Movement 1968,* p. 283.

12. *Current Digest of the Soviet Press,* XX (August, 1968), pp. 10-11.

13. *K Udalostem v Ceskoslovensku: Fakta, dokumenty, svedectvi tisku a ocitych svedku* "Concerning the Events in Czechoslovakia: Facts, Documents, Testimony from the Press and Eyewitnesses") translated from Russian (Moscow: 1968), p. 55.

14. Jaroslaw Piekalkiewicz, "Public Political Opinion in Czechoslovakia During the Dubcek Era," in his and E.J. Czerwinski, eds., *The Soviet Invasion of Czechoslovakia: Its Effects on Eastern Europe,* Praeger Special Studies in International Politics and Public Affairs (New York: Praeger Publishers, 1972), pp. 3-42. Also see Ithiel de Sola Pool, "Public Opinion in Czechoslovakia," *Public Opinion Quarterly,* XXXIV (Spring, 1970), pp. 14-15.

EPILOGUE

1. See the TASS communiques of August 21 and 22, 1968, and *Pravda's* lengthy editorial of August 22, 1968, in *Current Digest of the Soviet Press,* XX (September 11, 1968), pp. 3 and 5-14, respectively.

2. The occupation by Soviet forces of editorial offices during the week of invasion was reported in the extra editions of Prague dailies which were printed and distributed clandestinely throughout the week.

3. Quoted in Donald R. Shanor, *Soviet Europe* (New York: Harper & Row, 1975), p. 76.

4. *Mlada fronta* (Second Extra Edition), August 21, 1968, p. 1.

5. *Rude pravo* (Extra Edition), August 21, 1968, p. 1.

6. *Zemedelske noviny* (Extra Edition), August, 21, 1968, p. 1.

7. *Svobodne Slovo* (Extra Edition), August 22, 1968, p. 1.

8. Shanor. *Soviet Europe,* p. 103.

9. See for instance the story published by *Zemedelske noviny,* August 27, 1968, in Robert Little, ed., *The Czech Black Book,* prepared by the Institute of History of the Czechoslovak Academy of Sciences (London: Pall Mall Press, 1969), pp. 234-35.

10. Conditions of the Moscow Protocol appear in Pavel Tigrid, *Why Dubcek Fell* (London: Macdonald, 1971), Appendix A, pp. 210-14.

11. From *Mlada fronta,* August 31, 1968, as quoted in Little, ed., *The Czech Black Book,* p. 284.

12. From *Literarni listy* (Extra Edition), August 28, 1968, as quoted in *Tribuna,* May 28, 1969, p. 11.

13. *Sbirka zakonu Ceskoslovenske socialisticke republiky* ("Collection of Laws of the Czechoslovak Socialist Republic"), No. 127/1968, p. 346.

14. *Reporter,* February 28, 1969, p. 8.

15. *K Udalostem v Ceskoslovensku: Fakta, dokumenty, svedectvi tisku* a ocitych svedku ("Concerning the Events in Czechoslovakia: Facts, Documents, Testimony from the Press and Eyewitnesses") translated from Russian (Moscow: 1969), p. 58.

16. *Listy,* November 7, 1968, p. 1.

17. *Zpravy,* February 1, 1969, pp. 2, 7.

18. *Rude pravo,* November 28, 1968, p. 2; *Rude pravo,* November 29, 1968, p. 2.

19. A translation of the letter appears in Ivan Svitak, *The Czechoslovak Experiment 1968-1969* (New York: Columbia University Press, 1971). p. 233.

20. "O tisku, rozhlasu a televizi" ("Concerning the Press, Radio and Television") *Novinar,* XX, No. 12 (1968), p. 420.

21. *Ibid.,* p. 422.

22 "Aktiv prazskych novinaru v Lurene" ("The Activ of Prague Journalists in Lucerna") *Novinar,* XX, No. 12 (1968), p. 414.

23. *Reporter,* April 10, 1969, p. 1.

24. *Rude pravo,* May 17, 1969. The article later appeared in Ustredi Novinaru CSSR, *Novinari a jejich organizace v krizovem obdobi* ("Journalists and Their Organization in the Period of Crisis") *Novinar,* XXIII, No. 9 (Supplement, pp. 18-20.

25. *Rude pravo,* July 3, 1969, p. 3.

26. For a concise account of political arrests and trials during 1971 and early 1972, see Adam Roberts, "Czechoslovakia: trials without 'show'," *World Today,* XXVIII (March, 1972), pp. 93-98.

27. Oldrich Svestka, "Nejdulezitejsi ukoly hromadnych sdelovacich prostredku" ("The Most Important Tasks of the Mass Communication Media") *Novinar,* XXV, No. 2 (1973), p. 8.

28. *The Times* (London), April 23, 1975, p. 9.

29. Edward Taborsky, "Czechoslovakia under Husak," *Current History,* LXX, (March, 1976), p. 117ff.

30. Zdenek Horeni, "Celem k Zivotu, Celem k Budoucnosti" ("Facing Life, Facing the Future") *Sesity novinare,* IX, No. 1 (1975), pp. 6-7. In his article "The Profession of Journalism in Poland: A Profile," *Journalism Quarterly,* XLIV (Spring, 1972), pp. 123-28, Stanislaw Skrzypek notes that of the 4,800 members of the Polish Journalists' Association at the end of the 1960's, more than 58 percent had a university education.

31. See for instanceVladimir Hudec, "Fakulte Zurnalistiky do Vinku" ("Toward the Journalism Faculty's Future") *Novinar,* XXIV, No. 11 (1972), pp. 9-11, and CC CSSN, "Koncepce Ideove Vychovne Cinnosti a Jeji Nejblizsi Ukoly" ("The Concept of Ideologically Educational Activity and its Nearest Tasks") *Novinar,* XXIV, No. 10 (1972), pp. 7-9.

32. Quoted in Horeni, "Celem k Zivotu, Celem k Budoucnosti," p. 6.

APPENDICIES

APPENDIX I: Tables

TABLE I
DEVELOPMENT OF THE MASS MEDIA IN CZECHOSLOVAKIA 1948-1960

Year	Number of Daily Newspapers	Daily Press Run of All Daily Newspapers	Number of Periodic Titles	Newsprint Consumption (in metric tons)	Number of Radio Licenses	Number of Television Licenses
1948	21	2,475,000	1,031	40,447	2,108,000	—
1949	18	2,250,000	1,393	41,640	—	—
1950	18	2,230,000	1,971	40,327	2,297,000	—
1951	18	2,050,000	2,290	42,406	2,545,000	—
1952	11	2,010,000	2,591	36,057	2,608,000	—
1953	12	1,820,000	2,728	31,608	2,676,000	—
1954	12	1,780,000	2,608	30,776	2,745,493	3,833
1955	13	1,875,000	1,398	30,724	2,880,400	32,119
1956	14	1,990,000	1,451	34,000	3,013,318	75,934
1957	15	2,170,000	1,478	37,500	3,150,426	172,782
1958	15	2,285,000	1,490	40,800	3,317,179	327,861
1959	17	2,603,000	1,429	44,286	3,427,466	518,987
1960	21	3,053,000	1,230	48,136	3,530,418	794,898

Sources: *Novinarsky sbornik,* VI, No. 2 (1961), pp. 121-44; United Nations. *Statistical Yearbook* (New York: Statistical Office of the Department of Economic and Social Affairs, 1951-1954.)

TABLE 2
TOTAL NUMBER OF NEWSPAPERS AND PERIODICALS 1961-1970

Year	Number of Titles Published			Number of Issues Printed (in thousands)		
	CSSR	Czech lands	Slovakia	CSSR	Czech lands	Slovakia
1961	1,220	945	275	1,605,941	1,234,390	371,551
1962	1,336	1,060	276	1,645,250	1,255,852	389,398
1963	1,314	1,031	283	1,615,896	1,239,941	375,955
1964	1,299	1,015	284	1,693,119	1,289,699	403,420
1965	1,286	998	288	1,810,216	1,366,971	443,245
1966	1,247	964	283	1,893,500	1,429,009	464,491
1967	1,204	971	233	1,866,930	1,413,354	453,576
1968	1,403	1,147	256	1,974,055	1,494,634	479,421
1969	1,589	1,265	324	1,875,175	1,418,280	456,895
1970	1,412	1,067	345	1,773,540	1,316,602	456,938

Totals do not equal totals of following tables because miscellaneous category has not been included.

Source for this and the following tables: *Statisticka rocenka Ceskoslovenske Socialisticke Republiky* ("Statistical Annual of the Czechoslovak Socialist Republic") (Prague: SNTL, 1962-1971).

TABLE 3
DAILY NEWSPAPERS 1961-1970

Year	Number of Titles Published			Number of Issues Printed (in thousands)		
	CSSR	Czech lands	Slovakia	CSSR	Czech lands	Slovakia
1961	24	16	8	1,158,566	900,001	258,565
1962	24	15	9	1,185,585	906,676	278,909
1963	25	15	10	1,185,879	908,832	277,047
1964	26	15	11	1,245,177	945,553	299,624
1965	27	15	12	1,333,870	1,001,638	332,232
1966	27	15	12	1,381,798	1,035,970	345,828
1967	28	16	12	1,359,616	1,023,217	336,398
1968	28	16	12	1,419,286	1,065,533	353,753
1969	33	20	13	1,270,085	952,612	317,473
1970	31	19	12	1,203,945	892,783	311,162

TABLE 4
WEEKLY NEWSPAPERS AND PERIODICALS 1961-1970

Year	Number of Titles Published			Number of Issues Printed (in thousands)		
	CSSR	Czech lands	Slovakia	CSSR	Czech lands	Slovakia
1961	471	370	101	330,815	241,724	89,091
1962	499	394	105	334,090	248,505	85,585
1963	494	391	103	304,765	231,035	73,730
1964	507	401	106	319,622	240,416	79,206
1965	506	393	113	339,113	254,526	84,587
1966	444	338	106	377,725	284,240	93,485
1967	266	183	83	367,586	274,461	93,124
1968	304	210	94	391,777	292,223	99,554
1969	313	213	100	439,385	331,200	108,185
1970	308	203	105	413,303	300,776	112,527

TABLE 5
BIWEEKLY NEWSPAPERS AND PERIODICALS 1961-1970

Year	Number of Titles Published			Number of Issues Printed (in thousands)		
	CSSR	Czech lands	Slovakia	CSSR	Czech lands	Slovakia
1961	223	160	63	55,524	44,568	10,956
1962	241	176	65	61,952	50,289	11,663
1963	233	163	70	60,023	48,369	11,654
1964	192	130	62	59,936	49,229	10,707
1965	174	112	62	61,719	49,796	11,923
1966	157	97	60	61,351	51,124	10,227
1967	108	80	28	61,994	50,195	11,799
1968	130	110	20	68,086	54,284	13,802
1969	199	150	49	82,222	65,158	17,064
1970	173	123	50	71,877	55,576	16,301

TABLE 6

MONTHLY PERIODICALS 1961-1970

Year	Number of Titles Published			Number of Issues Printed (in thousands)		
	CSSR	Czech lands	Slovakia	CSSR	Czech lands	Slovakia
1961	332	257	75	58,235	45,498	12,737
1962	379	308	71	60,746	47,728	13,018
1963	382	305	77	62,375	49,048	13,327
1964	385	304	81	65,109	51,451	13,658
1965	382	305	77	66,910	52,700	14,210
1966	392	313	79	67,949	53,398	14,551
1967	477	396	81	71,348	59,681	11,667
1968	529	443	86	74,266	62,989	11,277
1969	593	494	99	70,385	58,465	11,920
1970	507	398	109	69,293	56,121	13,173

APPENDIX II: Select List of Newspapers and Periodicals Published in Czechoslovakia during Spring 1968

Czech Dailies

Name	Publishing Organization, (1) Place of Publication	Circulation (2)
Ceskoslovensky sport (Czechoslovak Sport)	League of Physical Culture (Prague)	168,200 (165,000)
Jihoceska pravda (South-Czech Truth)	KSC Regional Committee (Ceske Budejovice)	58,501 (54,000)
Lidova demokracie (People's Democracy)	People's Party (Prague)	168,366 (152,300)
Mlada fronta (Young Front)	Central Committee of the Union of Youth (Prague)	316,831 (269,800)
Nova svoboda (New Freedom)	KSC Regional Committee (Ostrava)	142,028 (133,300)
Pochoden (Torch)	KSC Regional Committee (Hradec Kralove)	61,718 (62,000)
Prace (Labor)	Central Council of the Revolutionary Trade Union Movement (Prague)	420,099 (301,800)
Pravda (Truth)	KSC Regional Committee (Pilsen)	67,600 (60,000)
Pruboj (Break-through)	KSC Regional Committee (Usti nad Labem)	75,260 (75,000)
Rovnost (Equality)	KSC Regional Committee (Brno)	131,154 (124,000)

(1) Unless otherwise stated, the publication listed is the official organ of the publishing organization.

(2) The first figures represent actual press runs of Wednesday, March 27, 1968. Those in parentheses designate projected press runs for this period as planned by the Postal Press Distribution Agency. Source: Boleslav Rohac, "Jak dal v rozvoji tisku" ("How to Proceed in the Development of the Press.") *Novinar*, XX, No. 5 (1968), p. 154.

Name	Publishing Organization, Place of Publication	Circulation
Rude pravo (Red Right)	Central Committee of the KSC (Prague)	979,013 (910,300)
Svoboda (Freedom)	KSC Regional Committee (Prague)	68,834 (69,700)
Svobodne slovo (Free Word)	Socialist Party (Prague)	180,594 (145,350)
Vecerni Praha (Evening Prague)	Prague Municipal Council of the KSC (Prague)	126,125 (99,480)
Zemedelske noviny (Agricultural News)	Ministry of Agriculture and Nutrition (Prague)	251,746 (234,000)

Slovak Dailies

Name	Publishing Organization, Place of Publication	Circulation
Hlas ludu (People's Voice)	KSS Regional Committee (Bratislava)	44,976 (42,750)
Lud (People)	Revival Party (Bratislava)	23,239 (17,700)
Praca (Labor)	Slovak Council of the Revolutionary Trade Union Movement (Bratislava)	170,370 (149,600)
Pravda (Truth)	Central Committee of the KSS (Bratislava)	278,750 (254,400)
Rolnicke noviny (Farming News)	Commission of the Slovak National Council for Agriculture and Nutrition (Bratislava)	87,554 (82,600)
Rude pravo (Red Right)	Central Committee of the KSC (Bratislava)	39,700 (39,000)
Smena (Shift)	Slovak Committee of the Union of Youth (Bratislava)	172,669 (128,980)
Smer (Direction)	KSS Regional Committee (Banska Bystrica)	45,126 (42,800)

Name	Publishing Organization, Place of Publication	Circulation
Sport (Sport)	Slovak Committee of the League of Physical Culture (Bratislava)	66,391 (62,000)
Uj szo (New Word)	Central Committee of the KSS (Bratislava) (In Hungarian)	77,640 (76,200)
Vecernik (Evening Paper)	Bratislava Municipal Council of the KSS (Bratislava)	41,947 (41,000)
Vychodoslovenske noviny (East-Slovak News)	KSS Regional Committee (Kosice)	66,297 (49,950)

Weekly Newspapers and Periodicals

		Language
Casopis University Karlovy (Charles University Periodical)	Charles University Faculty of Enlightenment and Journalism (Prague) (fortnightly)	Czech
Ceskoslovenska televize (Czechoslovak Television)	Program news of the National Television Network (Prague)	Czech
Ceskoslovensky rozhlas (Czechoslovak Broadcast)	Program news of the National Radio Network (Prague)	Czech
Dikobraz (Porcupine)	Satirical and humor magazine of the Central Committee of the KSC (Prague)	Czech
Hospodarske noviny (Economic News)	Economic journal of the Central Committee of the KSC (Prague)	Czech
Katolicke noviny (Catholic News)	Peace Movement of the Czechoslovak Catholic Clergy (Prague)	Czech
Katolicke noviny (Catholic News)	Society of St. Adalbert, Trnava (Bratislava)	Slovak
Kulturni tvorba (Cultural Creation)	Political-cultural tabloid of the Central Committee of the KSC (Prague)	Czech

Name	Publishing Organization, Place of Publication	Language
Kulturny zivot (Cultural Life)	Union of Slovak Writers (Bratislava)	Slovak
Kvety (Blossoms)	Illustrated magazine of the Central Committee of the KSC (Prague)	Czech
Literarni listy (Literary Pages)	Union of Czechoslovak Writers (Prague)	Czech
Mlady svet (Young World)	Illustrated magazine of the Union of Youth publishing house (Prague)	Czech
Nove slovo (New Word)	Organ of politics, culture and economics of the Central Committee of the KSS (Bratislava)	Slovak
Obrana lidu (People's Defense)	Ministry of Defense (Prague)	Czech
Reporter (Reporter)	Union of Czechoslovak Journalists (Prague)	Czech
Rohac (Stag Beetle)	Satirical and humor magazine f the Central Committee of the KSS (Bratislava)	Slovak
Sloboda (Freedom)	Freedom Party (Bratislava)	Slovak
Slovenka (Slovak Woman)	Illustrated magazine of the Union of Czechoslovak Women in Slovakia (Bratislava)	Slovak
Student (Student)	Central Committee of the Union of Youth (Prague)	Czech
Svet socializmu (World of Socialism)	Slovak Committee of the Czechoslovak-Soviet Friendship League (Bratislava)	Slovak

Name	Publishing Organization, Place of Publication	Language
Svet sovetu (World of the Soviets)	Czechoslovak-Soviet Friendship League (Prague)	Czech
Svet v obrazech (World in Pictures)	Illustrated magazine of the Union of Czechoslovak Journalists (Prague)	Czech
Televizia (Television)	Program news of the National Television Network in Slovakia (Bratislava)	Slovak
Ucitelske noviny (Teachers' News)	Ministry of Education and the Union of Employees in Education, Science and Culture for Slovakia (Bratislava)	Slovak
Ucitelske noviny (Teachers' News)	Ministry of Education and the Union of Employees in Education, Science and Culture (Prague)	Czech
Vlasta (a woman's given name)	Illustrated magazine of the Union of Czechoslovak Women (Prague)	Czech
Volkszeitung (People's Newspaper)	Central Council of the Revolutionary Trade Union Movement (Prague)	German
Zivot (Life)	Cultural, entertainment illustrated of the Central Committee of the KSS (Bratislava)	Slovak
Zivot strany (Party Life)	Journal for Party functionaries published by the Central Committee of the KSC (Prague) (fortnightly)	Czech

Name	Publishing Organization, Place of Publication	Language
	Monthly Publications	
Cerveny kvet (Red Flower)	Literary magazine published by Profil Publishing House (Ostrava)	Czech
Ceska literatura (Czech Literature)	Czechoslovak Academy of Sciences (Prague)	Czech
Czechoslovak Life	Illustrated magazine published by Orbis Publishing House (Prague)	English French Italian Swedish
Czechoslovak Youth	Central Committee of the Union of Youth (Prague)	English French German Spanish
Dejiny a soucasnost (History and the Present)	Cultural and historical review published by Orbis (Prague)	Czech
Democratic Journalist	International Organization of Journalists (Prague)	English French Russian Spanish
Divadlo (Theater)	Union of Czechoslovak Theater Artists (Prague)	Czech
Ekonomicka revue (Economic Review)	Popular scientific review of the Socialist Academy (Prague)	Czech
Ekonomicky casopis (Economic Periodical)	Slovak Academy of Sciences (Bratislava)	Slovak
Film a doba (Film and Time)	Journal of cinema art published by Orbis (Prague)	Czech
Host do domu (Guest for the House)	Journal of literature, the arts and criticism published by the Union of Czechoslovak Writers' publishing house (Brno)	Czech

Name	Publishing Organization, Place of Publication	Language
Impuls (Impulse)	Journal of literary criticism and theory published by the Czechoslovak Book Center (Prague)	Czech
Mezinarodni politika (International Politics)	Journal of international politics of the Socialist Academy (Prague)	Czech
Mlada tvorba (Young Creation)	Magazine of literature and the arts published by the Union of Slovak Writers' publishing house (Bratislava)	Slovak
MY (We)	Political and cultural magazine of the Central Committee of the Union of Youth (Prague)	Czech
Nova mysl (New Thought)	Theoretical and political organ of the Central Committee of the KSC (Prague)	Czech
Novinar (Journalist)	Union of Journalists (Prague)	Czech
Plamen (Flame)	Journal of literature and the arts published by the Union of Writers (Prague)	Czech
Politicka ekonomie (Political Economy)	Economic Institute of the Czechoslovak Academy of Sciences (Prague)	Czech
Pravnik (Lawyer)	Review of the State and Law Institute of the Czechoslovak Academy of Sciences (Prague)	Czech
Pravny obzor (Legal Review)	State and Law Institute of the Slovak Academy of Sciences (Bratislava)	Slovak
Sesity (Notebooks)	Literary magazine for youth published by the Union of Writers (Prague)	Czech

Name	Publishing Organization, Place of Publication	Language
Sesity novinare (Newsman's Notebooks)	Union of Czech Journalists (Prague)	Czech
Solidarity	Organ for Czechoslovak-African Relations published by Orbis (Prague)	English French
	Bimonthly Publications	
Ceskoslovensky casopis Historicky (Czechoslovak Historical Journal)	Historical Institute of the Academy of Sciences (Prague)	Czech
Orientace (Orientation)	Literary review published by the Union of Writers' publishing house (Prague)	Czech
Revue dejin socialismu (Review of the History of Socialism)	Institute of History of the KSC (Prague)	Czech
Sociologicky casopis (Sociological Review)	Scientific, Philosophy and Sociology Board, Academy of Sciences (Prague)	Czech
Svetova literatura (World Literature)	Review of foreign literature published by Odeon Publishing House (Prague)	Czech

SELECT BIBLIOGRAPHY

Books and Monographs

Bergman, Philip. *Self-Determination: The Case of Czechoslovakia 1968-1969.* Lugano, Switzerland: Gassi, 1972.

Bjorkegren, Hans. *Aleksandr Solzhenitsyn. A Biography.* Translated by Kaarina Eneberg. New York: Third Press, Joseph Okpaku Publishing Co., 1972.

Busek, Vratislav and Spulber, Nicolas, eds. *Czechoslovkia.* New York: Frederick A. Praeger for the Mid-European Studies Center of the Free European Committee, 1957.

Buzek, Antony. *How the Communist Press Works.* Praeger Publications in Russian History and World Communism, No. 147. New York: Frederick A. Praeger, 1964.

Czerwinski, E.J. and Piekalkiewicz, Jaroslaw, eds. *The Soviet Invasion of Czechoslovakia: Its Effects on Eastern Europe.* Praeger Special Studies in International Politics and Public Affairs. New York: Praeger Publishers, 1972.

Djilas, Milovan. *The Unperfect Society: Beyond the New Class.* Translated by Dorian Cooke. New York: Harcourt, Brace & World, 1969.

Dolejsi, Vojtech. *Noviny a novinari: Z poznamek a vzpominek.* ("Newspapers and Newsmen: From Notes and Recollections.") Prague: Nakladatelstvi politicke literatury, 1963.

Ello, Paul, ed. *Dubcek's Blueprint for Freedom.* London: William Kimber, 1969.

Fleron, Frederic J., Jr., ed. *Communist Studies and the Social Sciences: Essays on Methodology and Empirical Theory.* Chicago: Rand McNally, 1969.

Golan, Galia. *The Czechoslovak Reform Movement: Communism in Crisis 1962-1968.* Cambridge: Cambridge University Press, 1971.

Golan, Galia. *Reform Rule in Czechoslovakia: The Dubcek Era 1968-1969.* Cambridge: Cambridge University Press, 1973.

Goldstucker, Eduard. *Na tema Franz Kafka: clanky a studie.* ("On the Theme of Franz Kafka: Articles and Studies.") Prague: Ceskoslovensky spisovatel, 1964.

Hajek, Jiri. *Mytus a realita ledna 1968.* ("Myth and Reality of January 1968.") Prague: Svoboda, 1970.

Hamsik, Dusan. *Spisovatele a moc.* ("Writers and Power.") Prague: Ceskoslovensky spisovatel, 1969.

Hamsik, Dusan. *Writers Against Rulers.* Translated by D. Orpington. Vintage Books. New York: Random House, 1971.

Hermann, A.H. *A History of the Czechs.* London: Allen Lane, 1975.

Hopkins, Mark W. *Mass Media in the Soviet Union.* New York: Pegasus, 1970.

Inkeles, Alex. *Public Opinion in Soviet Russia: A Study in Mass Persuasion.* Cambridge: Harvard University Press, 1951.

International Press Institute. *"Svoboda" The Press in Czechoslovakia 1968.* Zurich: IPI, 1969.

Ionescu, Ghita. *The Politics of the European Communist States.* New York: Frederick A. Praeger, 1967.

Ionescu, Ghita and de Madariaga, Isabel. *Opposition: Past and Present of a Political Institution.* Harmondsworth, England: Penguin Books, 1972.

Janos, Andrew. "Group Politics in Communist Society: A Second Look at the Pluralistic Model." *Authoritarian Politics in Modern Society: The Dynamics of Established One-Party Systems.* Edited by Samuel P. Huntington and Clement H. Moore. New York: Basic Books, 1970.

Jilemnicky, Frantisek and Stejskalova, Eva, comps. *Noviny a Casopisy v Ceskych Krajich 1969-1971.* ("Newspapers and Periodicals in the Czech Lands 1969-1971.") Prague: Statni knihovna CSR — Narodni knihovna, 1971.

Journalist M (Maxa, Josef). *A Year Is Eight Months.* Garden City, N.J.: Doubleday, 1970.

K Udalostem v Ceskoslovensku: Fakta, dokumenty, svedectvi tisku a ocitych svedku. ("Concerning the Events in Czechoslovakia: Facts, Documents, Testimony from the Press and Eyewitnesses.") Translated from Russian. Moscow: 1968.

Kaplan, Frank L. "The Czech and Slovak Press: The First 100 Years." *Journalism Monographs*, No. 47 (January, 1977).

Klimes, Vladimir. *Pocatky ceskeho a slovenskeho novinarstvi.* ("The Beginnings of Czech and Slovak Journalism.") Prague: Orbis, 1955.

Kohout, Pavel. *From the Diary of a Counterrevolutionary.* Translated by George Theiner. New York: McGraw-Hill, 1972.

Kusin, Vladimir V., ed. *The Czechoslovak Reform Movement 1968.* Proceedings of the Sminar held at the University of Reading on 12-17 July, 1971. Santa Barbara, Calif.: ABC-Clio Press, 1973.

Kusin, Vladimir V. *The Intellectual Origins of the Prague Spring: The Development of Reformist Ideas in Czechoslovakia 1956-1967.* Cambridge: Cambridge University Press, 1971.

Kusin, Vladimir V. *Political Grouping in the Czechoslovak Reform Movement.* London: Macmillan, 1972.

Lavine, Isaac Don. *Intervention.* New York: David McKay, 1969.

Liehm, Antonin J. *The Politics of Culture.* Translated by Peter Kussi. New York: Grove Press, 1972.

Little, Robert, ed. *The Czech Black Book.* Prepared by the Institute of History of the Czechoslovak Academy of Sciences. London: Pall Mall Press, 1969.

Mayer, Milton. *The Art of the Impossible: A Study of Czech Resistance.* A Center Occasional Paper, II, No. 3. Santa Barbara, Calif.: Center for the Study of Democratic Institutions, 1969.

Mnacko, Ladislav. *Opozdene reportaze.* ("Belated Reports.") Prague: Ceskoslovensky spisovatel, 1964.

Mnacko, Ladislav. *The Seventh Night.* Translated from Slovak. London: J.M. Dent & Sons, 1969.

Olson, Kenneth E. *The History Makers: The Press of Europe from Its Beginnings through 1965.* Baton Rouge: Louisiana State University Press, 1966.

Oxley, Andrew; Pravda, Alex; and Ritchie, Andrew. *Czechoslovakia: The Party and the People.* London: Penguin Press, 1973.

Passin, Herbert. "Writer and Journalist in the Traditional Society." *Communications and Political Development.* Edited by Lucian W. Pye. Studies in Political Development, No. 1. Princeton, N.J.: Princeton University Press, 1963.

Paulu, Burton. *Radio and Television Broadcasting in Eastern Europe.* Minneapolis: University of Minnesota Press, 1974.

Prirucni slovnik naucny. ("Encyclopedia of the Czechoslovak Academy of Sciences.") 4 Volumes. Prague: Academia, 1962-1967.

Remington, Robin Alison, ed. *Winter in Prague: Documents on Czechoslovak Communism in Crisis.* Cambridge, Mass.: The M.I.T. Press, 1969.

Salomon, Michel. *Prague Notebook: The Strangled Revolution.* Translated by Helen Eustis. Boston: Little, Brown and Co., 1971.

Schmidt, Dana A. *Anatomy of a Satellite.* Atlantic Monthly Press Book. Boston: Little, Brown and Co., 1952.

Schwartz, Harry. *Prague's 200 Days: The Struggle for Democracy in Czechoslovakia.* London: Pall Mall Press, 1969.

Selucky, Radoslav. *Czechoslovakia: The Plan that failed.* Translated by Derek Viney. London: Thomas Nelson and Sons, 1970.

Seton-Watson, Hugh. *East Europe Between the Wars 1918-1941.* Harper Torchbooks. 3rd ed. Revised. New York: Harper & Row, 1967.

Shanor, Donald R. *Soviet Europe.* New York: Harper & Row, 1975.

Siebert, Fred S.; Peterson, Theodore; and Schramm, Wilbur. *Four Theories of the Press.* Urbana: University of Illinois Press, 1963.

Skilling, H. Gordon. *Communism National and International: Eastern Europe after Stalin.* Toronto: University of Toronto Press, 1964.

Skilling, H. Gordon and Griffiths, Franklyn, eds. *Interest Groups in Soviet Politics.* Princeton, N.J.: Princeton University Press, 1971.

Souckova, Milada. *A Literary Satellite: Czechoslovak-Russian Literary Relations.* Chicago: University of Chicago Press, 1970.

Statisticka rocenka CSSR. ("Statistical Annual of the Czechoslovak Socialist Republic.") Prague: SNTL, 1962-1971.

Svaz Ceskoslovenskych Spisovatelu. *IV. Sjezd Svazu ceskoslovenskych spisovatelu/Protocol/Praha 27.-29. cervna 1967.* ("Fourth Congress of the Union of Czechoslovak Writers/Minutes Prague, June 27-29, 1967.") Prague: Ceskoslovensky spisovatel, 1968.

Svaz Ceskych Spisovatelu. *Ustavujici Sjezd Svazu ceskych spisovatelu ve dnech 31.5-1.6.1972.*("Institutional Congress of the Unionof Czech Writers during May 31 - June 1, 1972.") Prague: Svoboda, 1972.

Svitak, Ivan. *The Czechoslovak Experiment 1968-1969.* New York: Columbia University Press, 1971.

Szulc, Tad. *Czechoslovakia Since World War II.* New York: Viking Press, 1971.

Taborsky, Edward. *Communism in Czechoslovakia 1948-1960.* Princeton, N.J.: Princeton University Press, 1961.

Tejkal, Karel. *Rozhlasove zpravodajstvi: K nekterym problemum rozhlasove specificnosti.* ("Broadcast Reporting: Toward Some Problems of Broadcasting Specification.") Prague: Statni pedagogicke nakladatelstvi, 1967.

Thomson, S. Harrison. *Czechoslovakia in European History.* Hamden, Conn.: Archon Books, 1965.

Tigrid, Pavel. *Why Dubcek Fell.* London: Macdonald, 1971.

Ustav Dejin Komunisticke Strany Ceskoslovenska. *Prirucni slovnik k dejinam KSC.* ("Encyclopedia of the History of the KSC.") 2 Vols. Prague: Nakladatelstvi politicke literatury, 1964.

Zacek, Joseph F. "Nationalism in Czechoslovakia." *Nationalism in Eastern Europe.* Edited by Peter F. Sugar and Ivo J. Lederer. Far Eastern and Russian Institute Publications on Russia and Eastern Europe, No. 1. Seattle: University of Washington Press, 1969.

Zartman, I. William, ed. *Czechoslovakia: Intervention and Impact.* Studies in Peaceful Change. New York: New York University Press, 1970.

Zeman, Z.A.B. *Prague Spring.* New York: Hill and Wang, 1969.

Zenkl, Petr. "Communist Seizure of Power and the Press: Czechoslovakia, 1945-1948." *Communist Penetration and Exploitation of the Free Press.* Committee Print of the U.S. Congress, Senate, Committee on the Judiciary. Washington, D.C.: Government Printing Office, 1962.

Zieris, Karel F. *The New Organization of the Czech Press.* Translated by G. Bohdan. Prague: Orbis, 1947.

Zinner, Paul E. *Communist Strategy and Tactics in Czechoslovakia, 1918-1948.* Praeger Publications in Russian History and World Communism, No. 129. New York: Frederick A. Praeger, 1963.

Articles, Documents and Unpublished Materials

Barnard, Frederick M. "Between Opposition and Political Opposition: The Search for Competitive Politics in Czechoslovakia." *Canadian Journal of Political Science,* V (December, 1972), 533-52.

Black, Robert E. "Leftist Distorted Press Laws to Capture Czech Newspapers." *Journalism Quarterly,* XXXVI (June, 1949), 181-85.

Brenner, Vladimir and Hrouda, Milan. "Veda a vysokoskolske vzdelani v prestizi povolani." ("Scholarship and Higher Education in the Prestige of Occupations.") *Sociologicky casopis,* IV, No. 1 (1968), 43-54.

Brown, A.H. "Pluralistic Trends in Czechoslovakia." *Soviet Studies,* XVII (April, 1966), 453-72.

Brown, A.H. "Political Change in Czechoslovakia." *Government and Opposition,* IV (Spring, 1969), 169-94.

Budzislawski, Hermann. "Spisovatele a novinari." ("Writers and Journalists.") *Novinarsky sbornik,* I, No. 1 (1956), 21-28.

de Sola Pool, Ithiel. "Public Opinion in Czechoslovakia." *Public Opinion Quarterly,* XXXIV (Spring, 1970), 10-25.

Djilas, Milovan. "The Unquenchable Fires of Czechoslovakia." Translated by Michael M. Milenkovitch. *The Central European Federalist,* XVI (December, 1968), 8-11.

Dolejsi, Vojtech. "Patnact let novinarske organizace." ("Fifteen Years of The Journalists' Organization.") *Novinarsky sbornik,* V, No. 3 (1960), 354-75.

Dolejsi, Vojtech. "Zmeny ve strukture nasich redakci." ("Structural Changes in Our Editorial Offices.") *Novinarsky sbornik,* III, No. 4 (1958), 419-26.

Dresler, Jaroslav. "Writers in Czechoslovakia." *Survey* (London), No. 49 (October, 1963), 149-53.

Golan, Galia. "The Short-lived Liberal Experiment in Czechoslovak Socialism." *Orbis,* XIII (Winter, 1970), 1096-1116.

Goldschmidt, Jiri. "Skola pro Africke novinare." ("School for African Journalists.") *Svet v obrazech,* XXI, No. 43 (1965), 19.

"Government Affairs." *News from behind the Iron Curtain,* II (September, 1953), 12.

Hajek, Hanus. "Czechoslovakia — A Late Thaw." *Current Affairs Bulletin* (Sydney), XXXIII (February 17, 1964), 99-112.

Hajek, Hanus. "Czechoslovakia — occupation and after." *Current Affairs Bulletin,* XLIII (January 13, 1969), 50-64.

Havlicek, Dusan. "Czechoslovak Mass Media in 1968." Paper presented at the proceedings of a seminar held at the University of Reading (England), July 12-17, 1971.

Helesic, Frantisek. "K problematice prace redakce Rudeho prava na prelomu 20. a 30. let." ("Problems Surrounding the Work of Rude pravo's Editorial Office at the End of the 1920's and Beginning of the 1930's.") *Sesity novinare,* III, No. 3 (1968), 33-68.

Helesic, Frantisek. "Komunisticti novinari a levicova kultura." ("Communist Newsmen and Leftist Culture.") *Sesity novinare,* III No. 3 (1968), 83-131.

Helesic, Frantisek. "Rude pravo v obdobi upevnovani panstvi burzoazie a docasne stabilizace kapitalismu v Ceskoslovensku (Cast druha)." (" 'Red Right' and the Period of the Bourgeoisie's Consolidation of Power and the Transitory Stabilization of Capitalism in Czechoslovakia — Part Two.") *Novinarsky sbornik,* V, No. 3 (1960), 315-47.

Horeni, Zdenek. "Celem k Zivotu, Celem k Budoucnosti." ("Facing Life, Facing the Future.") *Sesity novinare,* IX, No. 1 (1975), 5-12.

Hrabanek, Jan. "Press and Editorial Rights in Czechoslovakia." *Democratic Journalist,* XV (July-August, 1967), 88.

Hudec, Vladimir. "Fakulte Zurnalistiky do Vinku." ("Toward the Journalism Faculty's Future.") *Novinar,* XXIV, No. 11 (1972), 9-11.

Jancar, Barbara. "The Case for a Loyal Opposition Under Communism: Czechoslovakia and Yugoslavia." *Orbis,* XII (Summer, 1968), 415-40.

Jezdinsky, Karel. "Impact of Mass Communications Media on the Czechoslovak Reform Movement of 1968." Paper presented at the proceedings of a seminar held at the University of Reading (England), July 12-17, 1971.

Jones, Christopher, D. "Autonomy and Intervention: The CPSU and the Struggle for the Czechoslovak Communist Party, 1969." *Orbis,* XIX (Summer, 1975), 591-625.

Kaplan, Frank L. "The Communist International's Press Control from Moscow." *Journalism Quarterly,* XLVIII (Summer, 1971), 315-25.

Kaplan, Frank L. "The Writer as a Political Actor in Czechoslovak Society: A Historical Perspective." *East European Quarterly,* VII (September, 1973), 199-220.

Korecky, Jan. "Novinarska organizacia na Slovensku v rokoch 1945-1950 (sic'." ("The Journalist Organization in Slovakia Between 1945-1950 (1960).") *Novinarsky sbornik,* VII, No. 1 (1962), 72-84.

Kusak, Alexej. "Na vychode republiky." ("In the East of the Republic.") *Kvety,* Nos. 39-47, September 29-December 24, 1955. (A nine-part series appearing under the same title.)

Lakatos, Michal. "Dvatsad rokov budovania socialistickej demokracie." ("Twenty Years of Building Socialist Democracy.") *Pravny obzor,* XLVIII, No. 5 (1965), 265-74.

Lakatos, Michal. "K niektorym problemom struktury nasej politickej sustavy." ("Toward Some Problems of the Structure of our Political System.") *Pravny obzor,* XLVIII, No. 1 (1965), 26-36.

Mares, Vaclav E. "Czechoslovakia Three Springs Later." *Current History,* LX (May, 1971), 282-307.

Mond, George and Richter, R. "Writers and Journalists: A Pressure Group in East European Politics." *Journalism Quarterly,* XLIII (Spring, 1966), 95-106.

Roberts, Adam. "Czechoslovakia: trials without 'show.'" *World Today,* XXVIII (March, 1972), 93-98.

Roberts, Adam. "Socialist Conservatism in Czechoslovakia." *World Today,* XXVI (November, 1970), 478-88.

Ruml, Jiri. "Mych dvacet let." ("My Twenty Years.") *Reporter,* February 28-March 6, 1968, 5.

Sbirka zakonu a narizeni republiky Ceskoslovnske. ("Collection of Laws and Statutes of the Czechoslovak Republic.") No. 101/1947, pp. 519-24; No. 184 1950, pp. 716-17; No. 81 1966, pp. 433-37; No. 84/1968, p. 238; No. 127/1968, pp. 346-47.

Schwartz, Morton. "Czechoslovakia: Toward One-Party Pluralism?" *Problems of Communism,* XVI (January-February, 1967), 21-27.

Sedlacek, Jan E. "Tisk — jako nastroj ekonomicke propagandy." ("The Press — As an Instrument of Economic Propaganda.") *Novinarsky sbornik,* X, No. 4 (1965), 483-85.

Shaffer, Harry G. "Out of Stalinism." *Problems of Communism,* XIV (September-October, 1965), 31-40.

Sik, Ota. "The Economic Impact of Stalinism." *Problems of Communism,* XX (May-June, 1971), 1-10.

Simakova, Marie. "Noviny a interview." ("Newspapers and the Interview.") *Novinarsky sbornik,* X, No. 4 (1965), 437-46.

Sip, Emil. "How the press won its freedom." *IPI Report,* XVI (April, 1968), 4-5.

Skilling, H. Gordon. "Communism and Czechoslovak Traditions." *Journal of International Affairs,* XX, No. 1 (1966), 118-36.

Skilling, H. Gordon. "The Formation of a Communist Party in Czechoslovakia." *American Slavic and East European Review,* XIV, No. 3 (1955), 346-58.

Storkan, Karel. "Promeny publicistiky." ("Transformations in Journalism.") *Sesity novinare,* II, No. 4 (1968), 31-47.

Sumavska, Libuse. "Pohled na vyvoj ceskeho tisku od r. 1945." ("A Glance at Development of the Czech Press from 1945.") *Novinarsky sbornik,* X, No. 1 (1965), 9-16.

Sylla, J. "The Periodical Press in the People's Democratic Republics." *Gazette*, VI, No. 2 (1960), 181-197.

Taborsky, Edward. "Czechoslovakia under Husak." *Current History*, LXX (March, 1976), 114-18, 134-35.

Taborsky, Edward. "Czechoslovakia's Abnormal 'Normalization.'" *Current History*, LXIV (May, 1973), 207-11, 229.

"Television in Eastern Europe." *Eastern Europe*, XV (April, 1966), 12-15.

UV CSSN (Central Committee of the Czechoslovak Union of Journalists). "Koncepce Ideove Vychovne Cinnosti a Jeji Nejblizsi Ukoly." ("The Concept of Ideologically Educational Activity and Its Immediate Tasks.") *Novinar*, XXIV, No. 10 (1972), 7-9.

Velen, Victor A. "Czech Stalinists Die Hard." *Foreign Affairs*, XLII (January, 1964), 320-328.

Vesely, Jaroslav. "Vyvoj ceskoslovenskeho tisku, jeho struktura a perspektiva." ("Development of the Czechoslovak Press, Its Structure and Perspective.") *Novinarsky sbornik*, VI, No. 2 (1961), 121-44.

Wehr, Paul. "Responding to Invasion: Czechoslovakia, 1968." Paper presented at the 67th Meeting of the American Sociology Association, New Orleans, Louisiana, August 28-31, 1972.

Zaninovich, M. George and Brown, Douglas A. "Political Integration in Czechoslovakia: The Implications of the Prague Spring and Soviet Intervention." *Journal of International Affairs*, XXVII, No. 1 (1973), 66-79.

Newspapers and Periodicals Consulted

Czech and Slovak publications:

Ceskoslovensky novinar, Czechoslovak Life, Democratic Journalist, Historicky Casopis, Host do domu, Kulturni tvorba, Kulturny zivot, Lidova demokracie, Listy, Literarni listy, Literarni noviny, Mlada fronta, MY, Nova mysl, Novinar, Novinarsky sbornik, Otazky zurnalistiky, Plamen, Politika, Praca, Prace, Pravda (Bratislava), *Prispjevky k dejinam KSC, Reporter, Rude pravo, Sesity novinare, Student, Svobodne slovo, Tribuna, Universita Karlova, Vecerni Praha, Zemedelske noviny, Zitrek, Zivot strany.*

Other publications:

Christian Science Monitor, Current Digest of the Soviet Press, East Europe, The Economist, Gazette, The Guardian, Los Angeles Times, The New York Times, Problems of Communism, Survey, The Times (London), *Svedectvi* (Paris-based periodical), *Zpravy* (Warsaw Pact command newspaper published during invasion and initial period of occupation), Radio Free Europe reports and monitoring service.

INDEX